Bricks Matter

WILEY & SAS BUSINESS SERIES

The Wiley & SAS Business Series presents books that help senior-level managers with their critical management decisions.

Titles in the Wiley & SAS Business Series include:

For more information on any of the above titles, please visit www.wiley.com.

Bricks Matter

The Role of Supply Chains in Building Market-Driven Differentiation

Lora M. Cecere
Charles W. Chase, Jr.

WILEY

John Wiley & Sons, Inc.

Published by John Wiley & Sons, Inc., Hoboken, New Jersey.
Published simultaneously in Canada.

For general information on our other products and services or for technical support, please contact our Customer Care Department within the United States at (800) 762-2974, outside the United States at (317) 572-3993 or fax (317) 572-4002.

Wiley publishes in a variety of print and electronic formats and by print-on-demand. Some material included with standard print versions of this book may not be included in e-books or in print-on-demand. If this book refers to media such as a CD or DVD that is not included in the version you purchased, you may download this material at http://booksupport.wiley.com. For more information about Wiley products, visit www.wiley.com.

Library of Congress Cataloging-in-Publication Data:
Cecere, Lora M.
    Bricks matter : the role of supply chains in building market-driven differentiation / Lora M. Cecere, Charles W. Chase.
        pages   cm. — (Wiley & SAS business series)
    Includes index.
    ISBN 978-1-118-21831-0 (cloth); ISBN 978-1-118-28272-4 (ebk.); ISBN 978-1-118-28294-6 (ebk.); ISBN 978-1-118-28472-8 (ebk.)
        1. Business logistics.   I. Chase, Charles W.   II. Title.
    HD38.5.C343   2012
    658.7—dc23
                                                            2012037486

Printed in the United States of America
10 9 8 7 6 5 4 3 2 1

This book is dedicated to first-generation supply chain pioneers.

Contents

Foreword

Historically, successful companies were typically known for their marketing expertise or technological innovation. Today, great companies are also defined by supply chain excellence. Throughout my 40 years at Procter & Gamble (P&G), I watched the concept of a well-run supply chain evolve from one that was barely on anyone's radar screen to one that is front and center as part of any company's business strategy.

The fact that supply chain management is now an academic discipline further changes the game. PhDs enter the market with strong business backgrounds; they bring a new and an important focus to topics such as data synchronization, information systems, and demand shaping—the horizontal structures within a supply chain organization.

While it is gratifying to see this evolution, part of the challenge is integrating this data-driven approach with an appreciation for what, in my opinion, makes a great supply chain organization great: a foundation of functional excellence. The vertical supply chain functions—manufacturing, logistics, engineering, procurement, and quality—are what allow a company to leverage the capabilities that information can provide. A company's synchronization and information systems may be the best in the world, but without outstanding execution and support, systems alone cannot deliver.

The companies that view both elements as essential—cutting-edge systems and strong functional organizations—are the companies that knit the horizontal and vertical together in ways that truly add value to the business.

The second challenge I see is one that is critical to every business: leadership. Just as any company is always tweaking its marketing or innovation strategies to better anticipate and respond to marketplace dynamics, its supply chain strategies need to evolve as well. It is the supply chain leader's job to recognize how things are changing, where they are going, and when it is time to tear down and rebuild.

While we like to think that our people on the ground are best positioned to identify what is not working or what could work better, in my experience that is not how it happens. Organizations, by nature, generate inertia; there is always a tremendous investment in the status quo. The supply chain leader must be the one to take on transformation—the organization simply won't go there on its own.

I served as P&G's global product supply officer from 2001 through 2011. One example of rethinking our organization resulted in the creation of centralized purchasing spend pools; another was the consolidation of P&G's planning function within the supply chain organization. In both cases, each of our business units was managing these activities in its own way. The redesign led to increased scale and flexibility, greater focus, and stronger supply chain capabilities.

Another critical and closely related element of supply chain leadership is perspective: supply chain excellence is about continual improvement. To be clear, we sometimes innovate with big ideas that have immediate impact; however, that is rarely the case. Supply chain organizations are large and complex; they require persistent, day-in and day-out focus. The core work of creating a world-class supply chain is a journey.

I would also like to say a few words about culture, and the power that comes from building an entire organization focused on excellence. A strong supply chain culture starts with communication—making sure that people understand the business need and how their roles within the supply chain support and drive the business. It requires leaders who see themselves as coaches—leaders who explicitly model what "good" looks like and show up as being there to help solve problems.

A strong supply chain culture is about cultivating people with a healthy dissatisfaction, people who believe that what is good enough—or even great—today isn't good enough for tomorrow. When you develop a critical mass of people who take ownership for their results, that is when magic happens. When everyone is pulling in the same direction, people transcend their functional boxes because they are aligned to a bigger idea—a larger vision of success.

I am proud to have been a part of Procter & Gamble's supply chain journey—a journey outlined here. This is the right place to start. I know from experience that it works.

I wish each of you success on your quest for a world-class supply chain. As you progress, remember that it is a journey, not a sprint. It requires leadership, tenacity, a deep understanding of the fundamentals, and a commitment to be in it for the long haul.

R. KEITH HARRISON
Retired Global Product Supply Officer
Procter & Gamble

Preface

We firmly believe that bricks matter. Behind every shipment, there is an order. It is satisfied by a manufacturing and a logistics process. The customer's expectation is that the order will be perfect. Getting it right requires the alignment of the organization from the customer's customer to the supplier's supplier. It sounds easier than it is.

Supply chain management is three decades old. It is still evolving. While the term *supply chain* was used in logistics and warfare for decades prior, 2012 is the 30th anniversary of the use of the term *supply chain* in commercial manufacturing.

Over the three decades, the processes have changed greatly. Technology has been a major driver. Connectivity, business analytics, and e-commerce increased the pace of fulfillment and the customers' expectations. While clicks (the world of the Internet) are sexier than bricks (the world of fulfillment), companies cannot move forward without effective and efficient operations.

Like the annealing of steel, the processes were challenged and refined by many forces. This included the evolution of global markets and increasing business complexity. Many companies failed first before they could go forward. The greatest moves forward came not from success, but from failure. Material event after material event created a boardroom understanding of why bricks matter. This book is a synopsis of this journey.

For manufacturers, retailers, and distributors, the supply chain is business. The book is a compilation of stories, quotes, and anecdotes. The stories are rich. In telling them, we tried to make it anything but mundane. To understand the evolution, we interviewed 75 supply chain pioneers, and analyzed 25 years of financial data. We wanted to understand why the supply chain matters today, and how companies need to prepare for the next decade. The book is dedicated to the first-generation supply chain pioneers that cobbled together those first processes.

The book also predicts the future, giving advice to supply chain teams on the evolution of processes for 2020. To run the race for Supply Chain 2020, these teams have to have the right stuff. They must have the right balance between flexibility and strength, they have to be balanced in their approach between go-to-market strategies and fulfillment activities, and they need a clear understanding of supply chain strategy. This requires a multiyear road map and a cross-functional understanding.

It also requires an understanding of the future of technologies. The road before us will be quite different from the road that got us here. The world of big data, the Internet of Things, new forms of predictive analytics, and the evolution of digital manufacturing offer great promise. The adoption of new technologies is part of winning the race for Supply Chain 2020.

When we submitted the abstract of this book to many publishers, to celebrate this 30-year journey of supply chain management, we were told that it was "boring." Publisher after publisher turned us down. However, we persevered. We think it is an important story. It is the progression of the manufacturing age of business, the underpinning of the middle-class economy, and the essential component of many new business models.

Writing this book took six months. It would not have happened without a team of people. We would like to thank Regina Denman, Michael Hambrick, Heather Hart, Marie LeCour, Abby Mayer, and Jill Smith for their patience and help. Without this team, the book would not have happened.

CHAPTER **1**

Why Bricks Matter

*We had to learn supply chain practices. We then had to
unlearn them as technologies evolved, and then relearn
them based on new capabilities.*

—First-Generation Supply Chain Pioneer

The story is old. When generations come and go, at the end, the
bricks remain. They last through the ages. They are a symbol of
prosperity, solidity, and strength. Found in many forms, they
give a culture countenance. This book is a variation on this old theme.
In the end, *bricks matter*.

The foundation of business is built on *bricks*. Manufacturing plants,
warehouses, and sales operations centers are built to deliver on a
brand promise. Each is run by people. Collectively, their effectiveness
can make or break a company's ability to fulfill customer promises. To
drive success, these processes need to be synchronized. They need
to be carefully architected and adapted to meet strategy. The design
has changed over time as business complexity increased.

In business, while there are fads, true value is built through continuous improvement of processes to deliver real products to real people along with market differentiating services to build brands. To make
year-over-year progress, companies learn—although, sometimes the

hard way—that the ability to successfully deliver on the brand promise requires proficiency in supply chain management.

———————————

I found Rome a city of bricks and left it a city of marble.

—*Augustus*

———————————

The term *supply chain* is not new. It is fundamental to military strategy. It was the difference between winning and losing in the Napoleonic wars and the Battle of the Bulge in World War II. The application of supply chain practices as a fundamental business process is newer. First coined in 1982 to be used as an overarching business concept, it is now 30 years old. Over the last three decades, it has morphed in definition.[1]

No two companies today define it the same, nor will they agree on what *good* looks like. The definitions are as varied as ice cream flavors in a local shop.

The goal of this book is to share the insights of what has been learned over the course of these 30 years. In this book, we do not debate the ideal supply chain or the flavor of the month. Instead, we give insights on the evolution of the processes, share the stories of success and failure, and prognosticate on the future of tomorrow's supply chains.

To help the reader not familiar with supply chain vernacular, here we start with a definition. For the purposes of this book, we define the term *supply chain* as "the process of organizational alignment to effectively manage the flows of cash, product, and information from the customer's customer to the supplier's supplier."

Success depends on both vertical processes (within a function) to drive operational excellence and horizontal processes (across functions) to ensure alignment within the organization. Excellence happens when there is orchestration of the trade-offs to the business strategy.

Supply chains make good companies great; however, ensuring this happens is easier said than done. As shown in Figure 1.1, each company has an effective frontier: a unique set of trade-offs to manage to improve business outcomes.

Over the last 30 years, supply chains have become more complex with implications for cost, working capital, social responsibility, and product quality. These interactions involve thousands of trading partners in interconnected and ever-changing relationships that stretch around the globe. Excellence is defined through trade-offs on the effective frontier.

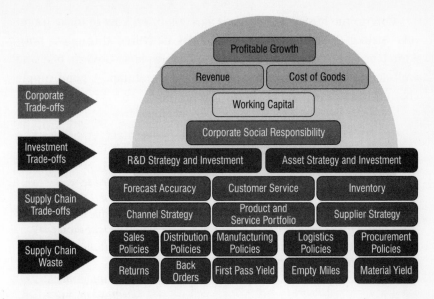

Figure 1.1 The Supply Chain Effective Frontier

The challenges are many. Time and clock speed pressures are high. Cultural differences are a hindrance. Data latency is a problem. The impacts on economic growth are far-reaching. It is a complex system with complex processes with increasing business complexity. This management is intricate. There is not one supply chain. Companies find that they have five to seven unique supply chains to be managed simultaneously. These systems need to be knitted together into business process outcomes.

Although it is easy to understand the increasing business process complexity, the key to supply chain success is a true understanding of the supply chain as a system, and learning how to make the right choices on business complexity to drive true lasting value. Today, there are 3,500 companies greater than $1 billion in revenue working on improving the supply chain response. There is no company that feels that it has it nailed. There are no best practices. Instead, the processes are evolving.

▶ THE MISSION

Supply chain leaders manage complex systems with complex processes with increasing complexity. Leaders orchestrate the trade-offs vertically and horizontally to deliver the business strategy. Laggards let the supply chain whip them around.

Core to the business strategy is agreement on how to make trade-offs. Strong decision-making capabilities delivered through a horizontal process characterize supply chain leaders. Governance and well-defined decision-making processes are essential. A good supply chain translates to good business.

Once I was asked to shut down a manufacturing facility. I had worked with the people in the factory for many years. As we rolled out the lay-off packages and talked about why we needed to relocate the factory, no one liked it; but everyone understood it. I was okay until we leveled the building, and I sat on the rubble of the bricks that once was a vibrant entity of people making real things day after day. It was then that I cried. I was all alone sitting on the bricks remembering what had been.
—*Director of Supply Chain Management,*
Chemical Industry

Most companies understand that supply chains have complex processes. They also know all too well that the underlying processes are growing more complex. They live it every day. However, what most companies fail to realize is that supply chains are *complex systems* with *finite trade-offs*. These choices happen up and down the supply chain. Leaders make them consciously while laggards make them by default. They are both horizontal (cross-functional) and vertical (within a function). They are also intra-enterprise (within the company) and inter-enterprise (external to the company within a trading network).

Each supply chain has a unique potential. As shown in Figure 1.1, the business choices are intrinsically linked at multiple levels.

The approach needs to be holistic. Some typical trade-offs include:

- The proliferation of products and services will increase demand error, raise inventory levels, and decrease asset utilization.
- An extreme focus on cost will decrease customer service and increase inventory levels.
- New products will increase forecast error, inventory, and supply chain waste.
- A singular focus on asset utilization will increase inventory and decrease customer service.

- An increase in customer service will increase cost, decrease asset utilization, and increase inventory levels.
- Shortening working capital cycles will increase cost.
- Lengthening the manufacturing and delivery supply chain cycles will increase working capital and decrease customer service.
- Increasing manufacturing quality hold times will increase inventory levels, increase working capital, and decrease customer service.

For each supply chain, the impact is different. There are no hard-and-fast rules. The trade-offs of customer service, forecast accuracy, and inventory are the easiest to understand. Through continuous improvement programs, employee training, investments in technology, and alignment of metrics, the core of the supply chain can be improved.

In setting targets for the supply chain, leaders use advanced modeling tools to understand their specific supply chain potential. Modeling helps organizations see the impacts of business changes through *what-if analysis*. This analysis allows companies to set realistic and holistic metric targets. Leaders use the same metrics but different targets for each supply chain team. The determination of supply chain potential cannot be accomplished through spreadsheets. As a result, companies working on improving supply chain capabilities need to invest in business analytics for supply chain modeling. Without this modeling, the goals are unclear. They cannot be rolled up horizontally across the organization or vertically from region to global.

There is no magic wand or easy button. Companies cannot wish things to happen; instead, leadership happens through hard work. It is about building the organizational muscle to raise this effective frontier. It requires strength, balance, and flexibility. Results happen over many years. Progress is not linear. Supply chain leaders set targets consciously and align metrics systematically with a focus on balance. Supply chain laggards let their supply chain whip them around.

Time is money. If we could take one day of transit time out of the supply chain, we could free up $1 billion in cash. Unfortunately, we cannot.

—*Chief Financial Officer, European Operations,*
High-tech and Electronics Manufacturer

IMPLICATIONS

Implications matter. The business impact of the evolution of supply chain practices is far-reaching. To support the evolution, an entire ecosystem of software, consulting, and hardware companies dedicated to improving supply chain processes evolved.

The use of these technologies enabled growth in global markets, accelerated new product introductions, and drove more-informed decision making within the company. As computing power grew and connectivity increased, process and technology innovation accelerated. Although progress has been made, this journey is far from over. Today, there is a plethora of solutions for cloud-based computing, big data supply chains, mobility, and advanced analytics for learning systems. The greatest concentrations of solution providers building technologies for supply chain management are in Germany, India, and the United States.

To improve the processes, and to conquer new opportunities, corporate spending has been significant. Over the past 20 years, manufacturing organizations have spent 1.7 percent of revenue on new forms of information technology (IT) to improve visibility, accelerate decision making, and drive insights. This spending has had a profound economic impact on the gross domestic product (GDP) of nations and on the business results of manufacturing companies.

I remember the early days of supply chain management, when we typed our own letters, mailed them in paper envelopes, and went to our office for a conference call. Today, we communicate globally in real-time anywhere. E-mail has replaced inter-office mail and our handheld devices define where we will have our next conference call. So much has changed.
—First-Generation Supply Chain Pioneer

Not all supply chains are created equally, and not all industries perform at the same level. High-tech, chemical, and consumer products supply chains are the most mature. The industries of automotive, pharmaceutical, and retail lag the rest.

There is an inverse relationship between margin and supply chain excellence. When margins were tight, supply chains got better. The combination of product life cycle changes, commodity margin pressures, and product proliferation put pressure on organizations to improve the processes quickly. Throughout this book, you will see that manufacturers with the tightest margins defined wave after wave of supply chain process excellence.

In today's world, *clicks* are sexier than *bricks*. There is a fascination with online presence. Social and e-commerce news grabs headlines while the traditional manufacturing processes are largely taken for granted. Delivery through the supply chain is assumed. Supply chain processes are not sexy. The pioneers did not earn the seven-digit salaries of the Wall Street financial executives. However, the supply chain was and still is the silent enabler behind great companies, world economies, and successful communities. It created viable brands and defined world economies.

The bricks of the supply chain are analogous to the children's story *The Three Little Pigs*. When a supply chain is done right, it makes companies stronger to withstand the storms and volatility of the global economy. When it is done wrong, companies fold against the winds of market changes. The best supply chains are built with a clear understanding that bricks matter.

Supply chains made hastily will fail. They are unequal to the test of demand volatility. They cannot meet the challenges of global risk management or the pressure to produce new products quickly to enter a new market. It is only when the supply chain is made of the right bricks that it can maximize opportunity and weather market-to-market volatility.

BUILDING THE RIGHT BRICKS

The bricks pave the evolution of supply chain processes. In the 30-year evolution, as shown in Figure 1.2, three types of bricks mattered: the right use of assets or *buildings*; expansion into Brazil, Russia, India, and China (BRIC countries) and the *knowledge* to build supply chain processes.

Published in England in 1886 by James Orchard Halliwell-Phillips, the tale of the *Three Little Pigs and the Big Bad Wolf* tells the story of bricks. This well-known story begins with three little pigs being sent out into the world by their mother to "seek their fortune." The first little pig builds a house of straw, but a wolf blows it down and the pig runs to his brother's house. The second pig builds a house of sticks and when he sees his brother he lets him in, with the same ultimate result. Each exchange between the wolf and the pig has a chant:

> "Little pig, little pig, let me come in."
> "No, no, not by the hair on my chinny chin chin."
> "Then I'll huff, and I'll puff, and I'll blow your house in."

The third pig builds a house of bricks and when he sees his brothers he lets them in. The wolf fails to blow down the house of bricks. The wolf then attempts to trick the little pigs out of the house, but the pigs outsmart him at every turn. Finally, the wolf tries to come down the chimney only to find that the pigs have placed a pot of boiling water in the fireplace. The wolf comes down the chimney, lands in the pot of hot water, and is cooked.

Brick 1: Effective Asset Strategies: The Buildings

The effective use of assets starts with supply chain design. In the early days of supply chain management, manufacturing and distribution processes were insourced. Companies owned their bricks and mortar, and products were made and sold within the same region. Today's supply chain is largely outsourced. Manufacturing and distribution

Figure 1.2 Bricks Matter

centers are operated by third parties and the flow of goods and services use many modes of transportation to cross multiple international borders to enter global markets.

Most companies inherited their supply chains. The active design of supply chain networks is relatively new. In the first 20 years, the placement of factories, the design of distribution centers, and the selection of suppliers were not critical. Today, the design is paramount.

As global trade barriers tumbled, the design of the supply chain needed to be more flexible. It needed to flex on many dimensions to take advantage of the lower costs of labor, to build the capability to enter new markets, or to drive the opportunities for tax incentives and rebates. As a result, today's companies focus on more frequent network design and the building of processes to support manufacturing and logistics outsourcing. Planning becomes more important.

Despite the increased outsourcing and growing complexity of production and distribution processes, companies quickly learn that while they may outsource the bricks of their supply chain, they cannot outsource the responsibility. Many companies have learned this lesson the hard way through failure.

As a result, they have stumbled forward. As companies have outsourced the supply chain, they have had to build inter-enterprise processes to ensure that they are able to achieve better levels of quality, customer service, and corporate social responsibility through their network as they did when all functions reported through their organization. As a result, the focus of the supply chain has become outside-in.

Today, it is focused on not just building chains but also on the design of agile networks.

As companies outsource, they quickly learn that relationships matter. The nodes of the network are only as effective as the trading partner relationship. As a result, the sharing of information and the alignment of incentives increase in importance. This is the mortar between the bricks.

To effectively use assets, supply chain leaders have found that they cannot be insular. They have found that they must tear down the bricks between the silos of their own internal organizations to stretch across networks to build lasting supply chain processes. The walls of these functional silos are difficult to break down, but they must be dislodged to build the end-to-end supply chain. For, it is now not just a company's bricks, but the responsibility for all the assets of the extended network that is paramount.

Brick 2: Right Expansion into BRIC Countries

Through the last decade, the largest contribution of the supply chain team was driving growth in emerging economies. These teams powered growth in the emerging countries of Brazil, Russia, India, and China. They fought the corruption of Russia, battled the compliance barriers of Brazil, and embraced the sheer enormity of China and India. These were greenfield start-ups (built from the ground up).

From our supplier's supplier to our customer's customer, our supply chain in Brazil is 200 days long. When we started, we projected capacity for five years. Due to exceptional growth, we found that we exceeded our usable capacity within one year. We were in trouble. To build a new plant in Brazil takes two years. The application process is tough. We have to get approval from three of the 13 ministries within Brazil before we can start the process. As a result, we built capacity in China and ship the product to Brazil to satisfy the burgeoning needs.

—Second-Generation Pioneer, Chemical Industry

The biggest hurdle was human. Within these geographies there was little to no understanding of supply chain processes. Factories had to be built, and teams had to be hired and trained. Companies forged new partnerships and adapted to new forms of logistics infrastructure. Each country had a unique story and set of obstacles. Coca-Cola's failure in India spurred progress on social responsibility while Wrigley's success in China redefined processes with distributors. It is one of the reasons that McDonald's succeeded in India while Kentucky Fried Chicken failed. Success in emerging markets gave InBev the funds to purchase Anheuser-Busch.

Globalization is a process of the past, present, and future. The work is not done. It is still a challenge, and of growing importance for companies to drive growth.

CASE STUDY

EXPANSION INTO BRIC COUNTRIES: MCDONALD'S

McDonald's operates in 119 countries serving 68 million customers on a daily basis. The company stayed true to the brand promise while recognizing the different local preferences for taste. In Norway, McDonald's offers a McLaks (a salmon and dill burger); in Uruguay, the menu features a McHuevo (a burger topped with an egg); whereas in Japan, the company serves Ebi Filet-O (a shrimp burger). In Germany, McDonald's serves beer. In India, the menu is free of beef and pork products. The menu is local. The supporting supply chain was designed to support country-specific taste preferences. Many times this was done in regions where the suppliers and the supporting infrastructure did not exist. In each region, the supply chain pioneers identified and qualified suppliers and built logistics infrastructure to deliver the redefined McDonald's experience.

Contrast this with the story of Kentucky Fried Chicken (KFC). KFC opened in India at the end of the twentieth century only to leave the market. The company made two mistakes: the menu was not localized to recognize regional taste preferences and the supporting supply chain of suppliers was inadequate. The company reentered the Indian market in 2004 with a new menu focused on meat-free rice dishes, wraps, and spices more in line with Indian taste preferences.

Brick 3: Knowledge: Building Effective Supply Chain Processes. Putting Value in Value Networks

The last brick is knowledge. It is building the right supply chain processes. While the definition of supply chain excellence has changed over the last 30 years, leaders have progressed through stages as shown in Figure 1.3. There are five phases: the efficient, the reliable, the resilient, the agile, and the aligned supply chain. For most, the agile and the aligned supply chain are aspirational. (The agile supply chain is often termed *demand driven* and the aligned supply chain is termed *market driven*.)

While companies attempted to implement best practices over the last 30 years, they are now grappling with the fact that many Y2K projects built an efficient supply chain without resiliency. These investments made the supply chain strong, but not agile. Today, most companies have processes that can respond, but cannot adapt. They are too rigid. They cannot sense and adapt to market shifts. This is the basis of the drive to create market-driven value networks.

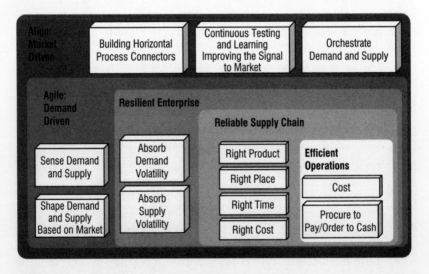

Figure 1.3 The Evolution of Supply Chain Process Excellence

A LOOK AT HISTORY

No two supply chains are alike. They come in many forms and definitions. While companies may argue on the definition of a supply chain, no one in manufacturing and distribution organizations will disagree that it matters. Over the last 30 years, it has become clear that supply chain practices both build and destroy brands. While failure can have a quick and deleterious impact, success can be seen only over many, many years. Although the stories of the losers fill headlines, the untold story is the one of quiet leaders using supply chain processes over the course of many years to improve corporate viability.

This book shares insights from these stories. To write this book, we interviewed 75 supply chain leaders from a variety of industries. These pioneers charted the path. They worked in apparel, automotive, chemical, consumer products, and high-tech and electronics industries. To better understand the evolution of supply chain management, we asked them three questions:

1. In your career, what were the primary tipping points?
2. How do you define supply chain excellence?
3. Who does it best? And why?

During the last six months of 2011, we captured their experiences to understand the evolution. Here, we tell their stories.

SUPPLY CHAIN PIONEERS: THE TIPPING POINTS

In the interviews, when we asked the pioneers about the major tipping points of supply chain management, there was no quick answer. They struggled to answer the question. There were so many changes that happened concurrently that it was hard for them to cite just one. In the discussions, they acknowledged that the changes were fast and furious. The major tipping points happened simultaneously in the forms of technology, globalization, and changes in transportation. In the interviews, it was hard for the pioneers to separate them; but when pressured, collectively they outlined the major tipping points as shown in Figure 1.4.

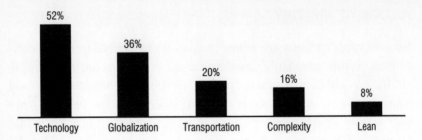

Figure 1.4   Major Tipping Points for Supply Chain Management Processes

When the pioneers recount their stories, they all agree that in the beginning, the emphasis was on manufacturing efficiency. The most efficient supply chain was believed to be the most effective supply chain. Supply chain practices evolved primarily to make manufacturing even more efficient.

When the practices started, there were islands of automation. No pioneer could have imagined the world today where data is anytime and anywhere.

In the early years, the personal computer was a rarity. The early processes were paper-based. The phone was stationary. Intercompany communication was completed by letter or telex. As computing power became a reality, it spawned a series of focused applications for the factory, transforming business-to-business interactions and improving the speed of data.

In this period, process innovation flourished. The major tipping points for the period of 1987 to 1999 are shown in Figure 1.5. The concept of just-in-time (JIT) manufacturing to manage the flow of inbound materials with suppliers reduced waste and improved the speed of receipt. The application of optimization techniques to improve factory scheduling using the theory of constraints (TOC) improved asset utilization and reduced manufacturing changeover times. Both were major steps forward. In this period, the first vestiges of a supply chain organization appeared in the form of a few specialists reporting to the leaders of manufacturing. In these early days, manufacturing centers operated as islands of isolated data.

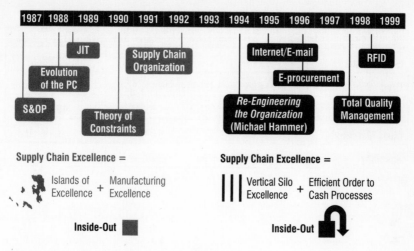

Figure 1.5 Supply Chain Tipping Points 1987–1999

As companies focused on year 2000 process readiness, the rate of technology change accelerated within organizations. What started as a simple initiative—to be sure that the computer systems could handle a time designation change with Y2K—became the focus of large-scale process transformation efforts. This period laid the foundation for the modern supply chain. While the prior period automated the factory, this coordinated effort focused on improving order-to-cash and procure-to-pay processes. Strong processes were built within the functions of source, make, and deliver to support the growing complexity of serving multinational supply chains.

The Internet along with Y2K was the perfect accelerant. The two forces intertwined to reshape and transform both business-to-consumer and business-to-business relationships. The most profound effect was in retail. As shown in Table 1.1, the Internet sparked a new channel that outpaced the growth in traditional store formats. While the uninformed might conclude that the growth of e-commerce made *bricks* obsolete, in reality, the opposite was true. Successful companies transformed their traditional supply chains to meet the new requirements of this growth channel. It required new bricks, new processes, and a business transformation.

Table 1.1 Growth of the E-commerce Retailer as a Business Model

Retail Channel	2000–2004	2005–2009	2010–2012
E-commerce	15.7%	16.0%	26.6%
Drug	14.8%	19.7%	9.5%
Grocery	12.2%	21.5%	19.6%
Mass Merchant	30.6%	9.6%	9.1%
Specialty	14.7%	12.2%	3.0%

Research from financial analyses of retail annual reports for the period 2000–2012

CASE STUDY

THE TALE OF TWO E-COMMERCE START-UPS: AMAZON AND WEBVAN

In 1997, Amazon and Webvan were both e-commerce retail start-ups. Amazon built distribution and fulfillment capabilities as the company grew, while Webvan drove massive capital investments to operate a 336,000-square-foot warehouse in Oakland, California. This distribution center was designed to process volumes equivalent to 18 supermarkets. In 1999, Webvan contracted with Bechtel to build 26 new fulfillment centers. This building project did not materialize because the company closed for business in 2001. Webvan is now owned by Amazon.[2]

In this period, interest in business-to-business trading exchanges skyrocketed; however, growth in these ventures fell short of expectations. While business-to-consumer business models flourished, business-to-business models were overhyped and often underdelivered.

In many ways, it was a new gold rush. The promise was high, but the underlying technologies were too immature to make it a reality. As a result, none of the industry analyst firms correctly predicted the future. In 2000, Gartner Group predicted that 7,500 to 10,000 trading exchanges would evolve by 2002. Similarly, Jupiter Research forecasted that the technology spending in business-to-business marketplaces would increase from $2 billion in 2000 to $81 billion in 2005.

In reality, less than 2 percent of the trading exchanges provided value to the extended supply chain over the course of the next decade. They were not a major factor in the evolution of supply chain processes.

CASE STUDY

THE TALE OF TWO TECHNOLOGY E-COMMERCE BUSINESS-TO-BUSINESS START-UPS: E2OPEN AND TRANSORA

In 2000, trading exchanges were proliferating. Market hype was at an all-time high when E2open and Transora opened their doors for business. Both companies were founded as business-to-business trading exchanges to improve supply chain visibility, drive network collaboration, and improve trading partner relationships. The similarities stopped there. E2open was funded by eight major high-tech companies. The initial funding was $200 million and the design was for it to be a private company that would go public. Transora was founded by 50 large consumer products manufacturing companies. It raised $240 million in four months.

We are well financed and strategically positioned to shape our own destiny in a way other business-to-business exchanges cannot. With this venture, old economy companies are becoming new economy leaders.

—Judy Sprieser, Executive Vice President of Sara Lee and Chairwoman of the early Transora steering committee

You will not be able to perform, compete, and survive in our industry if you are not participating in an electronic marketplace. It's that simple. We will not allow Transora to fail.

—Anthony Simon, President of Marketing Foods Division, Unilever[3]

While Transora struggled to find a successful business niche, E2open completed an initial public offering (IPO) in 2012 after delivering annual revenues of $55.5 million in 2011. Today, E2open has successfully diversified to multiple industries serving more than 32,000 trading partners. Transora, in contrast, merged with 1SYNC in 2005, and is seldom mentioned today in the industry.

The race for global expansion also spurred supply chain spending. Companies felt since they were forced to spend on Y2K that they might as well get more value for the investment by improving their global processes. Not all companies moved at the same pace, but the impact of the rollout of new technologies coupled with the global expansion was staggering. Armies of people worked on system implementations. Many companies today are still digesting the technology investments from this period of time.

It was a boom-and-bust cycle. In this period, talent shortages in information technology coupled with large IT investments for year 2000 readiness raised the stature of the chief information officer (CIO). Multimillion-dollar investments in IT infrastructure were made based on a handshake, and hundreds of consultants were trained to implement new technologies to improve supply chain management. Good talent was hard to find. As a result, many process compromises were made.

Growth in new markets was the rallying cry. To satisfy the demand following this period, supply chains processes were challenged to transition from regional, multinational organizations to a more global footprint. Focused on global growth serving multiple channels, teams were defined in-country to serve new customers. Employees were relocated to be in-country to build processes, teams, and infrastructure.

Connectivity was a strong enabler. With the growth of the Internet, friction was taken out of the supply chain. New processes evolved to better serve business-to-consumer (B2C) and business-to-business (B2B) relationships. In this period, millions of dollars were spent on B2B connectivity, enterprise resource planning (ERP), and e-commerce initiatives. Most were hastily implemented. These tipping points are shown in Figure 1.6.

While the primary impetus for global supply chains was the penetration of new markets, the second thrust to be global was driven by the lower cost of labor. For laggards, it was a pure labor arbitrage strategy.

To take advantage of the lower cost of labor, companies redesigned their supply chains and transformed the supporting logistics systems. Supply chains became longer. Air shipments, cross-border transport, and improvements in labeling were enablers. As supply chain planning grew in importance, it spurred the development of multiparty supply chain visibility systems.

In the last five years, escalating costs, material scarcity, and global warming concerns have further redefined supply chain practices. Because of the increasing volatility of demand and supply, the focus has been on the development of processes and on the organizations that can adapt to change. The new goal is greater agility to flex with market changes and business directives. This new era has also demonstrated the need to define the socially responsible supply chain.

> *No real impact can be made in a supply chain in less than three years. It takes time.*
> *—Marty Kisliuk, Director of Global Operations and Business Development, FMC Corporation Agricultural Products Group*

As a result, the focus of supply chain processes is shifting from inside-out to outside-in. To connect a network of smaller networks of suppliers, logistics providers, and third-party manufacturers, there is a shift from a vertical focus or building functional excellence in operations to the building of horizontal processes to connect value networks. In this transition, companies learn that they must break

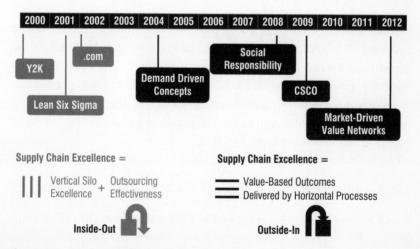

Figure 1.6 Supply Chain Tipping Points 2000–2012

down the bricks between the silos of the organization to build effective networks.

We used to see trade-offs in commodities. One would go up and one would offset it by going down in price. This is not so anymore. In the last two years, all we have seen is up. All commodities are going up at the same time.

—*Vice President and CIO,*
Fortune 500 Food Manufacturer

The future of a supply chain lies in the definition of these outside-in processes. It will drive new business models. Just as Amazon, Apple, Dell, and Walmart used supply chain management to define new business models of the past, new leaders will seize these shifts to power innovation.

The ability to sense and shape while listening and learning will define the supply chain of the future. Supply chain leaders are currently ushering in the era of big data, predictive analytics, and learning systems. The future will belong to those that understand the basics of what has happened in the past but can see the potential of the future.

MEET THE PIONEERS

Underneath the evolution of process and technology are the stories of people. It is about individuals who never dreamed that they would spend their careers in supply chain management. For these pioneers there were no yellow brick roads, or clear paths. Instead, they stumbled forward. These pioneers learned lessons through doing. Slowly, the processes evolved. And as they evolved, the pioneers transformed supply chain processes brick by brick.

1980–1990: First Generation of Supply Chain Pioneers

These leaders were from engineering backgrounds. Within their companies, they were thrust into the world of supply chain management from either manufacturing or procurement roles. When they started, there was no supply chain organization or defined process. In this era, manufacturing was king and supply chain processes were designed to support manufacturing efficiency programs. These leaders often led the charge for continuous improvement programs. They became pioneers by default, not by choice.

These pioneers were primarily male. They were seasoned. Their hands were calloused. Most had spent many years wearing hard hats and safety shoes. The culture was no-nonsense. They joked about using slide rules in college and knew what it was like to stand long hours on a factory floor. They focused on the adoption of new practices and technologies to improve time to market, to schedule transportation, to reduce product variation, and to plan manufacturing production.

As processes in manufacturing matured, companies realized that the goal of supply chain excellence could not be met only by working manufacturing processes in isolation. Instead, they envisioned an end-to-end value chain that could stretch from the customer's customer to the supplier's supplier. They hit their heads on the walls that formed around organizational silos.

The technology evolution—personal computers, in-memory processing for advanced analytics, client/server architectures to support networked employees, increased global connectivity, and e-commerce and business-to-business connectivity—was a steady drumbeat for process innovation and redefinition. These pioneers remember when memos were written by hand, letters were mailed through interoffice mail, and the phone was hardwired to the office wall.

They defined the processes and installed the new technologies. Each one, in his or her own way, fought for recognition. They wanted organizations to see the greater whole and create a supply chain organization. Most of these pioneers are now retiring. They are currently worried about where the next generation of supply chain leaders will come from. As they end their careers, three concerns weigh heavy on their minds:

1. These pioneers believe that an understanding of manufacturing processes is critical to being a great supply chain leader. With the outsourcing of manufacturing, they wonder how companies will train the next generation of supply chain leaders.

2. With the growing demand for supply chain skills, they worry how their companies will attract and retain the right talent.

3. As the educational processes shift from an engineering degree to a business background, they worry about the systems understanding of the third and fourth generations of supply chain pioneers.

Someone is sitting in the shade today because someone planted a tree a long time ago.

—*Warren Buffett*

1990–2000: Second Generation of Supply Chain Pioneers

The second generation of supply chain professionals acted as the boots on the ground for the expansion of supply chain practices into BRIC (the emerging economies of Brazil, Russia, India, and China) countries. They were the implementers of global processes and systems to penetrate new markets. They were the builders of supply chain organizations in new countries.

As they built the infrastructure of the global supply chain, they shuttled their families from country to country. The pace was fast, and the challenges diverse, but they kept their eye on the prize. Their goal was to build market domination to drive growth.

With backgrounds in either engineering or business, this generation was more diverse than the first. There were more women. It was more multicultural. The organizations had greater cultural diversity and the processes spawned the need for academic programs to support the growing need for talent. These pioneers defined cross-functional supply chain processes into finance, procurement, and sales. They built trading relationships and implemented planning systems.

They cut their teeth on Year 2000 programs. Many were hired to help implementation teams test new systems and prepare for possible Y2K failure. Out of this work, they designed and built e-business programs with trading partners and championed new ways to connect and improve procurement processes.

The second generation was mentored by the first. When they started their careers, there also was no supply chain organization.

There was no standard career path. They both witnessed and shaped the evolution. They saw the supply chain organization rise from the functions of procurement and manufacturing to own their own seat at the table with other operations leaders. Today, these pioneers are the new leaders of supply chain organizations in the Fortune 500. There is now a supply chain leader on the board of directors of 6 percent of the Global 1000.

These pioneers built training programs for new employees in emerging economies. Talent development, metrics alignment, and the building of stable relationships in these emerging economies became the secret to success.

2000–2010: Third Generation of Supply Chain Pioneers

The third generation of supply chain leaders is just entering the workforce. Many of these pioneers are new graduates. They have completed a four-year college degree or advanced studies in the field of supply chain management. They are the first generation of college graduates to deliberately choose supply chain management as a career path.

As they enter the workforce, the processes are now clearer, the technologies are more mature, and the career paths well defined. They are entering the profession as the first generation of supply chain pioneers retires. Life looks good for the third generation. There are more jobs than available candidates. Projects are numerous and exciting work abounds.

They are culturally diverse. Their backgrounds are more business than hard-core engineering. The legacy of the second generation's work surrounds them. However, their environment is rife with change management issues. As companies try to define supply chain excellence, the third generation often finds themselves inserted as reluctant peacekeepers to arbitrate between the functions of sales, marketing, manufacturing, distribution, and procurement. They are also often the voice of reason and conscience of the supply chain pushing for a faster pace in the definition of corporate social responsibility programs.

As students during the economic downturn, they have experienced high unemployment firsthand. They are happy to have a job. Most have friends that could not find employment, and they are excited to be entering a field where there are more job openings than qualified applicants. However, naivety reigns. They struggle to understand why the processes that they learned in school are so different from those in the real world.

Very, very few people could appreciate the bubble. That's the nature of bubbles—they're mass delusions.
                                                    —*Warren Buffett*

They are more aware of social technologies than the first two generations. They are often found on Twitter, Facebook, and Pinterest. They are pushing for companies to open up firewalls to enable access to social networks. This generation are the early adopters of mobile devices. They want access of systems beyond corporate firewalls, and they struggle to understand why the technologies that they work with are not easier to use.

2010–2020: Fourth Generation of Supply Chain Pioneers

The fourth generation of supply chain leaders is currently studying in college. They tend to be good at math, love computer gaming, and are active on social networks. They will bring a new view to supply chain management. They will push for technologies to be more visual, socially aware, and action-oriented. They will strive for improvements in corporate social responsibility.

Expect these employees to question the status quo. They carry two to three mobile devices and are connected at all times. They will take the supply chain from near real-time to real-time. Their focus will be on process reinvention. They will push to reduce data latency and improve the use of data.

They will be less accepting of the current levels of waste in the supply chain. Their focus will be on scarcity of materials and improving human welfare. They will be pushing to redefine commonly accepted processes for returns, scrap, and rework.

This will be the first generation to witness homegrown teams in emerging economies. No longer will the definition of the supply chain be dependent on expatriates. They will hire talent directly from home-grown educational programs in the evolving economies of Brazil, Russia, India, and China.

When this fourth generation enters the workforce, there will be less of a gap in their academic teaching to real-world practices. The career paths will be established and this book will seem archaic. We write this book to ensure that they understand the stories of the pioneers and can learn from history.

WHY IT MATTERS

The supply chain failures grab headlines. Success in the supply chain happens slowly over many years, but when a leader stumbles the impact on the balance sheet is pervasive. Much of the public understanding of supply chain management comes from reading about the failures. When companies with names like Apple, Boeing, Cisco Systems, Coca-Cola, ConAgra, Hershey, Johnson & Johnson, Ericsson, Mattel, Nestlé, Nike, PepsiCo, Sainsbury's, and Western Digital make headline news due to supply chain failure, it is hard to not pay attention. Each time these premier brands stumbled, failed, and learned new lessons, the bar on supply chain excellence was raised.

Companies stumbled in two areas: process evolution and technology implementations. These failures drove improvements in supply chain excellence. The pace of change from failure was much faster than from success.

Supply Chain Process Failures Leading to Financial Balance Sheet Disclosure (Material Events)

Supply chain failures affect each company differently. Rarely does a company tie balance sheet write-offs explicitly to supply chain failures, but recent annual reports provide a multitude of examples of where supply chain process mistakes were material events on corporate balance sheets.

- **2007**. ConAgra results in fiscal 2007 included a statement that "the impact of approximately $30 million due to the peanut butter recall, reflected as a reduction of net sales of $19 million, and an increase of $11 million in cost of goods sold."

- **Fiscal 2007**. Mattel stated, "Product recalls reduced gross profit by approximately $71 million. The costs can be further quantified as increased sales and administrative costs by $35 million, reduced net sales by approximately $48.9 million, increasing cost of sales by approximately $22 million and finally increasing ad and promotion expenses by $5 million. Regionally, U.S. operating income decreased by $30 million while International operating income decreased by an even greater $47 million."

- **2009**. Boeing stated that "research and development expense included $2.7 billion of production costs related to the first three flight test 787 aircraft that cannot be sold due to the inordinate amount of rework and unique and extensive modifications that would be made to the aircraft."

- **2010**. The Kellogg Company Annual Report stated that "Kellogg's cereal primarily manufactured in the United States was recalled due to an odor from waxy resins found in the package liner. Total charges were $46 million with a $.09 impact on earnings per diluted share."

- **2011**. Toyota's annual report stated that "Toyota announced four separate recall events. Net revenue in 2010 was down 8.9 percent compared to 2009. Although it is difficult to definitively separate out flagging sales numbers as a result of the economic downturn versus the recall issues, in fiscal 2011, Toyota had an approximately ¥100.0 billion increase in [operating] costs related to recalls and other safety measures conducted to heighten the level of reassurance for customers."

- **2011**. Western Digital's quarterly earnings report announced that the company had experienced "$199 million in charges and expenses relating to flooding in Thailand."

A negative supply chain event permeates financial returns. When there is a supply chain disruption, the affected company's share price drops 9 percent on average below their comparative peer group benchmarks. When there is a failure, companies do not recover quickly. Based on multiple studies by the Georgia Institute of Technology in 2005 to 2009, we know that the average stock return of those suffering from a disruption is almost 19 percentage points lower relative to the benchmark group over a two-year period following the disruption.[4]

The incidence of material failures has grown exponentially over the decade. The number of product recalls grew tenfold and the impact of corporate sustainability decisions filled the news. Why the increase? The processes of supply chain management have become more expansive with greater importance to both corporate balance sheets and reputation.

The stories of success make fewer headlines. There is no easy correlation between supply chain excellence and financial balance sheet returns. As a result, success is hard to measure. Instead, it becomes the organizational muscle providing year-over-year work resilience.

It is also a story of process innovation. The transformation happens slowly through the combination of discipline, training, and careful design. We share the stories of success at the end of this chapter.

Failures in IT Project Implementation

Companies also stumbled in the implementation of information technology (IT) systems. One by one, over the course of 10 years, projects failed. No industry went unscathed. The reasons for failure were repeated. The stories are now legend. The list of failures includes great names: Allied Waste, FoxMeyer Drugs, Hershey, Hewlett-Packard, Goodyear, Kmart, Nike, Sainsbury's, Waste Management, and Whirlpool. Here are excerpts from the news:

- **1996**. In 1994, FoxMeyer Drugs, with revenues of $5 billion, was the fourth largest U.S. pharmaceutical distributor. In 1996, the company was bankrupt. The fall was largely due to an IT project named Delta III that was kicked off in 1993. The original project was scoped to cost $65 million and deliver $40 million in annual cost reductions. Problems arose when the actual project costs spiraled to more than $100 million and resulted in a $34 million inventory write-off. The company was sold to McKesson Corporation for $80 million in cash.
- **1999**. The Hershey announcement in September 1999 made headline news. The original $112 million project was expected to go live in April 1999, but a number of complicating issues pushed the implementation back three months. The company

failed to implement a big bang project (three systems in one implementation) in one of their busiest seasons. As a result, the company was short in inventory to deliver $100 million of customer orders at Halloween. Hershey's stock price tumbled 8 percent; and in October 1999, the company reported a 12.4 percent drop in quarterly sales.[5]

■ **2000.** A $400 million upgrade to Nike's supply chain systems resulted in $100 million in lost sales and a 20 percent stock dip. The reason given by Philip Knight, then Nike's chairman and CEO, was "complications arising from the impact of implementing our new demand and supply planning systems and processes."[6]

As software project failures made front-page news, the tit for tat between the software providers and the industry leaders became the new soap opera.

There's no way that software is responsible for Nike's earnings problems.
    —Greg Brady, President, i2 Technology
    (Nike's supply chain vendor), in 2001

I guess my immediate reaction is: This is what we get for $400 million?
    —Philip Knight, Chairman and
    Chief Executive Officer, Nike

■ **2004.** In September 2004, CEO Carly Fiorina stated that Hewlett-Packard (HP) had "executed poorly on the implementation of an order-processing and supply chain management system." She partly blamed the problems for a $400 million third-quarter revenue shortfall within HP's enterprise servers and storage group. The company had completed 34 similar migrations, but the 35th failed. Three senior leaders were fired.[7]

■ **2005.** Sainsbury's had exceptional expenses of £145 million in information technology and £119 in supply chain costs following the implementation of a new supply chain system.

■ **2007.** After two years of attempted implementation of an ERP project, Allied Waste Industries pulled the plug on a $130 million system. Following suit, Waste Management cancelled a $250 million project after spending $45 million.

■ **2008**. In the second quarter of 2008, Levi Strauss Company's net income dropped by 98 percent because of the failure of an IT project for ERP. Three U.S. distribution centers were forced to close for a full week and the company took a $192.5 million hit to its bottom line. David Bergen, chief information officer, was forced to resign.[8]

■ **2009**. At the end of 2009, Comfort Corporation announced that the company had abandoned its plan to implement an integrated suite of ERP software and recognized asset impairment charges of $27.6 million. One shareholder's SEC filing deemed that it was "indicative of extremely poor judgment by management."

These examples of failures in IT implementation are now pages of history. However, if we step back and look at the mistakes holistically, there are four lessons:

1. **Approach new technologies with caution**. The supply chain is the lifeblood that supplies goods and services to customers. Without it there is no revenue. Major projects need to be approached with caution. In an attempt to meet return on investment (ROI) pressures, many of these projects were under-scoped and understaffed.

2. **Test software. Take the proven route**. Software sales cycles are long and complex. To shorten them, software sales personnel sell the promise and the hope of the project to top executives, short-circuiting the sales processes. As a result, 60 percent of these projects were sold to executive teams without proper testing by their supporting IT departments. As a result, many of the technology failures were due to project commitments made by unknowing leaders to buy software that was just not ready.

3. **Penny-wise and pound-foolish**. Over the course of time, companies have focused on shortening implementation cycles. However, there is often more risk than benefit in shortening the cycle. In this type of implementation, change management issues abound. While many companies focus on the "technology implementation," the larger risk lies in the management of change associated with technology adoption.

4. **A weak link**. Many of the projects implemented in this period were hastily defined and implemented. Knowledge of software and supply chain systems was scarce and the rate of change was rapid. Today's supply chain leader has inherited many of these poorly designed systems from the prior decade.

SUPPLY CHAIN PROCESS EVOLUTION

Supply chain processes are evolving. The definition of supply chain processes started within the company's processes of manufacturing or distribution. Today, the center is stronger than the ends. The vertical processes are stronger than the horizontal. As shown in Figure 1.3, the steps are progressive with each step building and encompassing the prior.

First Shift in the Supply Chain Process: The Efficient Supply Chain

In the beginning, supply chain excellence was defined as the lowest manufactured cost. The belief was that supply chain excellence could be achieved by sweating the assets. This set of beliefs formed the foundation for the efficient supply chain. Through the evolution of supply chain processes, costs were reduced, inventory levels lowered, and waste eliminated; however, each company reached a point where they could no longer just cut costs without trading off service to customers. They had reached their effective frontier.

Early pioneers fought hard battles with finance teams that did not understand the concepts. IT projects were implemented with overinflated commitments that were not grounded in reality. In the early days, the principles of supply chain trade-offs and the effective frontier were difficult to conceive. The singular focus on costs resulted in failures in customer service. These failures drove organizations to define supply chain excellence as a reliable supply chain to focus on closing multiple gaps:

- **A shift in the goal of continuous improvement programs**. In this period, there was a belief that savings from operations could self-fund growth. At first, it worked. However, as the company reached its effective frontier of trade-offs, these continuous improvement programs became largely shell games of trade-offs between functions. Net new savings and true impact on the bottom line became more and more difficult to achieve.

- **Recognition of multiple supply chains**. As companies matured, they also realized that they had not one but multiple supply chains. Each supply chain had unique rhythms and cycles requiring design from the outside-in (from the market back).
- **Need to build supply chain talent**. There was a need for a supply chain organization that could span the organization to build a guiding coalition: leaders that could credibly drive the discussion. This led to building of the supply chain organization and the need to hire and train the second generation of supply chain professionals. There is now a supply chain organization in over 83 percent of North American manufacturing and distribution corporations.

As shown in Figure 1.7, there is a new door for the supply chain leadership team. Most of these supply chain organizations

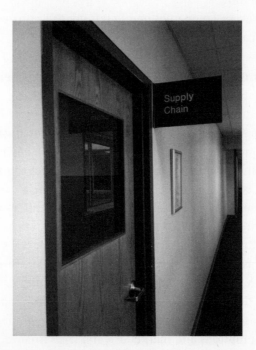

Figure 1.7 The Evolution of the Supply Chain Organization

are complex, operating in matrixed structures. The channel organization fans out to encompass multiple selling groups in a decentralized organization while the procurement organization usually aggregates spend into a central organization.

Second Shift in the Supply Chain Process: The Evolution of the Reliable Supply Chain

The lack of reliability to deliver customer service was the Achilles' heel of the efficient supply chain. This realization gave rise to the concepts of the reliable supply chain. With this shift, the focus changed to balancing costs with reliability in customer service. The goal of this new supply chain direction was the right product at the right place at the right time at the right cost. In this process evolution, companies focused on improving the decision support systems to increase the potential, or the effective frontier, of the supply chain. This included the implementation of deep analytics for inventory optimization and factory scheduling.

In this process, companies had to rethink their processes and close some major gaps:

- **Rethinking the goal**. There was a general belief that the best supply chain is a tightly integrated supply chain. As companies worked on the implementation of processes to become more reliable, they found tight integration was not always beneficial. Planning grew in importance and there was a need to focus on what-if analysis and simulation to test for reliability. Each planner needed his or her own workbench to test the feasibility of solutions and these solutions required a different technology configuration.
- **Redefining forecasting**. While many companies in their quest for efficiency embarked on a one number forecasting program, they quickly found that this was too simplistic. Instead, they found that they needed a common plan (not one number) with role-based views for sales, marketing, and manufacturing based on assumptions and market drivers. The visualization of a common plan by role with agreed assumptions increased supply

chain reliability. They also discovered that each type of forecast within the organization has a distinctively different data model, bias, granularity, and time horizon. (We share more about this evolution in Chapter 3.)

■ **Need for a supply chain strategy**. As companies worked on the definition of supply chain excellence, it became clear that there was a needed layer of definition between business strategy and supply chain planning. This spawned work on supply chain strategy documents to drive alignment and clarify cross-functional direction. Without this clarity, functions within the organization aligned on functional goals that were a barrier to building a reliable supply chain system. Today, only 5 percent of companies feel comfortable with their level of supply chain strategy.

Between 2000 and 2010, there were many market shifts, and companies found that without the ability to sense and adapt to market conditions, the reliable supply chain was not sufficient. In 2000, Cisco Systems was caught in the downturn of the e-commerce bubble. As a result of not sensing demand changes, the company was forced to write off $2.25 billion in inventory in 2001. This loss taught the company an important lesson. The redefinition of supply chain processes to be more resilient enabled the company to sense and withstand the downturn of the Great Recession of 2008.

It is now known as business continuity. In 2011, Intel lost $1 billion in revenue, and the Japanese auto industry lost ¥450 million in profit due to the Thailand floods.

In contrast, also in 2008, the leaders in the chemical supply chain learned a tough lesson. The magnitude of the economic downturn caught all by surprise. For example, DuPont, a supply chain leader five steps back in the supply chain serving the automotive and construction industries, was forced to shut down one-third of its factories in 2008. As demand was translated across the long supply chain through conventional processes, the dominos started to fall. The business impact was pervasive with an employee restructuring program in both 2008 and 2009. The strength of the DuPont supply chain team was able to drive cash flow improvements and cost savings to stem the losses.

In December 2008, DuPont announced plans to address rapidly deteriorating market conditions and strengthen the company's future competitiveness. Plans are focused on generating cash by better aligning cost, working capital and property, plant and equipment expenditures to the revised demand signals of the fourth quarter. These plans include a restructuring program with associated fourth quarter pre-tax charge of $535 million, with expected pre-tax savings of about $130 million for 2009, and about $250 million annual savings thereafter. The company also outlined 2009 plans to achieve $1 billion in net working capital reduction and a 10 to 20 percent reduction in capital spending.
—DuPont, 2008 Annual Report

Shuttering factories in 2008 for DuPont was serious business. The company is known for excellence in process reliability. It owns and operates factories in some of the most challenging chemical environments. The company is a supply chain leader. To ensure that this would not happen again, DuPont used the downtime in the factories to train employees on the principles of supply chain management. The focus was on the redesign of the processes to sense and adapt more quickly to market changes. The principles of supply chain agility grew in importance. Today, the company is actively building market-driven value networks.

Throughout the economic downturn, companies one by one gained a deeper understanding that the reliable supply chain was not sufficient. As a result, the demand-driven concepts gained greater adoption in the building of a resilient supply chain.

Third Shift in the Supply Chain Process: Building the Resilient Supply Chain. Absorbing Demand and Supply Volatility

Like the story of the three little pigs, supply chain leaders wanted to build supply chains that could withstand the winds of demand volatility or the pressure of supply disruption. These supply chains were built to sense outside-in and change the supply chain response based on market conditions. Supply chain leaders that built resilient supply

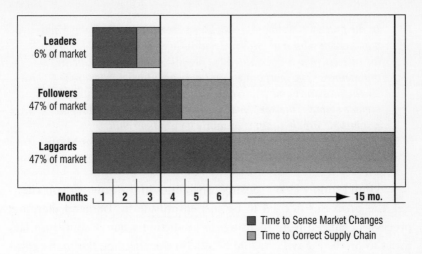

Figure 1.8 Great Recession: Leaders Corrected Five Times Faster

chains decreased the latency—or time to sense—demand and supply changes. Based on a qualitative survey of 60 Fortune 500 companies in the Great Recession, we find that companies that were better at demand sensing were able to sense market changes three times faster and align their total supply chains five times faster (see Figure 1.8) in response to market demand.

In this stage, supply chain leaders defined process excellence by minimizing data latency from both buy- and sell-side markets to drive a near real-time response. In the process, supply chains became networks. In the adaptive, or demand-driven supply chain, companies increased sensing capabilities and infused the processes of source, make, and deliver into the discussions with both buy- and sell-side trading partners. These top-to-top meetings and relationships became more data driven. The metrics changed. Procurement discussions focused on total landed cost rather than just purchase cost, and suppliers were incented to contribute through innovation networks and alignment to corporate social responsibility (CSR) programs. Scorecards and performance management processes evolved. The focus evolved to building win-win partnerships through supplier development programs.

In the process of writing this book in a center seat on a flight, I had a discussion with a physician. I was writing intently, and it piqued his interest. When I explained the premise of the manuscript, he commented, "Isn't corporate social responsibility an oxymoron?" He then laughed and retorted that he was not sure what was the greater obstacle, the "ox" or the "moron." I smiled. Building the responsible supply chain is certainly a paradigm shift.
—Lora Cecere, Coauthor, Bricks Matter

To build supply chain sensing capabilities in the downstream channel, the processes needed to be turned outside-in. Demand planning processes changed from focusing on predicting what to ship from factories to predicting what would be sold in the channel. For many companies, this made the investment that they had made in the integrated supply chain and multiyear ERP programs obsolete. It was no longer sufficient to be tightly integrated to order and shipment processes. Instead, the company needed to define the process of demand translation: the translation of market demands to supply operations with minimal latency. These processes were built on channel data, not corporate history. Demand architectures needed to be built to sense and then translate the meaning of channel or downstream data.

In the process, these leaders realized that sensing without changing the response was insufficient. They needed to be more adaptive. They needed internal processes that could flex and adapt with market changes. As companies experienced high levels of demand and supply volatility, they realized that they needed to embed mechanisms into the processes to ensure profitability. As a result, they invested in the processes of revenue management and demand shaping to deliver the adaptive supply chain. These leaders learned the hard way that it was not sufficient to just sense the change, but they needed to actively shape the outcome.

My supply chain planners used to work for NASA. They are scary smart. They say market sensing in supply chain management is tougher than what they did at NASA.
—Supply Chain Leader,
North American Manufacturing Company

Fourth Shift in the Supply Chain Process: Building the Adaptive Supply Chain. Becoming Demand Driven

In the *adaptive supply chain,* the processes first sense and then shape demand based on revenue management practices. This is sometimes termed a *demand-driven supply chain.* Demand shaping includes the active processes of new product launch, price management, trade promotion management, marketing and advertising, and incenting sales against revenue management processes. They design processes outside-in and evaluate what really matters to customers. Companies that mature in this capability usually are also mature in the processes of analyzing customer profitability through cost-to-serve analysis and looking at product profitability to determine the right product portfolio. They actively manage complexity.

> We introduce 15 to 20 mobile phones a year. This can only happen if there is cross-functional alignment.
>
> —*Chief Financial Officer,*
> *High-tech Manufacturer in Europe*

This stage of development requires tight integration of the research and development (R&D) efforts into the supply chain processes. Since 60 to 80 percent of the costs of a product are defined in a new product launch and many supply chain networks are defined at the time of launch, in the maturation of these processes, companies need to carefully define the coupling of cross-functional, horizontal processes. This includes the integration of the processes of sales and operations planning (S&OP) with R&D stage gate planning and CSR with supplier development programs. This integration is even more critical in heavily regulated industries like pharmaceutical, agro sciences, and aerospace and defense supply chains. If these companies do not get it right at product launch, they have a difficult time amending the process later.

In this stage of supply chain development, one of the toughest change management issues is the role of sales in driving a profitable demand response. Most sales organizations are incented on volume and not profitability. There is a strong resistance to shape demand unless the incentives are aligned to focus on selling a profitable unit. This is a change management issue worth fighting. As the adaptive supply chain evolves, leaders find that one of the largest impacts is improved customer service and the reduction of the cost of sales as a percentage of revenue. Customer satisfaction improves and the dialogue is now focused more on what the customer values versus internal self-serving metrics.

Today when it comes to improving sales, a dollar spent on improving the supply chain of our customers is worth three spent in trade promotion management.
—Vice President of Supply Chain, Consumer Products

As the networks within the supply chain coalesce, demand, supply, and innovation networks begin to overlap. Companies learn that a customer is not just a customer; and that a supplier is not just a supplier. A customer may also be a supplier and a supplier may also be a strong contributor of ideas through open innovation networks. A supplier and/or a customer may also be a provider of logistics services.

There is a misconception that these concepts apply to only consumer product value networks. This could not be further from the truth. In discrete industries, the demand signal is from contract to order. Based on the pipeline status in the contract cycle, advanced companies are able to better forecast and share product requirements with their suppliers. In 2012, the aerospace and defense industry is forecasting 50 percent greater demand. If production rates stayed constant, this would represent an eight-year backlog. Slowly the industry will adapt and increase production rates by 50 to 60 percent. In 2011, when PricewaterhouseCoopers (PwC) evaluated the readiness of suppliers in the value network to adapt to this level of change, the study revealed that 21 percent of the suppliers were at risk of failure.[9] Manufacturers are now more dependent on suppliers. The lack of capacity in today's aerospace and defense supply chain is driven by supplier capacity issues, not manufacturing.[10]

The largest benefit of a demand-driven value network is assessing and building the value network to meet upcoming demand. The use of technologies to sense market insights from unstructured data has helped companies to sense potential supplier failures before the issue percolated into the supply chain. As a result of its work in this area, Intel detected the potential failure of 9 suppliers in the Great Recession and Toyota sensed and prevented the failure of 300 suppliers following the Japanese tsunami in 2011.

Demand and sensing capabilities are important, but for most manufacturers they are still aspirational goals. This level of capability is far from mainstream. Today, only 6 percent of the Fortune 500 has the capability to decrease demand and supply latency.

Supply chain design and the architecture of supply chain strategy increases in importance. This changes from an ad hoc or annual process to be an integral part of the monthly S&OP process. Companies also learn that forecasting is more important than ever, but it needs a new focus. It is no longer about the accuracy and tight integration of numbers; instead, it is sensing market drivers, aligning on assumptions, and planning the network based on the predicted level of demand volatility.

The change in demand forecasting processes is a major change management hurdle for the traditional supply chain. The shift from a focus on history to a focus on market drivers, or to align on demand assumptions versus debating numbers, is a cultural redefinition.

Today, this stage of maturity is largely aspirational for most companies, and not well understood. It includes companies like Dow Chemical, Intel, Kimberly-Clark, LG Electronics, Procter & Gamble, Seagate, and Samsung.

Fifth Shift in the Supply Chain Process: Align the Supply Chain Market to Market. Become Market Driven

The market-driven supply chain is the future state aspiration for the supply chain leader. The concepts are based on building advanced processes to test and learn. These advanced analytics can power learning systems that continually sense, learn, and adapt.

These networks are termed *market-driven value networks*. Market-driven supply chains are adaptive networks that can quickly align organizations market to market focused on delivering a value-based outcome. They sense and translate market changes (buy- and sell-side markets) bidirectionally with near real-time data latency to align sell, deliver, make, and sourcing operations. The focus is on horizontal process orchestration. With the evolution of market-driven supply chains, companies can focus on delivering value-based outcomes through complex networks.

Traditional supply chains could not sense; instead, they had a fixed response that was often wrong and late. Despite what was happening in the market, the response remained the same. Likewise, supply chains were not built to test and learn. With the evolution of technologies for learning systems, supply chains can now orchestrate demand across the organization market to market while executing test and learn strategies. The response can be adaptive: multiple *ifs* can map to multiple *thens* to allow the supply chain to align, adapt, and learn. This last phase, the market-driven supply chain, is currently being designed by supply chain leaders.

The design of the market-driven supply chains is dependent on the building of value networks, strong horizontal processes, the redesign of forecasting and supply, and a retraining of the organization. (It should not be confused with a marketing-driven supply chain. In the marketing-driven supply chain, the focus is on an internal signal, not a market signal. And, it does not adapt horizontally market to market (buy-side to sell-side markets)). In contrast, the marketing-driven supply chain stretches horizontally across the extended supply chain from market to market.

▶ **DEFINITION**

Market-driven supply chains are adaptive networks that quickly align across an organization to sense and shape a market-to-market response. These processes are focused on delivering a value-based outcome. When successfully implemented, these supply chains sense and translate market changes (buy- and sell-side markets) bidirectionally with near real-time data latency to align sell, deliver, make, and sourcing operations to market conditions.

CASE STUDY

CARGILL BEEF

Cargill Beef is a market-driven leader. The company uses price optimization tools to evaluate the market potential for beef. Before the company decides what to package for the market, it first evaluates the market potential for each cut of beef and then optimizes how to harvest its inbound herds to maximize the opportunity and minimize the risk. There are 197 ways to cut up beef cattle. Because each breed of cow has a different potential or finite mix of products—steaks, ground beef, roast, and so on—Cargill uses the technology in sales and operations planning to drive rancher insights to define which breeds are best for customer demand. This process of being adaptable to trade-offs from market to market based on the use of optimization technologies is termed *demand orchestration*. It is a key capability requirement for market-driven leaders.

Today's Supply Chain Organization

Today, the concepts of market-driven value networks are aspirational. The supply chain organization is still evolving. No two companies have defined them alike. The most mature organizations design the supply chain from the customer's customer to the supplier's supplier. To maximize the potential, mature organizations have changed the organizational design: direct reporting of manufacturing and procurement functions into the same organization as distribution and customer service. When this does not happen, it is more difficult for the supply chain to reach full potential.

WHO DOES SUPPLY CHAIN BEST?

Supply chain excellence is defined by the ability to use the supply chain to deliver the business strategy. The maturity of process allows companies to improve the potential of the supply chain to maximize opportunity and mitigate risks while raising the effective frontier.

As companies mature, they want to know how their supply chain compares to others. They also want to know whether they are getting better or worse and what good looks like. They are hungry to know if they have reached their supply chain potential. While this sounds simple, the answers to these questions are not easy. The ability to get comparison data on supply chain performance is easier said than done.

While there are many services in the market that have evolved to share benchmark data, there are many pitfalls. Companies need to overcome five issues:

1. **Avoid self-reported data**. When companies self-report data, there is usually a bias or overstatement of results. Consequently, the best benchmarking source is either government-regulated financial reporting or the output from software as a service (SaaS)–hosted solution providers where data is a by-product of running the technology for a peer group of companies.

2. **Consistent definitions matter**. When it comes to supply chain benchmarking, the basics matter. Definitions, granularity, and frequency of the process need to align for data to be relevant.

3. **Common data model**. To be useful in benchmark comparisons, the planning systems need to have a similar data model. Very few companies have implemented planning in a similar enough manner to facilitate peer group benchmarking. For most, this is overlooked.

4. **Timeliness**. One of the issues with benchmarking is timeliness. Data gathered in snapshots—once or twice a year—are not very useful.

5. **Peer group**. An essential element to getting useful benchmark data is having a comparable peer group.

After considering the available options in the market, and judging them against these pitfalls, most companies will find that benchmark data available in the industry is expensive and usually not of a great value.

If we look at history, the early leader in a marathon is never the winner that finishes the race. Instead, the winner builds the skill, capability, and resilience to compete. Then based on their strategy, the athlete pushes over the finish line.
  —*Michael Noblit, Senior Vice President of Operations,*
  Samsung Electronics America

Companies also find, as they mature, that it is difficult to get the complement of metrics necessary to view the supply chain as a system. There are six metrics in supply chain management that are tightly woven with intrinsic trade-offs. These metrics are asset utilization, days of inventory (or inventory turns), forecast accuracy, customer service (on-time delivery of orders shipped complete), cost of goods, and revenue growth.

In conjunction with this benchmark data to determine supply chain potential, additional insights are gained through the understanding of supply chain cycles. In the supply chain, time is often money. There are 10 primary cycles to map:

1. **Order to delivery**. The time that it takes from order receipt to customer delivery.

2. **Order to cash**. The time from order receipt to payment.

3. **Manufacturing product cycle**. Each manufacturing line has a cycle of product families and the progression that makes the most sense for manufacturing. The manufacturing cycle wheel is the time for a company to progress through this logical grouping of products to minimize changeovers in manufacturing.

4. **Product shelf life cycle**. Not all products have equal shelf life potential. This cycle is the amount of time that a perishable product is viable to be sold.

5. **Product life cycle**. This is the expected time that a product will be available to sell in the market before being outdated with a new product. Margin is usually the highest at the initial launch.

6. **Procure to delivery**. This is the time to source raw materials and receive them at the inbound manufacturing location.

7. **Procure to pay**. It is the amount of time from the purchase of the raw material to the payment of the receipt of the material.

8. **Order latency**. By definition, it is the time from a channel purchase to order translation (visibility of the product's purchase in the channel). For a consumer products company the order latency is 7 to 14 days. For a chemical company, the order latency is often two to four weeks.

9. **Concept to launch**. The critical cycle for time to market is the time required to effectively launch a new product from the ideation and test phase to first-time manufacturing to launch into the market.

10. **Return to receipt**. It is the time to return a product and complete the transactions associated with the return.

To understand supply chain excellence, these 10 cycles need to be viewed together with the measurements from studying the supply chain effective frontier (Figure 1.1) (to determine supply chain trade-offs) for each supply chain. They need to be viewed by a peer group.

So, who does supply chain best? There are many attempts in the market to crown a supply chain leader; and while there are many methodologies attempting to define who does supply chain the best, they are inadequate. One methodology throws all companies into a spreadsheet and compares them on growth, inventory, and asset utilization and asks peers to rate the companies. This methodology has a number of problems. Supply chain excellence cannot be determined this simplistically. Instead, it needs to be evaluated in a stepwise holistic manner based on three criteria:

1. **Strategic alignment**. The supply chain should not be viewed in isolation from the business. This first measurement is perhaps the most important. It is the contribution of the supply chain team to the delivery of the business strategy.

2. **Year-over-year performance**. This is a year-over-year comparison of how a company performed against its peer group on the supply chain financial measurements of growth, revenue/employee, asset utilization, days of inventory, and cost of sales as a percent of revenue. To determine supply chain excellence, companies need to compare year-over-year performance of a similar company to its peer group for at least three to five years.

3. **By peer group**. Benchmarking needs to be against a comparable peer group. While leaders gain insights on innovative practices from other leaders in dissimilar peer groups, benchmarking performance needs to be compared within a peer group based on similar value chain definitions.

Benchmarking analysis is fraught with issues. Companies are not simple. They have multiple supply chains. The markets are dynamic. Companies are bought and sold. Product lines evolve. Channels ebb and flow. As a result, while companies want to benchmark and insights can be gained, definitive answers remain more of an art than a science.

MEET THE SUPPLY CHAIN LEADERS

In interviews, supply chain pioneers were asked, "When you think of supply chain excellence, which company comes to mind?" The first response by the supply chain leaders is that no one company stands above the rest. The collective opinion is that while individual companies do pieces of the supply chain well, there is no one company that does everything well.

In phone interviews, as the leaders think through their answer, they will often cite Apple's dominance in high-tech innovation, Dell's leadership in defining new business models, and Toyota's definition of lean processes. However, when the pioneers are pressed to name a single leader, one name is usually mentioned followed by silence: P&G is seen as the year-over-year leader by the pioneers. Apple is the second most often mentioned and Dell is third. The aggregate response of the supply chain pioneers is shown in Figure 1.9.

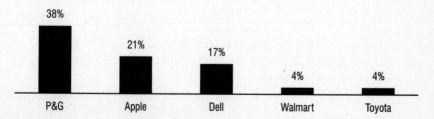

Figure 1.9 Who Does Supply Chain Best?

It is significant to note that each of these three companies pioneered both product and process innovation over the course of the history of supply chain management. They spawned new business models. For Apple to be successful, it required the definition of iTunes. Dell defined a make-to-order online business model. P&G's work on customer-driven supply chains drove market share.

Apple is a relative newcomer with few peer comparatives. P&G and Dell on the other hand have been focused on supply chain for many years with strong performance against their peer groups. We discuss P&G and Dell in the next section, and we share some insights on Apple in subsequent chapters.

PROCTER & GAMBLE: THE QUIET LEADER

Based on the evaluation by peers, over the course of the last 30 years, P&G is seen as the supply chain leader. With a dogged focus on the consumer, P&G has been on a mission to deliver a better response for shoppers in the store. The supply chain played a critical role in delivering on this brand promise.

Founded in 1837, the company closed fiscal 2011 with annual sales of $82.6 billion. Today, the company supports 300 brands in more than 80 countries. Twenty-two of the brands contribute more than $1 billion of annualized sales to the P&G topline.

The company has championed process innovation. In 2003, P&G introduced the term *customer-driven supply chain* to the market. It also pioneered top-to-top meetings with retailers, championed barcode product adoption, and automated store checkout in the late 1980s. In 2002, it built one of the first demand signal repositories to use channel data to sense demand.

Over (the past) nine quarters, we've organically added $7 billion to company sales. This is roughly equivalent to growing one Energizer and one Church & Dwight in a little over two years.
—Jon Moeller, Chief Financial Officer, Procter & Gamble,
Opening Statement at an Investor Conference, 2011

P&G is known for its brands and for delivery on the brand promise. The company's business strategy is enhanced by its supply chain efforts. As stated on P&G's website, the focus of its business strategy is:

- **More consumers**. We are improving more consumers' lives by innovating and expanding our product portfolio vertically, up and down value tiers. We continue to successfully develop and launch premium innovations focused on improving consumer value through enhanced performance. We are also serving consumers who are more price conscious through lower-priced offerings with superior performance versus other mid-tier and value-tier alternatives.

- **In more parts of the world**. We are improving lives in more parts of the world by innovating and expanding our existing product portfolio geographically into new markets. We are increasing our presence in developing markets and increasing the amount of sales from these markets by focusing on affordability, accessibility, and awareness of our brands.

- **More completely**. We are improving lives more completely by innovating to improve existing products and creating or entering adjacent categories. We are driving regimen use that broadens the occasions for which our brands can serve the needs of each consumer. By attracting new consumers into our existing brand franchises and broadening the products used by our current consumers, we are able to build scale, reduce costs, and profitably grow market share.

P&G was an early adopter of supply chain principles. The company was an early leader in the design of the supply chain organization. In 1985, the company moved source, make, and deliver teams to a single reporting relationship through one common organization globally. At the time, this organizational definition was unique and 10 years ahead of the market. Today, the organization operates in a matrix organization with four elements:

1. **Global business units** (GBUs) focus solely on consumers, brands, and competitors around the world. They are responsible for the innovation pipeline, profitability, and shareholder returns from their businesses.

2. **Market development organizations** (MDOs) are charged with knowing consumers and retailers in each market where P&G competes and integrating the innovations flowing from the GBUs into business plans that work in each country.

3. **Global business services** (GBSs) utilizes P&G talent and expert partners to provide best-in-class business support services at the lowest possible costs to leverage P&G's scale for a winning advantage.

4. **Lean corporate functions** ensure ongoing functional innovation and capability improvement.

This organizational structure enabled better alignment horizontally (across P&G's trading network) and vertically (within the company). It enabled the building of outside-in processes in global economies to sense demand and adapt the response. Consumer products companies are complex organizations. As each company in consumer products scrambled to enter the emerging economies of Brazil, Russia, India, and China, each company defined its supply chain organization differently:

- **Definition of global**. In this period, companies within the consumer products industry defined the term *global* differently. Most often it was not conscious. The definition evolved. The race was on. The definition was driven by a strong leader's vision.

  For P&G, it was by design. They moved quickly to build a global organization with a strong vision of global planning for local execution. They defined a matrix organization where global teams set standards, defined processes, and were trained to a common set of standards. While other companies had a global product footprint, and put strong energies into opening global channels, the organizational design for the supply chain team was different. For companies like Colgate, Johnson & Johnson, Kraft, and Unilever, the organization had strong regional autonomy. Companies like Campbell Soup, General Mills, Kellogg, and Kimberly-Clark were slow to create a global organization, and when they did it was primarily regional (North America and Europe).

- **Supply chain organization definition**. P&G was also an early mover to consolidate make, source, and deliver into a common organization. This holistic view enabled them to have a better discussion on trade-offs than their peers. In all of the other consumer products companies, as shown in Figure 1.10, there was stronger functional and regional autonomy. This made it more difficult to see and mobilize to take action on trade-offs. During the period 1985 to 2005, P&G was the only organization on the chart to have these supply functions reporting to one common global leader.
- **Technology selection**. Each of the companies also selected and adopted technology differently. While Colgate consolidated on a single vendor strategy, Unilever allowed the regions to select their own technologies. Unilever had lots of small projects with each region doing its own thing. In this period, P&G was consistently an early adopter of technology. It funded corporate development efforts and often worked with small vendors to drive innovation.

The company's progress in supply chain excellence is multidimensional. It is a business process innovator. As the reader will see in subsequent chapters, the company pioneered techniques in open innovation, global talent development, demand-driven manufacturing, and corporate social responsibility.

As technology matured, the possible span of control of a manager increased. . . . Technology enabled the effective management of larger teams.

—Keith Harrison, Global Product Supply Leader,
Procter & Gamble, 2001–2011

In preparation for this book, we looked at industry peer groups in automotive, apparel, high-tech and electronics, chemical, consumer products, and retail industries. In this data, we do not see another company that outpaced its peer group as fast as P&G did revenue/ employee and EBIT (earnings before interest and taxes)/employee over the last 20 years. We also do not see another leader within a peer group that demonstrated the capability to drive growth while maintaining inventory levels and reducing the cost of sales. These trends for consumer products companies are outlined in Figures 1.10 through 1.14.

P&G's supply chain leaders were among the early supply chain pioneers. They were primarily engineers. In conversations, they clearly understood that the supply chain was a system that had innate

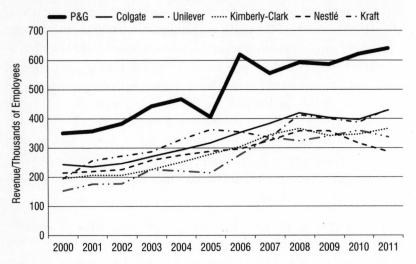

Figure 1.10 Comparison of Revenue/Employee for the Period 2000–2011

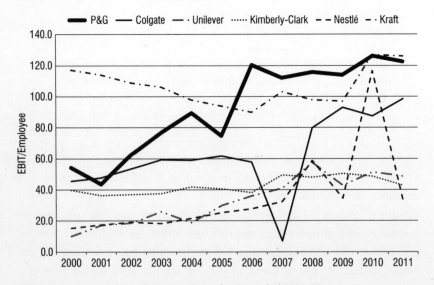

Figure 1.11 Comparison of EBIT/Employee for the Period 2000–2011

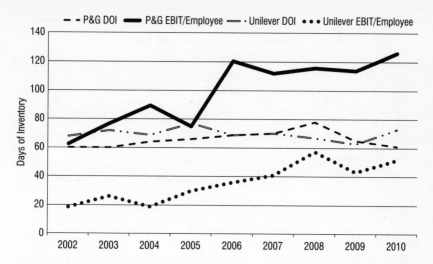

Figure 1.12 Comparison of EBIT/Employee Plotted against Days of Inventory for P&G/Unilever for the Period 2002–2010

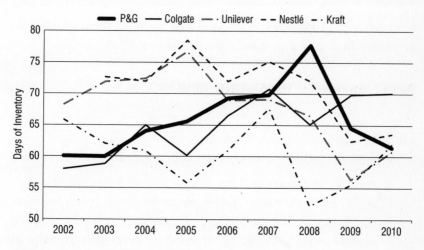

Figure 1.13 Consumer Products: Comparison of Days of Inventory for the Period 2002–2010

trade-offs between customer service, cost, asset utilization, and inventory. They attempted to redefine the potential of the supply chain by improving the effective frontier of their supply chain on many fronts: direct shipments to customers to reduce logistics costs, daily schedule changes at their factories to align to demand, co-located suppliers

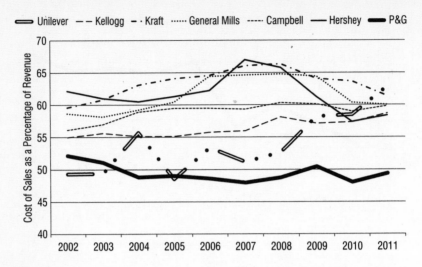

Figure 1.14 Consumer Products: Cost of Sales as a Percentage of Revenue for the Period 2002–2011

to improve the supply response, late-stage postponement to improve responsiveness, and a laser focus on continuous improvement.

APPLE AND DELL: INVENTING NEW MODELS

When asked, "Who does supply chain best?" the supply chain pioneers rated Apple and Dell as second and third in delivering supply chain excellence. In the design of their supply chains, there are many commonalities:

- **Process innovation**. Both Apple and Dell defined the supply chain to play a key role in delivering their brand promise. For Apple, one of the primary elements of delivering its brand promise was the design of iTunes. This innovative network to handle content and redefine the role of the supplier within this network helped to define the mobile experience. For Dell, it was the design of a make-to-order business model for online computer ordering that allowed customers to design their personal computer and track its progress through the value chain that drove market share.

- **Daily data used daily**. In each company, data matters. Dell and Apple run their supply chain on daily data used daily from the channel with a view from the outside-in. The leadership at both companies has valued data-driven decision making. They have each invested in systems to minimize data latency.

- **Integration with product innovation**. Each company values product innovation and has focused on building strong horizontal processes for the intersection of S&OP and new product launch.
- **Learning from failures**. Unlike P&G, both companies have stumbled in the last five years. Apple's supplier development issue bubbled up as a corporate social responsibility press issue with Foxconn in 2012. Likewise, Dell's challenge with channel redefinition that started in 2009 is ongoing.

When financial balance sheets are compared year over year, both companies have outperformed their peer groups. In Figures 1.15 through 1.17, Apple's and Dell's results are compared to their peer groups'.

When you contrast Apple and Dell to Motorola, it is easy to see why supply chain matters. The differences are many. Apple and Dell had a focused supply chain vision at the corporate level and it was embedded in the company strategy. Motorola did not. Motorola made

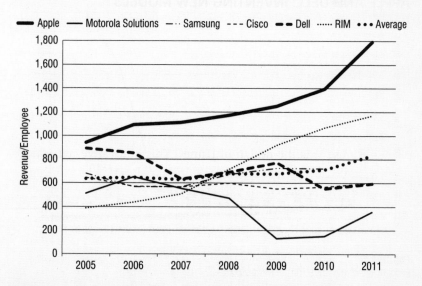

Figure 1.15 Comparison of High-Tech and Electronics Revenue/Employee for the period 2005–2011

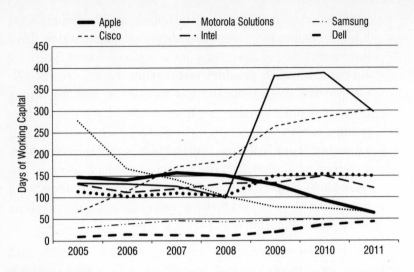

Figure 1.16 Comparison of Days of Working Capital in High-Tech and Electronics for the Period 2005–2011

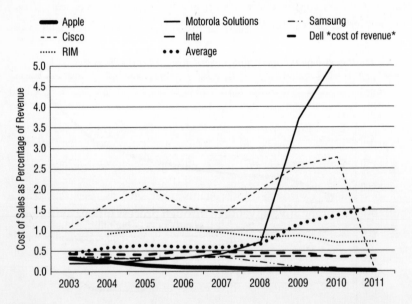

Figure 1.17 Comparison of High-Tech and Electronics Companies' Cost of Sales as a Percentage of Revenue for the Period 2003–2011

a choice to proliferate products without common platforms, and it did not define a supply chain for user-based content. As a result, the company lost its edge on innovation. The lack of downstream data sensing and advanced predictive analytics coupled with declining sales of new products caused Motorola to be hit hard by the recession. They were not able to weather the storm.

When we asked Dell founder, chairman, and CEO Michael Dell for his opinion, he replied, "Our supply chain has always enabled our business strategy—that is true of the early days of just-in-time manufacturing (the backbone of our direct model) to today's segmented and tightly integrated value chain that delivers a much broader portfolio of Dell solutions."

He continued, "It has been foundational for our success. For most of our company's history our direct business model—and the agile supply chain that drove it—were key differentiators for Dell. Constant feedback from our customers, partners, and suppliers gave us the insight that we needed to fine-tune our operations and deliver *only* the products and services that our customers wanted."

The big lesson for us was that the role of supply chain management goes beyond operational excellence and cost efficiencies. When done right, it enables new business models, creates competitive advantages in the marketplace and enhances brand equity for long-term customer value.

—Michael Dell, Founder,
Chairman, and CEO, Dell

In the balance sheet trends against peer groups, Dell and Apple both built a competitive advantage through process innovation. Today, supply chain excellence is no longer about operational excellence and costs; instead, when done right, it defines new business models and drives new forms of value.

The role of the supply chain is growing in importance. As product life cycles change, demand cycles get shorter, and supply chain cycles get longer, the supply chain needs constant alignment. For example, today, for a mobile phone or a personal computer, the time to manufacture and ship the product is one-third of the total life cycle. As a result, every step in the process is more important than before. It matters now more than ever.

TO DRIVE CHANGE

- Evaluate how the organization has defined supply chain excellence.
- Identify how many supply chains you have. Detail what is rewarded in each.
- Evaluate how the supply chain organization aligns with what you would like to reward.

SUMMARY

Today, with 30 years of supply chain history behind us, companies no longer have to stumble forward. Instead, they can harvest the insights from the pioneers and build value networks to drive lasting value.

In subsequent chapters, we share insights on five areas to start the journey. In Chapter 2, we discuss the growing importance of value networks. In Chapters 3 and 4, we share insights on demand and supply processes while in Chapter 5, we discuss how to make the right changes to define horizontal processes.

As many companies attempt to digest the multitude of technologies bequeathed to them from the prior generation of pioneers, it is a great time to reflect, to challenge traditional paradigms, and to make a fresh start. Historically, we have:

- **Tried to get precise on imprecise data**. Supply chains of the future will be based on ranges, they will dance agilely with error and adapt to changing supplier demands. The future is not the integrated supply chain; instead, it is about new forms of predictive analytics to deal with uncertainty.
- **Built efficient chains, but not effective networks**. As companies mature, they will realize that the future of their supply chains lies in the strength of the relationships at each end of the

value network. Today's supply chain has a strong center and weak ends. The ability to manage this holistically will define success and failure.

- **Focused inside-out, not outside-in**. As companies build sensing mechanisms, they will quickly learn that there is no place to put either demand or supply sensing data in traditional IT architectures. As a result, most will have to reimplement the technologies that they worked so hard to implement the first time.
- **Rewarded the urgent, not the important**. The natural inclination of the first-generation pioneers was to act. As technologies evolved to enable better planning, the tendency to reward the urgent over the important delayed the adoption of planning systems. As a result, companies rewarded reacting, firefighting, and jumping through hoops. The supply chains of the future will reward planning and the use of decision support tools.
- **Implemented projects without a holistic plan**. For most companies, the implementation of projects has been without a holistic plan. As companies now attempt to digest their many projects and technologies from the last 30 years, it will be hard for them to connect the dots and string them together. For many this will force reimplementation. Supply chain strategy matters more now than ever.

In the next chapters, we challenge these assumptions and share insights to help navigate the future.

NOTES

1. R. K. Oliver and M. D. Webber, "Supply-Chain Management: Logistics Catches Up with Strategy, Outlook, Booz, Allen and Hamilton, Inc." Reprinted in 1992 in *Logistics: The Strategic Issues*, ed. Martin Christopher, Chapman Hall, London, 63–75.
2. Amazon and Webvan Annual Reports, 2007–2009.
3. "Transora Is the Big Business Trading Exchange. But, What for Small Business?" Just-food, June 16, 2000, http://www.just-food.com/analysis/transora-is-the-big-business-trading-exchange-but-what-for-small-business_id94061.aspx.
4. Vinod R. Singhal, "The Effect of Supply Chain Disruptions on Long-term Shareholder Value, Profitability and Share Price Volatility," Ph.D. dissertation, Georgia Institute of Technology, Atlanta, GA, 2005.
5. Emily Nelson and Evan Ramstad, "Hershey's Biggest Dud Is its New Computer System," *Wall Street Journal*, October 29, 1999.

6. Thomas Wailgum, "10 Famous ERP Disasters, Dustups and Disappointments," CIO, March 24, 2009, http://www.cio.com/article/486284/10_Famous_ERP_Disasters_Dustups_and_Disappointments.

7. Patrick Thibodeau and Don Tennant, "HP's CIO Points to Internal Issues in ERP Project Snafus," *Computerworld*, September 27, 2004.

8. Bent Flyvbjerg and Alexander Budzier, "Why Your IT Project Might be Riskier than You Think," *Harvard Business Review* 89 (9), 23–25.

9. "Supply Chain Resilience 2011," Third Annual Survey, November 2011.

10. Josh Cable, "As Boeing and Airbus Ramp Up, It's Crunch Time for Aerospace Suppliers," *Industry Week*, March 10, 2012.

CHAPTER **2**

Building Value
Networks

You cannot save your way to value.

—Lora Cecere

While building the end-to-end value chain was their stated goal for the supply chain pioneers, it has not been their destination. Supply chain leaders have talked about building the end-to-end supply chain from the customers' customer to the suppliers' supplier for the last 30 years, but it is an unrealized aspiration. As we enter the fourth decade, the extended supply chain is an uncharted frontier. Conquering it will be a slow journey.

Let's start the discussion with definitions. When the supply chain is extended to a network of trading partners, it is termed a *supply network*. When the emphasis of this extended supply chain shifts from cost to value, it is called a *value chain*. When it becomes more strategic to the company, focused outside-in to drive value-based outcomes, it is termed a *value network*.

Here we discuss the journey from extended supply chains to value networks. We start with the discussion of how to move from a cost to value and then share insights on how to use this focus to build the right relationships. We then share lessons from the pioneers.

59

THE JOURNEY FROM COST TO VALUE

So, what is value? It can take many forms. Value happens when the supply chain is used to drive competitive advantage. The supply chain drives maximum value when it is aligned to the business strategy.

The best supply chains have a well-defined strategy to deliver the business goals to maximize value. They are fit for purpose. They are designed outside-in. Examples include the evolution of new business models, access to new channels and markets, acceleration of innovation, defining strategic sourcing relationships, or driving improvements in working capital. The options are many. In fact, there are so many possibilities that making a choice is sometimes an obstacle. Analysis paralysis can reign.

Cost savings are forgotten in a matter of months; the impact of creating value stays for many years.
—*William Cron, Senior Associate Dean for Graduate Programs and Research, Texas Christian University*

The Race to Become Global

Companies that committed to global growth early in the period from 2000 to 2005 accelerated corporate growth faster than their peer groups through the adoption of supply chain practices.

The changes happened quickly. In 1972, Richard Nixon and Henry Kissinger laid the groundwork for U.S. business expansion into China. In 1989, the fall of the Berlin Wall accelerated trade in the Eastern European block countries. Leadership in high-tech product innovation shifted from Japan to Korea in the late 1990s. The rise of the euro in 1998, and a single currency in Europe, changed the face of trade.

Changes in geoeconomic policy made expansion possible. Global brands were a new reality. While the first generation of supply chain professionals focused on the first brick of the supply chain—asset utilization—the second generation led the charge for the second brick of the supply chain. They were the boots on the ground to establish the global supply chain in emerging countries.

In the race to become global, there were multiple tipping points. New technology enabled new processes. For the first time, companies were able to plan globally to act regionally. These new technologies decreased the latency of data from weeks to days, allowing a near real-time status of orders, inventory, and shipments. Global visibility became a new reality. These changes widened the span of managerial control and improved organizational communication.

Global connectivity and the speed of communication also changed the dynamics of business. Air cargo became more widespread and a viable shipping method for international shipments. As the cost of computing decreased, data became more available, and information technology applications made it more usable. The investments in Y2K (year 2000) occurred at this dawn of global supply chain infrastructure.

The Stages

Supply chain globalization happened in multiple phases. The first stage was from 1999 to 2003. In this phase, companies opened regional offices, formulated channel strategies, and initiated work to open new channels. For some companies, global expansion was a drive to lower costs through the use of cheaper sources of labor; but for supply chain leaders, it was a quest for value.

To unleash the growth potential, supply chain processes needed reinvention. During this time, companies defined their global strategies and corporate processes. In this era, companies built teams and trained supply chain professionals.

Like a snake swallowing its dinner, companies are still digesting the myriad of technologies acquired in this period. The average company now has more than 150 distinctly different supply chain technologies. For example, only 27 percent of Fortune 1000 companies can easily measure total supply chain costs.

Companies are still rationalizing and stabilizing these global processes through supply chain centers of excellence and corporate initiatives. In the next decade, companies will capitalize on their supply chain investments of the prior decade. The promise of global market growth, as shown in Figure 2.1, is the driver.

Figure 2.1 Global Growth *Source:* "The World at Six Billion," United Nations, 2004; The World UN Population Assessment 2006; *Unsustainable World*, April 15, 2008, BBC

> *The biggest change for us was to migrate from a regional buy and sell model to a business model where we could design anywhere, ship anywhere, service anywhere. We wanted this to be one model of a car. We started in 2004, and we successfully built the first global vehicle in 2009 (OPAL Insignia).*
>
> —*CIO, General Motors*

Transitioning from Cost to Value

So, how do companies make the journey to build long-term value in their supply chains? How do organizations move from a myopic focus on cost to a more holistic view to drive value? There are three primary steps. The greatest impact happens when the following three steps are taken simultaneously.

Step One: Design for Value

As organizations mature, the conversations change. The discussion evolves from one only focused on cost to a more holistic picture of the supply chain adding value.

The degree of pace and change is based on organizational maturity. In the early stages of the supply chain (see Figure 1.3), teams are focused on transactional efficiency. The focus is on basic blocking and tackling. The focus is on improving the accuracy of the order-to-cash and procure-to-pay processes and getting the basics right in the areas of inventory management, logistics and delivery, and customer service. At this stage, the supply chain does not have the credibility to discuss anything other than improving the reliability of operations and reducing costs.

As team mature, they earn the right to talk about value. As the supply chain groups conquer the goal of delivering the right product to the right place at the right time at the right cost, they are able to engage in higher-level discussions. In the beginning, it starts as a cross-functional discussion of making the right trade-offs. At the next stage of the supply chain (resiliency), processes start to become horizontal and outside-in (market sensing). The focus then shifts to risk mitigation, demand sensing, and translation of market signals. At this stage, the organization slowly earns the right to improve the value in customer relationships. In our interviews of supply chain leaders, 80 percent of companies are working in stages 1 and 2 of the supply chain maturity model, as defined in Figure 1.3, and 15 percent are operating at stage 3.[1]

As the supply chain matures, supply chain leaders partner with the commercial teams to design outside-in processes that can better sense and shape demand. They use these insights to drive a more profitable response. In our interviews for this book, 5 percent of companies were at this stage of maturity, which is often termed *demand driven*.

With greater maturity, the company aligns the supply chain market to market to become market driven. In this stage, the supply chain senses buy- and sell-side market shifts and orchestrates trade-offs horizontally in a bidirectionally coordinated response. This represents less than 1 percent of companies interviewed.

Each stage requires progressive levels of outside-in thinking and design of horizontal processes. However, each level of maturity opens up new opportunities to add value—including driving innovation, creating new business models, and executing channel strategies—within the greater organization.

As the value discussion evolves, the need for a supply chain strategy becomes paramount. Business leaders want to know how they can align operational silos to improve the business strategy. This results in the development of a supply chain strategy. Figure 2.2 is a framework for this development.

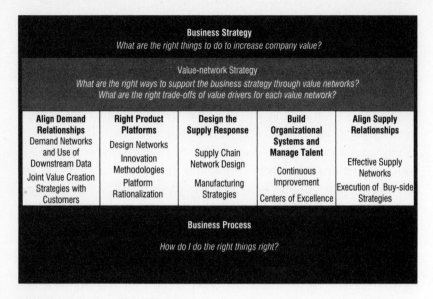

Business Strategy				
What are the right things to do to increase company value?				
Value-network Strategy				
What are the right ways to support the business strategy through value networks?				
What are the right trade-offs of value drivers for each value network?				
Align Demand Relationships	**Right Product Platforms**	**Design the Supply Response**	**Build Organizational Systems and Manage Talent**	**Align Supply Relationships**
Demand Networks and Use of Downstream Data	Design Networks	Supply Chain Network Design	Continuous Improvement	Effective Supply Networks
Joint Value Creation Strategies with Customers	Innovation Methodologies Platform Rationalization	Manufacturing Strategies	Centers of Excellence	Execution of Buy-side Strategies
Business Process				
How do I do the right things right?				

Figure 2.2 Supply Chain Strategy

The right place to start to maximize value is to design the supply chain. While most supply chain leaders believe that the starting place is process excellence, this is erroneous. The change from cost to value must start with strategy.

Step Two: Think Outside-in

Today's supply chain responds. It does not sense. It is a response based on internal data with no market sensing. If markets are stable, this is not a problem. However, if conditions are volatile—increases in competition, changing commodity prices, or significant changes in consumer confidence/economic cycles—this is problematic.

Market turbulence has increased. As a result, in 2011, 85 percent of companies experienced a major supply chain disruption. To drive resiliency and to improve supply chain reliability, companies must improve demand and supply sensing and drive dynamic decision making.

In stages one through two of the model outlined above (refer to Figure 1.3), the processes were designed inside-out: from the enterprise to the network. In this traditional design, the supply chain is insular. The supply chain is blind to what is happening in the market.

The only data used to make decisions is internal. Trading partner relationships are transactional. The parties share order-to-cash and procure-to-pay information, but little else. The focus is on transactional efficiency and cost mitigation. Processes are governed by inflexible rules. The organization responds, but it does not sense.

In stages three through five of the model, the processes become progressively outside-in (from the market into the enterprise). The focus shifts to the use of external data. To maximize value, companies focus on capturing market data with minimal latency at the lowest level of granularity and the highest level of frequency. The volume of data, the disparate data types, and the difference in data formats have given rise to data repositories for supply and demand market data. These repositories cleanse, harmonize, and synchronize data for enterprise usage. This shift to outside-in processes, the redesign of enterprise processes to sense before responding, is a major change management issue. It can also be painful. Why? In the evolution, companies find that many of the processes and technologies built over the last 30 years are obsolete.

Market sensing helps companies create and keep customers. As shown in Chapter 1, it lowers the cost of sales and general administration (SGA) expenses.

> The purpose of any business is to create and keep a customer.
> —Peter Drucker, Management Consultant

Step Three: Go Horizontal

To be effective at market sensing, companies have to build strong horizontal processes to connect downstream and upstream data. Traditionally, supply chain processes have evolved from vertical processes. These functional silos—source, make, and deliver—gave birth to supply chain management. However, this silo approach, and a focus on vertical excellence, is both a barrier and an enabler to maximize value and build strong networks. It is a conundrum. Companies need to build strong vertical silos to deliver operational excellence; but at some point in their maturity, they must "break the glass" and shift their focus to build horizontal excellence.

The shift from vertical silo excellence to building strong horizontal processes is necessary to connect the end-to-end supply chain. These horizontal processes help to drive alignment by translating market shifts into action. The driving forces include corporate social responsibility, revenue management, global tax efficiency, sales and operations planning, and supplier development. While excellence in vertical supply chain processes defined the first generation of supply chain excellence, the design and implementation of horizontal processes will define success for the third and fourth generations of supply chain professionals. We share insights on the design of horizontal processes in Chapter 5.

ALIGNING FOR SUCCESS

Leaders are still seeking a clear definition of supply chain excellence. Despite 30 years of investment in supply chain management, the definition is not clear. It remains a holy grail. In interviews, we asked, "What company defines supply chain excellence?"

Instead, of having one clear leader demonstrating supply chain excellence, the pioneers acknowledge that different companies have done *pieces* of the supply chain well. The examples are many. Walmart is known for everyday low costs. Procter & Gamble is famous for its customer-driven approach to redefining supply chains. Dell is remembered as a visionary for its definition of a new business model for online ordering of the personal computer. Amazon's leadership in transforming the e-commerce buying experience is legendary. Toyota is known for the development of lean practices. Intel is known for the advancement of supplier development and supply chain leadership training. The list goes on and on.

However, what is not clear to supply chain pioneers is how to manage day-to-day operations to drive value. In many ways, this race for supply chain excellence is analogous to competing in a triathlon. Why? A triathlon is a multisport event involving the completion of three continuous and sequential endurance events. The events can vary but are most frequently a combination of swimming, running, and biking. The goal is to be good, but not necessarily the best, at all three events. To prepare, the athlete needs to train for all three events, and during the competition, make the choice on trade-offs for the best finish.

Managing day-to-day operations in the supply chain is similar. The key to success is balanced leadership. Leaders excel at making these decisions. They understand that the most effective supply chain is not necessarily the most efficient. These leaders have also aligned the organization to a supply chain strategy to drive value. In this supply chain triathlon, while the events can vary by industry, the most common focus areas are the trade-offs among product costs, asset utilization, growth, and working capital. The potential of the supply chain is defined by the effective frontier of forecast accuracy, inventory requirements, customer service, and cost trade-offs (refer to Figure 1.1).

Just as an athlete is born with innate potential, the supply chain's potential is defined by this effective frontier. As the supply chain race progresses, the key decision is how to make sense of all the market data, and make the right choices to trade off these conflicting metrics to drive higher value through the execution of the supply chain strategy.

Like athletes preparing for a triathlon, companies have to train for each event. They have to be good at manufacturing and understand the levers of asset utilization. They have to have seamless order-to-cash and policies to drive customer service. Inventory policy, logistics strategies, and order execution have to be flawless. They need to sense market variability and understand the risk and opportunity with new product launches. There has to be clear governance of supply chain planning to execution. To be successful, the supply chain leader uses outside-in horizontal processes to make the right trade-offs against the supply chain strategy. It requires clean data with little latency, decision support tools, clarity on strategy, and alignment of the organization on what drives value in a value chain.

How Do I Transcend Supply Chain Design Concepts to Build Value Networks?

Supply chain processes are characterized by industry. The processes are very specific. As value chains are built, industries are coupled together to build extended supply chains. When industries focus on value-based outcomes, it is termed *value networks*.

The typical groupings are agricultural, aerospace and defense (A&D), automotive, consumer packaged goods, chemical, food and beverage, heavy and industrial equipment, high-tech and electronics (HT&E), hospitality, financial services, medical device, make-to-order discrete manufacturing, retail, oil and gas, semiconductor, pharmaceutical, software, and third-party logistics. (Note: There is no standard industry nomenclature for supply chains. These industry definitions will vary by source.)

To make a value network, trading partners from different industries form a chain and link together to drive an end-to-end supply chain solution. These links are forged to provide a set of products or services for the end customer. For example:

- **Defense and warfare value networks**. The combination of the armed services, government programs, A&D, logistics providers, and discrete manufacturers to provide goods and services for the deployment of effective missions.
- **Consumer-driven value networks**. The combination of retail, consumer manufacturers, logistics providers, and chemical suppliers to provide products for sale in retail channels.
- **Health-care value networks**. The combination of hospitals, clinics, insurance providers, medical device, and pharmaceutical companies focused on improving health-care services to patients.
- **Industrial value networks**. The combination of distributors, discrete manufacturers, industrial equipment companies, and logistics providers to service manufacturers, the building industry, and commercial operations.
- **Warranty value networks**. The service supply chain is often forgotten in the design of value networks. It includes service providers, airfreight forwarders, spare-parts distributors, and machine shops. Warranty claims are a valuable demand and supply sensing mechanism that can be tightly integrated for early warning and risk mitigation. Service policy is also a valuable differentiator.

Five Rules of Thumb

No matter which industry or which value chain, there are some common rules for the design of effective networks. Putting the pieces together in the right way is paramount to maximizing value. There are five rules of thumb:

1. **Variability increases with the number of nodes**. The more nodes that a value chain has in a design, the greater the variability, the more working capital required and the higher requirements for automation and supply chain visibility. Waste (unessential activities and costs) increases as the number of nodes increases. Whenever possible, look for opportunities to disintermediate the supply chain and reduce the number of nodes.

2. **Waste increases with the length of the supply chain**. The longer the supply chain, the more difficult it is to manage. Variability is amplified with each node. Long supply chains are the best fit for products with high volumes and low demand and supply variability.

3. **Coordination requirements increase with demand shaping and bifurcated trade relationships**. The greater the complexity in demand shaping and bifurcated trade arrangements (multiparty payments), the more important the need for value chain orchestration in the end-to-end value chain. The more complex multiparty payments are, the more waste in the network and the greater the issues with building strategic relationships. Demand shaping programs distort demand signals and increase supply chain risk.

   One of the most complex value chains for the distortion of trade is in the health-care supply chain. For example, the U.S. Medicaid drug rebate program applies rebate rules for new drugs, allowing states to collect on drugs provided through Medicaid's managed care organizations. The rules are changing and IT system flexibility is paramount. In the words of one medical device manufacturer, "If you have seen one rebate, you have seen one rebate." Why? Each is unique, and the process is complex. This company had 40,000 customers, 650,000 products, 30,000 contracts, 19 primary rebate types, 27 order types, and 12,000 types of sales. In Figure 2.3, the flows illustrate the complexity. Companies have inherited this design, but it is a barrier to progress. The future of health care will need to redesign these flows to improve value and reduce waste.

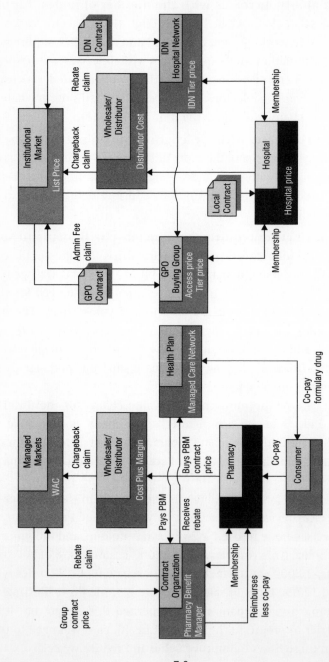

Figure 2.3 U.S. Medical Rebate System

There is a similar distortion in the consumer products value chain caused by trade promotion spending. The impact is significant. Promotion spending is the third line on the balance sheet of a consumer manufacturer. For the food retailer, this spending adds costs and shifts demand without adding value. Consider that Kroger, an $82 billion grocery retailer, reported a net profit of $1.1 billion in 2010 but received over $6 billion in trade allowances from suppliers.[2] When the food retailer makes more money on the buy rather than the sell, the focus for supply chain effectiveness is lost, the need to pursue new technologies is limited, and the execution at store level is problematic.

The practice of money passing hands as a tax does not create value. In addition, there are issues with execution. Based on in-store surveys, sensing of in-store data, and compliance audits, more than 45 percent of trade promotions in the consumer value chain are not executed at the store level. This leads to shopper frustration and failed promises.

4. **The more borders, the greater the cost and the increased need for coordination**. Each time that a supply chain crosses a country's border, there is increased need for compliance, security, and trade documentation. This has given rise to free trade zones and freight forwarding services; but in general, supply chain design should focus on fewer border crossings. Every time that a product crosses a border and is slowed down for inspection or incurs a fine or tax, there is a loss of value.

5. **Design for push and pull and push/pull decoupling points**. Like a tug-of-war, within the supply chain, there are push and pull relationships between trading partners at each node. For leaders, this is a conscious design element in the determination of supply chain strategy.

In general, a pull-based supply chain is easier to manage; however, it is not always realistic. For example, in process industries that are asset intensive—chemical or paper supply chains, where it takes days and weeks to start up a factory— a pull-based supply chain is not feasible. However, these process intensive companies can make improvements by designing push/pull decoupling points as part of a network strategy. This includes inventory postponement, the use of semifinished goods (intermediates and active ingredients), and common platforms for recipes for late-stage manufacturing. The push/pull nature of relationships can also change as demand and supply cycles shift with promotion, seasonality, and new product launches. They require ongoing design.

Within these value chains, change happens frequently. Relationships come and go. The value chain is characterized by the number of nodes in the network, the number and type of constraints, the variability of demand and supply, the rhythms and cycles of decisions, the products and shipments, and the latency of information. Five years ago, the design of supply chains and value networks was an ad hoc process. Today, over 35 percent of companies have planning teams to rationalize the design and refine the network for current conditions. In our interviews, we learned that these teams are growing in both size and importance.

A value network is a higher-level concept than a supply chain. It is a commitment by multiple parties to work together for a shared outcome. These relationships are more strategic and are governed by contracts, scorecards, and performance to compliance standards. These networks enable new capabilities. They allow the company to sense and adapt to market forces. They can bring new assets, capabilities, or intellectual property to the supply chain through joint innovation.

BUILDING OF VALUE NETWORKS

In the development of the supply chain strategy, there is a critical question for each company to answer. It is, "How and what should be outsourced?" Outsourcing to third parties can happen in all supply chain links—sales, distribution, manufacturing, procurement, and innovation—in building a value chain. It can add value, reduce costs, and improve time to market, but it increases the need for planning, supply chain coordination of day-to-day activities and inventory, and visibility. Although companies can outsource their day-to-day supply chain activities, they cannot outsource the responsibility for the outcomes. This additional layer of management and oversight is defined as network orchestration.

The questions surrounding outsourcing and the building of strategic relationships through value networks are answered in the development of the supply chain strategy. This is easier said than done. It is ongoing. Most supply chains are complex.

How Many Supply Chains Do I Have?

In the development of a supply chain strategy, executives encounter a gnarly issue. They struggle to answer the question, "How many supply chains do I have?" Most executives see them as a tangled, unruly, and knotted mass. Is it one? Or is it many? Over the history of supply chain management, this tangled mass has historically been treated as one supply chain; yet, supply chain professionals know intuitively that they do not have just one supply chain. They also know that if they could unravel them and better align their goals, that they could drive higher levels of supply chain performance. The question for most is, "How?"

The goal is to identify the number and types of supply chains to improve the supply chain response. Most organizations have five to seven supply chains. Each one can be at different levels of maturity. Each one can require its own response. In general, in the design of supply chains, there are three types. They can be characterized by the type of response:

1. **The efficient supply chain**. This supply chain is focused on the lowest cost/case. There are five characteristics. Demand and supply variability is predictable, volumes are high, supply chain reliability is high, demand-shaping activities are low, and the raw material costs are stable.

2. **The agile supply chain**. In the agile supply chain, demand and supply volatility are high and volumes are low. The agile supply chain is designed to deliver the same cost, quality, and level of service given the level of demand and supply variability. These supply chains are not the lowest cost, and must be redesigned continually as supply and demand volatility changes.

3. **The responsive supply chain**. The responsive supply chain is designed for short cycles. This supply chain has high volumes, but also high demand and supply variability due to factors like seasonality, weather, short life cycles, and high levels of demand shaping in the channel.

By definition, the responsive supply chain does not operate at the lowest cost. A premium is required to reduce the cycles in the supply chain. The issue for many supply chain leaders in the design and adoption of the responsive supply chain is quantifying the value of time. While many companies desire a supply chain with all three characteristics—efficient, agile, and responsive—it is not realistic. These three outcomes have distinctive trade-offs. It requires a choice. The potential of each one is driven by improving the effective frontier of forecast, customer service, and inventory trade-offs. The goal needs to be clear in the supply chain design, allowing the company to focus on the primary outcome. (We focus on the application of these concepts to manufacturing strategies in Chapter 4.)

The Journey

When asked, "How many supply chains does the team have?" often the supply chain group knows the answer intuitively. They look beyond items or assets. They think in terms of supply chain drivers and variability. It is a discussion of rhythms and cycles. The challenge is to have the entire organization think holistically and be inclusive of all supply chains when developing a design. Some examples are:

- **Agriculture**. These supply chains are driven by the dynamics of agricultural cycles—preparation, planting, harvest, and packaging—and weather. As a result, these supply chains need to be designed for agility around these four moments of truth.
- **Apparel**. The design of apparel supply chains typically boils down to three supply chain types: fashion, basic, and personalized items. Each of these supply chains has a different rhythm and cycle. The supply chain for basic items can be long and efficient. The supply chain for fashion items needs to be short and responsive based on the season. The supply chain for

personalized items needs to be agile. Each one needs a different type of supply chain design supported by the alignment of supply chain relationships and value networks.

■ **Food**. The food supply chain is usually defined by product handling characteristics. This could be the management of an expensive ingredient or a type of storage. In these supply chains, supply chain leaders will often speak of frozen, refrigerated, or dry supply chains. Alternatively, they may reference terms like *shelf-stable* and *short life cycle* or *open-code date supply chains*.

These supply chains are heavily driven by commodity markets and product handling considerations. The supply chain response will be driven by the input costs and the market opportunity. For example, a short life cycle supply chain with high volumes will need to be responsive whereas a product with a long shelf life supply chain and high volume can be designed for an efficient response.

■ **Consumer packaged goods (CPG)**. The most common type of CPG supply chain is based on flows: turn volume, promoted volume, and new product introductions. Turn volume (frequently ordered products with stable demand) supply chains are designed to drive an efficient response. Heavily promoted items require a responsive supply chain and new products need an agile supply chain. New product introductions introduce the greatest variability and risk. The challenge is adapting the supply chain over time as companies launch promotions and new products into the market.

■ **Consumer electronics**. These supply chains are often typed by the combination of variability (demand and supply) and life cycle. Supply chains focused on product delivery of items with short life cycles and high demand/supply variability need to be designed for agility. Products with long life cycles with low variability can be designed for efficiency. IBM, a leader in supply chain design, tackled this problem in an innovative manner. The company would launch products using in-house manufacturing assets with goals aligned around agility; as the product matured, the supply chain design would shift to be more efficient using third-party global manufacturing locations. The company was an early leader in recognizing that the long, extended supply chain was only effective when there was minimal supply and demand volatility.

■ **Discrete manufacturers**. These supply chains are often characterized by platforms (sometimes termed *programs*) and warranty/service agreements. For make-to-order discrete companies, the supply chains can also be defined by degree of configuration and labor input. A frequent mistake in these industries is to forget about the design of their service supply chains. In the design of these supply chains, the platforms and inputs need to be analyzed for variability and volume to determine if the outcome needs to be efficient (high volume with little variability), responsive (short cycles based on premiums), or agile (priced for quick turns and flexibility).

■ **Pharmaceuticals**. These supply chains are driven by usage. These companies often have three supply chains. There is a need for an efficient supply chain: products that have low variability and stable demand. There are products in the innovation pipeline or in clinical trials that depend on an agile supply chain. There is also a need for a high volume supply chain with high variability. Why? We will never be able to predict when the sun will shine for the sale of suntan lotion or when there will be a flu epidemic.

■ **Specialty chemicals**. These supply chains are often typed by active ingredients or molecules. Demand is usually predictable, and the focus is on the management of the supply chain by supply characteristic.

The key to supply chain excellence is typing the supply chain (recognizing the rhythms and cycles) and aligning the design of these cycles with the value-based outcome through relationship building in both channel and sourcing relationships. Leaders evolve the supply chain design over time, changing the goal based on market drivers. They use top-to-top meetings to define winning relationships at the ends of the many supply chains. It is an ongoing process.

BUILDING VALUE NETWORKS

Value networks do not just happen. Extending the supply chain outward from the enterprise through strategic relationships is an integral piece of the supply chain strategy. It takes time. It is a staged progression. Concentrated effort and a shared vision are essential. Network orchestration is critical.

To extend the supply chain from an internal to an external focus requires skills, incentives, resources, planning, and leadership. There are many stops and starts. Relationships need to be treated differently based on importance, capabilities, and strategic alignment. Before companies can build successful value networks, they have to be clear on what determines value in the supply chain strategy.

Three Primary Types of Extended Value Networks

There are three primary forms of networks to help the supply chain leader improve value: demand, supply, and innovation. These can operate singularly or together. They usually have a different flavor by industry.

The greatest and most lasting impact on value happens when they converge and support the supply chain strategy. We find that supply chain leaders are often good at all three types, while supply chain laggards have not begun to define these critical network relationships.

1. **Demand networks**. These outside-in networks improve the timeliness and depth of demand insights from the channel. They shorten the time to sense channel demand and improve demand shaping to drive a more profitable response. These are the most mature in consumer-facing value networks. Leaders include Apple, Dell, General Mills, Kraft, PepsiCo, Procter & Gamble, and Samsung.

2. **Supply networks**. Supply relationships focus on improving the effective sourcing of materials and services. In this type of network, the cycles and relationships of supply are designed to improve value. The most mature supply networks are found in discrete value networks of A&D, HT&E, and retail value chains. Leaders include Boeing, Food Lion, Herman Miller, Toyota, Walmart, and Walgreens.

3. **Innovation networks**. In the third type of network—innovation—the principles of open design accelerate the time to market for new products and business models. Innovation networks are not prevalent in one industry segment; instead, the presence of an innovation network is usually attributable to the legacy of an insightful leader. Companies demonstrating leadership in innovation networks include Boeing, Kraft, General Mills, Procter & Gamble, and Toyota.

Partnering to Maximize Value

Companies often go into these relationships haphazardly without designing for success. This can result in confusion, anxiety, false starts, or slower change than desired. Procter and Gamble (P&G), a leader in value chain relationships, learned this the hard way. Because of the lack of alignment, the company experienced five years of disappointing results in retail collaboration. From its work on the pilots, P&G learned to ensure that the organization was aligned on all elements at the *start* of the relationship to improve the odds of success. It successfully applied this learning to the implementation of efficient consumer response (ECR) relationships with retailers. This is summarized in Figure 2.4. As a result, P&G has ranked higher in managing retail relationships in third-party studies than any other consumer products manufacturer for the past 15 years.

Relationships come in many forms. Some, based on size or importance, are strategic. Most are transient and tactical. They can change over time. Trading partners can gain or lose power. Value network design is based on understanding both the nature and the power positions of the players. As a result, it is an ongoing exercise. Success in value networks never starts with process, people, or technology. It should always start with strategy. After a clear definition of the strategy, the process can be defined and value maximized.

Weathering the Changes over Time

In value chain relationships, shifts happen. These are continuous. And the design of the relationship needs to be ongoing. The team needs to

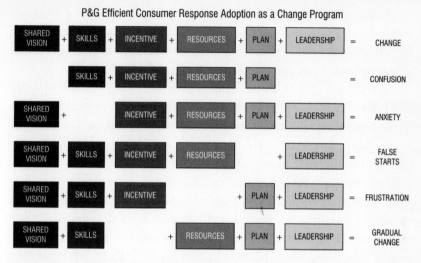

Figure 2.4 Organizational Alignment to Improve Value Chain Relationships
Source: Procter & Gamble, based on J. P. Kotter's framework

sense changes, to respect power positions, and to take advantage of opportunities.

The first is a change in power. This change can take many forms: regulations and compliance, preferential channel relationships, access to data, changes in technology, or company size. Examples include a pharmaceutical company losing or gaining patent protection. Eli Lilly, over the next seven years, will lose patent protection on drugs that accounted for 74 percent of its sales in 2009. This shift in patent protection will reduce Eli Lilly's power in the extended supply chain. Another example is access to preferential channel relationships or data. In 2011, AT&T was given exclusive channel rights to sell the iPhone for two years. Power shifted when this right was given to Verizon. Similarly, Walmart gained power in the grocery supply chain through the sharing of data with its suppliers.

The most pervasive power shifts are driven by technology. The changes in media—the shift from advertising on national television to micro-marketing—has transferred power in the consumer supply chain from manufacturer to retailer. The use of social technologies has shifted power from the retailer to the shopper. Apple's invention of iTunes consolidated power in entertainment. As these changes happen, the rhythms and cycles of the supply chains change, and the effectiveness of demand shaping programs change. This results in the rethinking of demand shaping tactics.

The second shift is *disintermediation*, or the change in the number and type of players in the value network. E-commerce enabled disintermediation and the creation of new business models. The changes in regulation in the U.S. telecommunications industry resulted in the redefinition of the structure of the value network.

Supply chain leaders move quickly to take advantage of power shifts and disintermediation. They also make supply chain design a priority. It becomes an end-to-end network modeling activity. They realize that as time progresses, value networks need to be modified, evolved, and upgraded. It also requires training and trading partner onboarding. Aspirations need to be continually aligned with capabilities. When capabilities are not equal to the task, supplier development efforts are used to help close the gap.

However, how do you make the design last? How do you maximize value? The key is the relationship design. Network relationships can only be sustained when there is a sustainable win/win value proposition between the two parties. The relationship needs to weather changes and transcend time. As power positions in the supply chain shift, it needs to adapt without breaking. If the value proposition is a one-sided view, or is not reevaluated on an ongoing basis, it will break.

The ends of the supply chain are fragile and the traditional definitions of customer relationship management and effective supplier relationship management are not designed to be value network adaptors. As value networks mature, new adaptors will evolve with a redefinition of enterprise architectures from the outside-in.

WHY ARE VALUE NETWORKS SO HARD TO BUILD?

The evolution of supply chain management practices to build effective networks is slow. It is painful and often not well understood.

Supply chains are complex. Today, companies span more markets. The need for market-segmentation is increasing. Companies have more products. Demand and supply cycles have greater volatility. Risks are higher. The race to become global, along with the acceleration of merger and acquisition (M&A) activities, has made organizations larger.

In parallel, companies have become more dependent on third-party trading relationships. Outsourced manufacturing and logistics are today's reality. Companies today find that they need to plan globally to execute locally across a diverse network bidirectionally; yet, the functional leaders are not incented to build value networks. To effectively plan, companies need to value the important, but the metrics reward the urgent.

Leaders look at the problem and wonder, "Why isn't it easier?" Supply chain collaboration to build the most effective end-to-end value network sounds simple, but it has not happened effectively. Why? There are some basic problems:

- **Frayed ends**. The ends of the supply chain are fragile. They lack alignment. This is especially problematic in two areas: sales and procurement. Sales organizations are typically incented on volume sold. As a result, the sales organization is rewarded for the transaction, not for driving value through the relationship. In a similar manner, the procurement organization struggles to drive value. The typical procurement organization is measured on landed cost. As a result, it is difficult to get organizational support in procurement for anything other than reducing costs.

- **Penny-wise and pound-foolish**. The natural tendency is for companies within a supply chain to compete instead of collaborate. Buying and selling relationships are managed for the lowest cost. This traditional focus on the transaction and driving the lowest cost does not translate to the highest value for both parties. While companies talk about corporate social responsibility, open design networks, quality, shared intellectual property, and service networks, few companies bring these factors into the buying decision. Leaders put their money where their mouth is while laggards talk about value and buy-on cost.

- **Clarity of supply chain strategy**. A value network is the alignment of the strategies and actions of multiple companies to deliver greater value. When successful, the sum is greater than the parts. The lack of a clear value chain strategy is problematic. Many well-intended organizations have disconnected processes, random projects, and no road map. Many consultants advise companies to start with a process, and as a result, the supply chain has many processes that are not aligned.

- **A focus within the four walls**. Traditionally, supply chain processes are focused on what a company can effectively accomplish within the company's four walls. (Examples of this include: Lean manufacturing, and multiyear technology projects [e.g., enterprise resource planning investments], and advanced planning system rollouts.) Millions of dollars are tied up in these traditional projects. As a result, the shift toward outside-in horizontal processes is slow. Value network investments for supplier relationship management for risk mitigation, effective corporate social responsibility, and safe and secure supply chains drive change toward the building of value networks but are progressing slowly.

- **Reward systems**. The emphasis is on the most efficient or lowest cost procure-to-pay and order-to-cash processes. While many companies have scorecards for suppliers and customers, at the end of the day, the majority of these scorecards are not used in the buying decision. As long as the buying and selling of goods is driven by lowest cost criteria, scorecards for social responsibility, customer service, and innovation will only be given lip service.

- **Competition**. The focus on the efficient transaction pushes costs and working capital backward in the supply chain. The realization that the most effective supply chain is not the most efficient is only understood by a few leaders.

We live in a world where supply chains, not companies, compete for market dominance. But companies often have diverging incentives and interests from their supply chain partners, so when they

*independently strive to optimize their individual objectives, the
expected result can be compromised.*

—Hau Lee, Stanford University

_____

A CLOSE-UP: TAKING A CLOSER LOOK AT A VALUE NETWORK WITHIN THE CONSUMER VALUE CHAIN

To illustrate these points, let's take a closer look at a specific industry—consumer products—and the dynamics of its underlying value network. The consumer value chain is composed of many companies. It stretches from the consumer through a network of retailers, manufacturers, and suppliers. Other industries—transportation, third-party logistics firms, freight forwarders, and marketing agencies—play supporting roles. It is not linear. Instead, it is a network of hundreds of companies. Each company within the chain operates multiple supply chains. The industry has worked hard to be collaborative; however, today few interactions are truly collaborative. They lack alignment and a win-win value proposition that can sustain the test of time.

One source of tension is market growth potential. The growth of the consumer manufacturing industry has been much slower than that of retail. While growth by retailers was regional, growth by consumer products was primarily in the emerging economies of Asia, Africa, Europe, and South America. As consumers tightened their wallets in the economic downturn, sales growth in the food and beverage products category increased.

The second is innovation. Although manufacturers and retailers agree that the lifeblood of the consumer products industry is innovation, there is tension. In the past 15 years, new items have grown from 7 to 15 percent of all items scanned into a consumer's basket and two-thirds of brand growth for the consumer manufacturer is derived from new product innovation. However, in the last 22 years, the average number of items in the average U.S. grocery store grew threefold. The number of items grew 10 times faster than retail store profit. As products have proliferated at the store, the retailer is struggling for space. This has led to frustration in top-to-top meetings between grocery

Table 2.1 Growth by Industry Sector of the Consumer Value Chain

Years	Average Year-over-Year Growth per Period				
	1990–1994	1995–1999	2000–2004	2005–2009	2010–2012
Grocery Retail	17.05%	42.46%	12.89%	8.76%	5.15%
Consumer Packaged Goods	2.12%	.84%	3.91%	7.26%	2.32%
Food and Beverage	3.68%	2.97%	8.13%	2.59%	4.27%

Source: Compiled information from financial balance sheets from 1990 to 2012 of Fortune 500 companies.

retailers and consumer manufacturers. There is a lack of alignment on the goal of how to best serve the shopper at the shelf.

If it were based on effort, the relationships should be stronger. There is no supply chain that has sponsored more industry programs to build value chain collaboration than the consumer-driven value chain. They were many. Over the last 10 years, there have been a myriad of programs to improve collaboration: ECR, collaborative forecasting and replenishment, the Voluntary Inter-industry Commerce Solutions Association, and the Foundation for Strategic Sourcing Association. However, the industry has made little progress. There are four fundamental issues:

Issue 1: True collaboration requires a sustainable win-win value proposition. The first issue is that the goals of the companies are not aligned within the value network. For a network to be successful, there needs to be a shared outcome with supporting metrics that are shared by all parties. True collaboration can only happen when there is a sustainable win-win value proposition. In Figure 2.5, we share a simplistic overview of this consumer value chain. The goals are not aligned. This can be rectified by having all of the parties in the value chain focus on a joint outcome. This is usually the "shelf" or the "basket."

Issue 2: Tackling demand distortion and waste. The number of nodes in the supply chain increases variability. Data latency and distortion happen in each step, or node, of the supply chain. In the building of value networks, the greatest potential value and usually

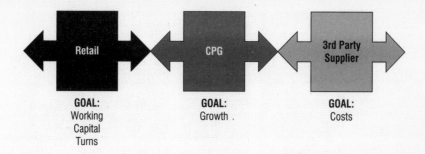

Figure 2.5   Goal Alignment, and the Lack thereof, within the Consumer Value Network

the least power to implement the necessary changes happens in the last link of the supply chain. In the consumer value chain, there are usually four parties in the value network: retailer, manufacturer, supplier, and logistics services provider.

Despite investments in technology and connectivity, companies within the consumer value chain have not reduced the bullwhip effect (distortion of the demand signal at each node) within their value network. This distortion coupled with the length of the supply chain (20 to 30 weeks) increases costs and waste for all parties. This is shown in Figure 2.6.

Note: The bullwhip effect and demand distortion worsens in the emerging economies of Brazil, Russia, India, and China.

The end result is an offset in the demand signal by days or weeks. It varies by organization, and it is a key parameter to correct to become market driven. Figure 2.7 is a depiction of the offset of the signal in a supply chain. By focusing on gaining a better understanding of channel data and correcting for the lag times in data latency, the company reduced shelf out-of-stocks at Walmart retail stores in 2010 by 60 percent. Companies like Kimberly-Clark, Kraft, and Procter & Gamble have found that out-of-stocks at the store level were four times worse than originally believed. Out-of-stocks can only be solved at a store level based on demand sensing of in-store data.[3]

The bullwhip impact varies both by industry and by geography. While it varies by company, the general trend in Table 2.2 illustrates the problem.

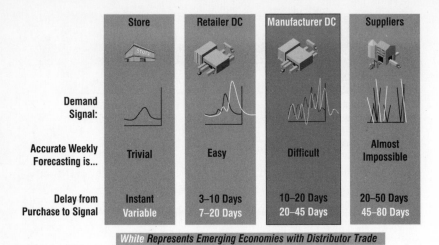

Figure 2.6 Demand Distortion (Bullwhip Effect) within the Food Manufacturing Network

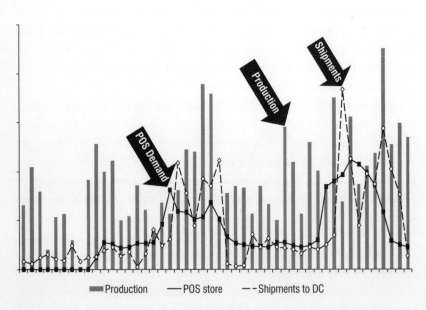

Figure 2.7 Traditional Supply Chains do not Respond Fast Enough with Market Data to Self-Correct

Table 2.2 Demand Latency and Demand Distortion in Food Manufacturing Channels

Supply Chain Type	Demand Latency from Shelf to Order	Order Cycle Time	Manufacturing Cycle
Modern Trade to Retail	10–14 days	3 days	10–20 days
Emerging Markets	40–48 days	1 day	30–40 days
Food Service	24–35 days	2–3 days	30–40 days

While companies know that there is waste between companies and the links of the supply chain, companies lack incentives to seize the opportunity. For example, in 2010, a major consumer products food company had an opportunity to implement a system to reduce shrinkage on short-code date products by 3 percent. The investment had a one-month payback. However, the project could not get funding. Why? The reason was clear: The dollars (savings) were not in any one person's budget. The chief financial officer would not approve the project without a definitive return on investment (ROI) from a specific budget within the company. In an industry forum, there was a group discussion on the need for a definitive return on investment to fund this type of pilot. The group laughed when one industry leader pushed back and said, "If my company needed a definitive ROI on technology then the company would never have invested in personal computers. We need to invest in the future. This is a form of innovation that we need to fund." However, for the specific company on stage, the project was not worth the fight. The distortion of the signal and the resultant shrinkage for write-offs was just accepted as a cost of doing business.

Issue 3: Joint ownership of value-based outcomes. In the consumer value network, in the period of 1985 to 2000, power shifted from the consumer manufacturer to the retailer. To better compete, the industry consolidated 57 companies into 10.

Recent trends in social media, e-commerce shopping, and product personalization have recently shifted power from the retailer to the consumer. As the power equation changed within the value chain, competition increased and margins became tighter. To improve competitiveness, the parties shifted the burden of the costs and working capital backward in the value chain.

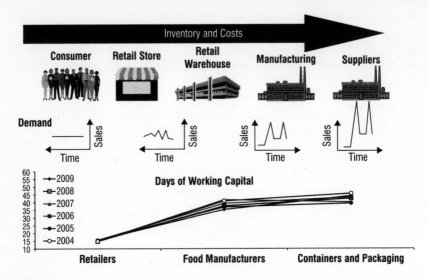

Figure 2.8 Working Capital within the Food Manufacturing Value Network

Retailers pushed supply chain costs back on manufacturers, and manufacturers pushed the costs back on suppliers. In Figure 2.8, the pushing back of inventory costs is detailed in the consumer value chain. This has happened, year over year, for the past 20 years. The cost of the total supply chain is going up. The irony is that the weaker players of this supply chain—both in brand presence and in cost of capital—are at the end of the chain. The second irony is that upstream companies are forced to eat these costs with a markup in yearly negotiations. Year over year, these added costs of inventory and write-offs become embedded in the cost of goods sold.

The pushing back of costs in the value chain makes the network more fragile and, ironically, as economic volatility increases and compliance regulations get more stringent (e.g., in this case, food safety legislation), the parties within the supply chain become more dependent on each other. In the Great Recession of 2008, suppliers at the end of the value chain felt the pinch more than at the front of the chain. Many ceased to exist. For example, Smurfit-Stone (a major supplier of corrugated paper boxes to the consumer manufacturer) went bankrupt. With increasing compliance and pending economic shifts, the entire value chain needs strong players.

Issue 4: Fragile ecosystem. If the supply chain was a play, the logistics providers would get the best supporting actor's award. With the problems with governmental regulation, rising energy prices, and declining infrastructure abound, capacity has tightened. As a result, volumes are half of pre-recovery levels from the recession; but the capacity, especially in air and truck logistics modes, is almost fully engaged. In North America, the recession had a devastating impact on capacity, removing 16 percent of available truckload capacity from the value chain. Leaders work to build strong ecosystems. Laggards work passively to minimize the impacts within their network, but do not take responsibility for the greater whole.

In the creation of value networks, the company's focus changes. It requires a holistic view. It becomes less tactical and more focused on driving long-term sustainable value. The supply chain can become the engine of growth. The network becomes the enabler. It is no longer about money moving from one company to another. Instead, it is a discussion of value.

Finance is the art of passing money from hand to hand until it finally disappears.
>   —*Robert W. Sarnoff, Chairman, RCA*

VALUE CHAIN CASE STUDIES

While companies talk about networks, the creation of demand, supply, and innovation networks requires focus, time, and effort over many years. Here we share case studies of three companies that drove success and follow with examples where failure in the network created market turbulence.

SUCCESS IN CREATING VALUE IN VALUE NETWORKS

One of the little-known facts about the success of Apple and Dell is the conscious design of their supply chains to use daily channel data daily. When they launched their new business models, they designed the processes to use daily demand data to build outside-in processes.

In interviews, no supply chain leaders in either company could imagine running operations without daily demand data. The insights to be gained from updated channel views are too important to managing a dynamic supply chain.

The use of daily data used daily as a demand feed is not unique to Apple and Dell. Another early adopter in the use of point of sale data was Scotts Miracle-Gro. The company markets and manufactures consumer lawn and garden products.

CASE STUDY

DEMAND NETWORKS: SCOTTS MIRACLE-GRO

In 2004, Scotts Miracle-Gro faced a crisis. Retailers were unhappy, sales were lagging, and on-shelf availability was an issue. Because of demand volatility (a combination of season, climate, weather, consumer preference and competitive behavior), Scotts' traditional supply chain systems were just not up to the task of delivering the right product at the right time at the right place. The lack of supply chain reliability had become a major issue in their three major retail relationships: Home Depot, Lowe's, and Walmart. This was significant. These three relationships represented more than 80 percent of the company's channel volume.

The company responded by building a demand network. This included item by store by day information for these three retailers. Using this data, sales teams were alerted within 24 hours on retail outages. Planning systems were redesigned to include daily in-stock analysis, seasonal planning, and sales reporting. The benefits were large. Shelf availability improved 50 percent, forecast error improved by 60 percent, and the company saved more than $4 million ($2 million from not having to transfer product from store to store and more than $2 million in rework charges). These changes also allowed them to improve order management.

Errors were reduced. In the prior system, more than 40 percent of the orders required manual adjustments to align orders with out-of-stock conditions. The design of the demand network used downstream data (point of sale and store demographic data) and outside-in processes to shorten the latency of demand data and improve replenishment.

In summary: A product category like lawn and garden care is a high volume product with variable demand due to weather, season, and pestilence. Shortening the time to sense channel demand is paramount in the design of a responsive supply chain like Scotts Miracle-Gro.

Supply Networks: Walmart Retail Link

Walmart now tops the Fortune 500 list. For the last 25 years, the company has outperformed competitors. One of the reasons is Walmart's investment in supply chain management. A competitive advantage is Walmart's building and usage of a supplier network termed *Retail Link*. Today, you would not think of being a supplier to Walmart without the use of the Walmart Retail Link.

Founded in Rogers, Arkansas, in 1962, the company has progressively invested in technology and new approaches. It was not a big bang approach but a steady investment that was focused on building sustaining value through the automation of stores and building supplier networks.

Early investments in inventory management were foundational. In 1975, the company installed inventory control systems to produce income statements for each store. This investment in store execution level to see inventory on a daily basis was an essential element for Walmart's soon-to-be supplier network. (For reference, today only 60 percent of North American grocery stores have perpetual inventory management systems installed at the store level.)

Subsequent investments formed the basis for the Walmart Retail Link. In 1977, the company implemented one of the first companywide computer networks to order merchandise from suppliers. In 1982, the company was an early adopter to use bar codes to scan point-of-sale data. In 1992, Walmart rolled out the Retail Link network system to strengthen supplier partnerships. The system provided daily data daily on sale trends and inventory levels. In 1996, Walmart made the Retail Link and electronic data interchange available via the Internet and began using the Internet as an application platform. In 2005, the Retail Link system had approximately 100,000 registered users running more than 350,000 queries a week.

Today, the Walmart Retail Link is a prerequisite to do business with Walmart for a supplier. It has also been adopted as an integral part of Walmart's global expansion. Each country has its own Walmart Retail Link providing daily data daily on sales (52 weeks of point-of-sale data), store insights with consumer demographics, perpetual inventory changes, store voids (no product available), and shifts in demand patterns.

In summary: Supplier networks can decrease the bullwhip effect in the supply chain and improve replenishment. The sharing of daily data daily

(Continued)

in the supply chain with suppliers can decrease demand latency by up to 80 percent. As a result, suppliers can see and respond to channel demand requirements more quickly.

Innovation Network: Procter & Gamble (P&G)

P&G's birth is a testimonial to the success in building value networks. The company was formed in 1837 when William Procter (candle maker) and James Gamble (soap maker) began to collaborate to get a better price on hog fat (a common raw material for the two companies). The company now has more than 300 brands—24 of the brands are billion-dollar brands—and the company operates in 180 countries.

The transformation in the last decade is also a testimonial to successful collaboration. When Alan George "A.G." Lafley—former chairman of the board, president, and chief executive officer of Procter & Gamble took the helm—he turned around the company with a focus on "the consumer is boss." He transformed the supply chain to focus on two moments of truth. The first moment of truth was at the shelf: "Did the product make the right impression?" The second was in the home: "When the consumer uses the product, will they be delighted?" (This is an early example of moving from inside-out to outside-in processes.) Using this strategy, sales doubled, profits quadrupled, and P&G's market value increased by more than $100 billion.

Lafley was also a strong believer in open design networks. Knowing that more than two-thirds of brand growth is derived from new product innovation, in 2001, he gave the research and development function a goal: source at least 50 percent of innovation from outside the hallowed walls of P&G. They forged a connect and development strategy and built processes to source new ideas from the outside. In less than four years, the P&G organization had met Lafley's goal of 50 percent outsourcing. It resulted in breakthrough ideas for Swiffer Dusters and Mr. Clean Magic Erasers. In later years, this strategy drove innovation in brand leaders like Olay Regenerist, Tide Total Care, and Cover Girl Lash Blast Mascara.

Currently, the team organization—with more than 100 people in global business development—has a new growth target to add $3 billion of revenue growth year-over-year. For the past 15 years, P&G has introduced 60 percent of the top-selling new products in consumer products, according to SymphonyIRI research (see Table 2.3).

P&G has also created $3 billion in sales for its Open Innovation partners. An example is Glad ForceFlex trash bags. This joint venture between

Table 2.3 Consumer Products New Product Innovation for 1997–2010

Top 25 Pacesetter Manufacturers 1997–2010			
Rank	Manufacturing Company	Total Year Company Revenue from New Product Pacesetters ($)	Number of New Product Pacesetters	# Top 25
1	**Procter & Gamble**	**$17,627,710,439**	**382**	**141**
2	Kraft Foods Inc.	$9,791,194,475	281	52
3	PepsiCo Inc.	$8,094,927,173	181	60
4	Unilever	$6,058,613,316	184	44
5	General Mills Inc.	$5,421,096,005	180	35
6	Nestlé S.A. Switzerland	$4,735,298,800	163	33
7	Kellogg Co.	$4,184,264,051	171	21
8	Kimberly-Clark Corp.	$3,391,925,317	36	13
9	Johnson & Johnson	$2,715,087,306	113	20
10	Coca Cola Co.	$2,647,374,368	52	22
11	ConAgra Foods Inc.	$2,566,940,193	73	17
12	L'Oreal USA	$2,295,480,077	129	25
13	Mars Inc.	$1,698,435,794	71	14
14	Campbell Soup Co.	$1,651,322,517	58	8
14	Colgate Palmolive	$1,592,370,625	59	17
15	SC Johnson & Son Inc.	$1,557,242,219	66	12
16	Pfizer Inc.	$1,462,252,586	50	13
17	The Clorox Company	$1,406,076,189	50	16
20	The Hershey Company	$1,342,897,373	44	7
19	H.J. Heinz	$1,316,583,147	41	7
22	Sara Lee Corporation	$1,274,393,963	41	8
21	GlaxoSmithKline PLC	$1,274,393,983	24	8
23	Group Danone S A	$1,239,919,405	30	12
24	Anheuser-Busch InBev	$1,150,624,790	22	9
25	Revlon Inc.	$868,781,141	43	5

Note: A SymphonyIRI Pacesetter is a product that achieved 7.5 million in first-year sales in the United States.
Source: Data courtesy SymphonyIRI Group, Inc., "SymphonyIRI New Product Pacesetters Report: A Look at 15 Years of History," 2011.

(Continued)

P&G and Clorox, which makes the Glad line of trash bags, was formed in November 2002 based on intellectual property from P&G. P&G also contributed global marketing expertise. Clorox brings its brand equity in the plastics category, focused R&D in plastics and resins, and the organizational structure for creating and distributing new plastic film products. Total Glad sales have doubled in the four years since the joint venture was formed, making Glad the second Clorox billion-dollar brand.

In summary: Open design networks can speed time to market and improve the innovation of breakthrough products. By the use of the network, companies can more quickly learn and seize innovation ideas. Innovation networks often go hand-in-hand with the design of supplier networks. As these networks evolve, suppliers want to contribute great ideas and be rewarded for them. As a result, it is important for R&D teams to work closely with procurement on the design of effective open innovation networks.

MISTAKES IN BUILDING VALUE CHAIN NETWORKS

Not all value chain initiatives are successful. Failure often teaches us more than success. The most well-known case studies of failure are Coca-Cola's creation of Coca-Cola Enterprises, Walmart's introduction of RFID, and the launch of the Boeing 787. Each story is a testimonial that despite the hype and promise of new ideas, what lasts is the building of true value in the value network. It has to be based on a sustaining win-win value proposition with trading partners.

CASE STUDY

DEMAND NETWORK FAILURE: COCA-COLA ENTERPRISES (CCE)

Coca-Cola Enterprises Inc. (CCE) was spun out of the Coca-Cola Company in 1986. The goal was to consolidate the many independent bottling groups in the Coca-Cola system. The secondary goal was to improve the asset efficiency of the parent company. On February 24, 2010, just four years after the creation of CCE, the Coca-Cola Company and CCE entered talks to sell CCE's North American division to Coca-Cola. Coca-Cola paid more than $15 billion dollars to reacquire CCE in North America, including redemption of Coca-Cola's 35 percent shareholding in CCE.

This was a public admission of demand network failure. With the creation of Coca-Cola Enterprises in 1986, Coca-Cola was the darling of Wall Street. The company divested assets to improve its return on assets and financial fundamentals. What was not obvious then—and is all too clear now—was that when a company sheds assets, it must redesign to sense and shape demand to drive market performance. The more extensive the supply chain and the more third-party nodes, the greater the challenge and the more critical it is to sense demand and service a network. Form needs to follow function. Alignment and strategy are essential.

Coca-Cola learned this the hard way. Battered by retail feedback (five years of falling scores on retailer surveys in North America), declining market share, and rising costs, Coca-Cola declared, "Enough!" It announced the repurchase of the bottler. There were three fundamental supply chain issues underlying the defeat:

1. **Goal alignment**. In the formation of CCE, the bottling operations were incented on volume. It sounded like a good idea then. Who could argue with pay based on more volume on the shelf? However, when carbonated beverage consumption changed due to consumer health and wellness preferences, the Coca-Cola Company wanted to power growth through selling more new products. Suddenly, there was a problem. The established incentives drove a volume-based response from CCE of more traditional Coca-Cola products. The incentives were not aligned to compensate the supply chain parties for the lumpier, lower volume demand patterns accompanying new product introductions (iced tea, juices, and flavored water). As a result, the company was not able to achieve the right balance between efficiency and innovation.

2. **Flexibility to morph outside-in**. When the Coca-Cola bottling system was defined, Walmart was a regional player. As Walmart gained power and established a national presence, a regional bottling system became a liability. Walmart wanted a more efficient and responsive supply chain. The company wanted one voice to the customer with flawless execution. The Coca-Cola regional system was riddled with goal alignment issues and could not meet the needs of its largest customer.

3. **Technology evolution and adaptation**. In the period of 2005 to 2012, while Pepsi proactively pursued the use of market sensing and downstream data technologies in the United States, Coca-Cola could not. While PepsiCo aggressively built sales overlay systems across the bottlers and pushed for the adoption of new technologies to sense

(Continued)

demand, Coca-Cola continued to struggle with alignment of the bottlers. The capability gap between the two companies on the use of downstream data to sense and shape demand created a competitive advantage for PepsiCo. The design of the PepsiCo supply chain system encouraged technology adoption outside-in while the design of the Coca-Cola supply chain system pushed from the inside-out.

In summary: While a company may shed assets, it must carefully craft strategies to ensure alignment, adaptation, and evolution across the entire network. It needs to start with the demand network and the building of winning channel relationships.

Supplier Network Failure: Walmart RFID

Walmart is the power broker of the consumer value chain. Traditionally, when Walmart said, "Jump!" the consumer manufacturer usually said, "How high?"

In June 2003, Walmart launched the start of a retailer compliance program stating that it would ask its top 100 suppliers to begin tagging pallets and cases with radio frequency identification tags (RFID). In 2004, the company began the RFID trial. Eight suppliers participated.

The effort was massive. It spawned an entire industry focused on RFID technology innovation. The race was on to lower the price of tags to make the effort affordable. However, this is a case study of Walmart trying to wield a big stick and force suppliers into compliance before the technology was mature enough to support the network. Supplier mandates for RFID usage and compliance fines went on for seven years before the company aligned expectations with technology capabilities. The steps of the pilot are a testimonial of why big sticks and one-way value propositions do not work. There was just no joint value proposition. The benefits went to Walmart, while the costs went to the suppliers; yet, Walmart was not willing to absorb the costs through price increases. The progression of events occurred over the past six years.

From 2004 to 2006, Walmart met with its top 100 and its next level of 200 suppliers in its Bentonville offices to lay out RFID tagging requirements and the timeline for compliance. Suppliers were told that by June 2005, RFID systems would be operating in up to six of its distribution centers and 250 stores. Walmart further said that it expected to be using this technology in up to 13 distribution centers and 600 Walmart and Sam's Club stores by the end of 2005.

When this did not work, Walmart grabbed an even bigger stick. To try to convince consumer products companies to comply, in 2005 Walmart sponsored a report from the University of Arkansas's Information Technology Research Institute, a part of the Sam Walton College of Business. The study focused on the potential benefit of RFID on reducing retail out-of-stocks (OOS). The researchers from the University of Arkansas concluded that RFID reduced OOS at store level by 16 percent over non-RFID based stores. Using this report, Walmart began the dictate for the next 200 suppliers. In April 2006, the dictates become stronger. Walmart stated that it "will phase out the use of Gen 1 tags in favor of Gen 2 by mid-year" and "will no longer accept the use of Gen 1 tags on the cases and pallets it receives from its suppliers after June 30."

Despite internal management changes, Walmart continued the support of the RFID program, but in a lower-key manner, until the issue hit the press. In February 2007, Walmart made the front page of the *Wall Street Journal* with an article titled, "Walmart's Radio-Tracked Inventory Hits Static." The article stated, "Walmart Stores Inc.'s next leap forward in ultra-efficient distribution is showing signs of fizzling," given a lack of internal progress in rolling out the technology and a lack of value for suppliers. The CIO of Sara Lee stated, "RFID isn't making sense at the current level of cost and performance."

Under market pressure, Walmart attempted to adapt. In October 2007, Walmart announced a major change in its RFID strategy, largely abandoning the initial pallet/case focus on shipments going to Walmart stores in favor of three focus areas: (1) shipments going to Sam's Club; (2) promotional displays and products going to Walmart stores; (3) tests to see RFID's impact in improving category management in select areas. "We're coming at RFID from a different angle," Walmart's VP of information technology, Carolyn Walton, stated at the EPC Global conference.

In January 2008, Walmart announced its first real compliance penalties for failure to tag products, specifically for shipments to its Sam's Club chain. Walmart said in a letter to suppliers that a failure to tag pallets sent to its distribution center (DC) in DeSoto, Texas, or directly to one of its stores served by that DC after January 31 would be charged a service fee, starting at $2 per untagged pallet on February 1, 2008, and capping at $3 per pallet on January 1, 2009.

In February 2009, Procter & Gamble issued a statement saying that after validating the benefits of RFID in merchandising and promotional

(Continued)

displays, it was ending its pilot program. The article was a public reversal of the Walmart RFID efforts.

In the design of this initiative, Walmart ignored the readiness of the technology. RFID technology, while promising, still was not ready for prime time. Reading RFID tags on metals and liquids was just not feasible. Tag costs were prohibitive, and the tagging of only Walmart products too expensive.

In summary: Changes in a value network have to drive a sustainable win-win value proposition. While Walmart had the power to drive change, it did not pay enough attention to the economics and physics of the supply chain to drive a win-win value proposition. Walmart made it a win-lose. Why? The price of tags and tagging products was high and the cost was being borne by the suppliers at the same time that Walmart was pushing for price reductions.

Innovation Network Failure: Boeing 787

Boeing is the world's largest aerospace company and leading manufacturer of commercial jetliners and defense, space, and security systems. Boeing's products and tailored services include commercial and military aircraft, satellites, weapons, electronic and defense systems, launch systems, advanced information and communication systems, and performance-based logistics and training. Boeing employs more than 170,000 people across the United States and in 70 countries. It is composed of two business units: Boeing Commercial Airplanes and Boeing Defense, Space & Security. Boeing has manufactured commercial jetliners for more than 40 years. With the merger of Boeing and McDonnell Douglas in 1997, Boeing's leadership in commercial jets, joined with the lineage of Douglas airplanes, gave the combined company a 70-year heritage of leadership in commercial aviation. Today, the main commercial products are the 737, 747, 767, and 777 families of airplanes and the Boeing Business Jet. New product development efforts are currently focused on the Boeing 787 Dreamliner, and the 747–8. The Boeing 787 is a long-range, mid-size jet airliner. It was unveiled on July 8, 2007, and was targeted to enter service in May 2008. It entered commercial service on October 26, 2011. The launch encountered numerous delays and was delivered three years after the promised date.

Attractive to the market, the Boeing 787 is a super-efficient airplane designed for passenger comfort. The fuel-efficient design enables the plane to fly with 20 percent less fuel consumption. On introduction, demand was high. Early orders exceeded expectations. Then the schedule started slipping. And orders were canceled. Negative press started to flow. What happened? How could the Boeing supply chain have such a major miss in a delivery?

The story is one of an innovation-driven company trying to collaborate with third-party suppliers to bring multiple innovative technologies—composites, new design, energy-efficient software, and more effective engines—to market simultaneously for the launch of a new type of aircraft. The revolutionary design was lightweight due to the extensive use of composite materials. Composite materials made up 50 percent of the aircraft, and the design of a one-piece fuselage eliminated 1,500 aluminum sheets and over 40,000 fasteners. This simplified the design and made it lighter to improve fuel consumption. Innovative engines from General Electric and Rolls-Royce enabled even greater fuel consumption savings.

The work started well. Boeing commissioned 50 suppliers at more than 130 sites around the world to design and assemble subassemblies for final assembly at Boeing's Everett, Washington, facility. The suppliers designed sub-components around the globe using a new computer-aided design solution.

The issue was one of holistic execution and quality control. The Dreamliner launch had multiple public delays due to a shortage of fasteners. Conflicting specifications, compliance issues, and coordination plagued the program, which translated into delay after delay. As a result, orders were canceled and renegotiated, and the schedule was pushed out.

In 2011, Boeing shipped three completed 787 planes and finished the year with 857 unfulfilled orders. The company publically stated, "Our goal in 2012 is to ensure that 787 production is stable and reliable, while maintaining focus on execution as we deliver an increasing number of airplanes across all our programs." Through a redesign of the supply chain, the company established goals to increase production of the 787 by 300 percent. To do this, the company invested in supplier assistance teams adding 200 engineers and supply chain specialists over the past two years to orchestrate the supplier network.

The company is learning from the mistakes in the production of the 787. The Boeing executive responsible for the 737 program was quoted as indicating that the company will take a "fundamentally different" approach with this new program. Rather than a top-down approach to setting supplier requirements and milestones, the company is actively

(Continued)

pursuing supplier development programs. This work will focus on ensuring that suppliers have the right skills, capabilities, and resources.

In summary: Boeing outsourced design and carefully architected a supply network to deliver a superior new aircraft. The focus was on features: the best engine, the lightest composites, and superior performance of each supplier's work on subassemblies. The new engines worked well, but the issue became one of network orchestration and management of the holistic design effort. The network was not set up for control of quality, manufacturing, and testing. As a result, quality control and design coordination plagued assembly. Boeing learned the hard way that the more outsourcing in a network, the greater the need for quality control processes to ensure network orchestration. While subassemblies manufacturing and supply can be outsourced, the process for network orchestration is essential. The coordination requirements are even greater when working on new products or new technologies. Although a company can outsource its network, it cannot outsource the responsibility for coordination.

RISK MANAGEMENT

As companies shift from a focus on internal operations to the coordination of value chain networks, both the opportunity and the risks increase. The number of inputs, the pace of change, and the challenge of coordination is exponential. Within the past five years, to answer this need, supply chain risk management practices have evolved. The greater the length and complexity of value networks, the greater the need for supply chain risk management practices. While catastrophic events like the floods in Taiwan, Hurricane Katrina, or the tsunami in Japan propel supply chain stories into global news, risk management needs to be a focused systemic process, not a knee-jerk reaction. Risk management is about the prevention of a crisis rather than just the response to one.

The secret to risk management is taking a holistic approach. The framework in Figure 2.9 gives an overview. It is not sufficient to focus only on the high probability, high impact events. Risks in all four quadrants need to be managed as a part of normal operations.

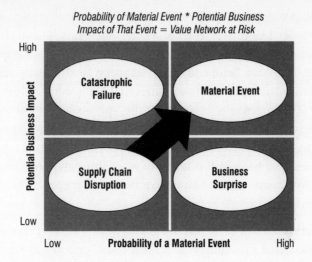

Figure 2.9 Risk Management Framework

As companies build value networks, they also need to build a risk management prevention system. The goal is to:

- **Minimize day-to-day incidents**. Process reliability and clear accountability is the foundation of a risk management program. Focus on process control and clarity on roles and responsibility.
- **Design to reduce risk**. Reduce the likelihood of high-impact, highly probable supply chain events and manage to eliminate periodic incidents and supply chain surprises.
- **Staff and plan for risk scenarios**. As the network is outsourced, the need for network orchestration increases. Since the building of networks is often a focused effort to reduce costs, companies new at building networks usually understaff coordination. As a result, the supply chain becomes more fragile.
- **Sense so as to reduce failures**. Companies good at risk management use network technologies to sense potential network failure before it occurs. When problems are discovered, teams are deployed to correct or help suppliers or channel partners before there is a network failure. When the Great Recession hit, Intel,

using supplier sensing, was able to get early alerts on potential supplier failure and avert a disaster. Increasingly companies are sensing supplier risk from public documents (e.g., legal action, patent filings, tax liens, and social networks) to drive early warnings.

■ **Know the options**. Companies that are good at reducing risks in value networks understand the options before the event or crisis occurs. The use of what-if analysis and scenario planning helps the company build playbooks of potential outcomes. These playbooks allow teams to work through potential options before a major issue helping companies to prepare. This reduces the time to act.

Preparing for risk in the extended supply chain is everybody's business. Established procedures, a control room or a control tower for visualization of global operations, and practiced drills are a necessity. This combination allows the organization to spring to action when a situation arises.

SHIFT TO VALUE-BASED OUTCOMES

The most lasting value in building networks happens when there is alignment in relationships to value-based outcomes. This happens when all parties in the extended supply chain are aligned to a common goal. This new definition redefines relationships, permeates processes, and gives companies new reasons to truly collaborate. Redefining traditional relationships from inside the supply chain is a Herculean task. The opportunities are few and far between; but when the shift happens, supply chain leaders should seize the opportunity. These opportunities to align supply chains to value-based outcomes are many: major disruptions, government regulation, or a disruptive technology. Some examples are:

■ **Performance-based logistics**. In this shift, the department of defense changed from purchasing airplanes and weapons defense systems to contracting for performance-based outcomes through third-party service providers. This was a dramatic change and transformed behavior. The rewards moved from the sale of the unit to up-time performance. The incentives for longevity changed contracts, design, and services.

- **Health and wellness in health care**. U.S. health-care costs are $2.2 trillion a year, approaching $8,000 per person or 16 percent of the economy. Solving the issues in the health-care value chain will be a monumental, if not an insurmountable, task. The greatest improvement could happen if a change is made from a focus on the patient and sickness to health and wellness. This focus from efficient sickness to health and wellness will alter the focus from the hospital to the use of sensing of wellness in a patient's home. It will change the services, products, and trading partners in the supply chain. The goal will shift to prevention.

- **Safe and secure food chains**. The global supply chain has created both problems and opportunities for food safety. Pending legislation will include serialized tracking of food products and improvements in track and trace through each stage of the process. The most problematic areas are the steps in manufacturing that change the state of the material—cooking, mixing, drying, batch filling—and involve multiple ingredients. To control these areas, companies will have to redesign the interface between manufacturing recipe control, the bill of materials, and product specifications. Food legislation to improve food safety from field to fork is imminent and fewer than 1 percent of food manufacturers are ready. The focus will move from selling products to ensuring the safety of the products sold. This shift will redefine supply chain networks and produce a new set of winners and losers.

- **Software solutions**. Companies no longer want to buy license software. The evolution of software as a service (SaaS) and iTunes concepts are shifting purchasing behavior. The shift is from a large purchase (license software model) to one of rental (incremental payments based on usage). This shift in the sale of enterprise software also redefines the customer relationship to drive higher levels of satisfaction and customer value.

  Software maintenance is currently 32 percent of a manufacturer's information technology budget. With the move to SaaS solutions, many companies can eliminate the maintenance charges and the headcount to service the software. It also increases a company's flexibility to stay current on new releases.

It also improves adaptability of the solution to deal with increasing importance of content. In the software value chain, content is growing in importance. Companies want software solutions that combine the right software and content to improve decision making. To date, there is no company that has been successful in producing both content and software. The transition from licensed software sales to SaaS sales has been made by fewer than 5 percent of licensed software companies.

Opportunities abound to power growth through value-based outcomes in value networks. We are slowly moving in this direction; however, it is a new frontier. As we move forward, we learn that we need new processes (such as risk management), and new systems for sensing and compliance. The processes move outside-in and horizontally making many of the traditional implementations of enterprise resource planning and advanced planning solutions obsolete.

CASE STUDY

TAIWAN SEMICONDUCTOR MANUFACTURING COMPANY (TSMC) REDESIGNING A VALUE NETWORK TO DRIVE VALUE-BASED OUTCOMES

Founded in 1987, TSMC was the semiconductor industry's first pure-play foundry. In this role, the company made no product of its own and focused all of its efforts in making semiconductor chips for third-party manufacturers. Today, the company is one of the world's largest foundries serving more than 450 customers and manufacturing more than 8,800 products for a variety of applications in computer, communications, and consumer electronics value chains.

The main thing that we have learned is that a foundry needs to be a service-oriented business, so we are molding ourselves into a service company.

Morris Chang, Chairman and CEO, TSMC

In the semiconductor industry, a foundry is a major investment with a short life cycle and high cost. A good rule of thumb in the industry is to plan for 18 months to build a foundry and 6 to 12 months to reach a level of production reliability. The capital cost to build a foundry has doubled with every two generations of semiconductor chip development.

It is a market with intense competition. In the period of 1997 to 2000, the company attempted to be the most efficient producer. However, TSMC quickly learned that the future success of the company was in the transition to service. As a result, the company has invested in a long lineage of service-based offerings to drive open-innovation for the customer's network positioning themselves as a partner, not a supplier or a competitor.

In 2001, the company launched an integrated library, Reference Flow, which had a single goal in mind: to provide the shortest time possible to design and ramp up the production of new products. These libraries were a network to support time to market for upstream customers. The library included TSMC-tested semiconductor designs and also validated the designs of third parties. By 2004, 75 percent of the TSMC customers used the company's library in their upstream designs. The company also launched services to reduce the costs of testing and introducing new techniques, like parallel mask production, to reduce the cycle time of wafer fabrication. It also developed direct communication systems to improve customer visibility for work-in-process material status and online testing results.

In later years, the company renamed the service the TSMC Open Innovation Platform. It retained many of the original concepts, but used more modern technology to enhance customer collaboration with suppliers on design. It is a substantiation of TSMC's Open Innovation model that strives to bring tighter thinking of customers and partners to drive a common goal of shortening design time, minimizing time-to-volume of innovation, and speeding time to market. Today, TSMC is the market leader in the global contract manufacturing semiconductor market with a 49 percent market share. The closest competitors have a 12 percent market share, demonstrating that companies win when they put more value in the value chain for trading partners.

TO DRIVE CHANGE

- Evaluate how value networks can improve supply chain excellence.
- Apply the five rules of thumb to network design.
- In building a value network, ask yourself, "What can I learn from the success and failure of others?"
- How do you reward sales and procurement?
- How does this need to change to improve the value in the value network?

SUMMARY

As competition increases, a company's first reaction is to tighten its belt and reduce costs. However, a company cannot save its way to value. Instead, the supply chain can be used to drive more value in the value chain through the design of differentiated products and services that can define unique value. To do this, consider the following:

- **Focus on value**. Make the transition from cost to value through the building of supply chain capabilities. This is a year-over-year transition that needs to be grounded in a supply chain strategy supported by corporate leadership.
- **Drive process innovation**. The building of global supply chains accelerates growth and supply chain maturity. Today, some of the most mature supply chains are the result of efforts of the global Fortune 500 establishing presence in emerging economies. Use the evolution of supply chains in emerging countries to drive process innovation and define new capabilities in relationships.
- **Relationships matter**. Design and implement value chains with a focus on building win-win value propositions aligned around value-based outcomes.
- **Build capabilities for network orchestration**. While you can outsource value chains, you cannot outsource the risk of the value chain. As the supply chain is outsourced, staff for value chain orchestration and process coordination.

NOTES

1. Supply Chain Insights Report, "Putting the Pieces Together," 2012.
2. Kroger Annual Report, 2011.
3. Philippe Lambotte, Kraft, Presentation to MIT Supply Chain Forum, Cambridge, MA, November 2011.

CHAPTER 3

The New World of Demand Management: Demand Sensing, Shaping, and Translation

You can't wish demand to happen. There are no magic wands or easy buttons.

—Charles Chase

The global marketplace is volatile, fragmented, and dynamic. Supply processes are more mature than demand. There is a larger gap to fill in the redefinition of demand processes to be market driven than in any other area of supply chain management.

To become market driven, companies need to identify the right market signals, build sensing capabilities, define demand-shaping processes, and effectively translate the demand signal to create a more effective response. This approach makes the 30 years of technology and process thinking by the first- and second-generation supply chain global pioneers obsolete.

Demand management processes are challenging. They are more difficult to get right than supply. Talent is scarce and the processes are evolving. Organizationally, the work on demand processes is fraught with political issues. (Demand processes are more politically charged than supply processes.)

As a result, many companies often want to throw in the towel. They want to forget demand and only focus on the redesign of supply processes to become more reliable, resilient, and agile. The list of possible projects is long and often includes lean manufacturing, cycle-time reduction, order management, or the redefinition of distribution center flows.

However, focusing only on supply has limited results. Supply-centric approaches can only impact business complexity. It cannot improve the potential of the supply chain as a complex system. Working supply processes in isolation to demand will drive up costs, increase working capital, and reduce asset utilization. The secret to building supply chain excellence is to build the right stuff in the demand management processes. Improvements in demand management will give the supply chain the right foundation to make effective trade-offs against the supply chain effective frontier (Figure 1.1).

▶ **DEFINITION**

A supply-centric approach cannot compensate for the lack of a strong demand management process.

The development of a demand management strategy is easier said than done. Demand management systems were designed for the supply chains of the 1990s when there was less complexity. Over the past decade, supply chains have become more complex because of consolidation through acquisition and globalization. Unfortunately, the evolution of demand management practices has not kept pace with business needs.

Historic approaches to demand management are not up to the task. As a result, companies are coming to the realization that the demand

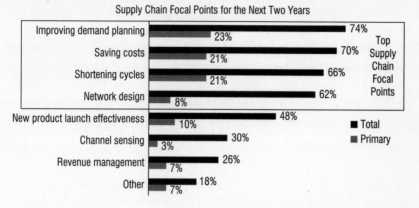

Supply Chain Focal Points for the Next Two Years

	Total	Primary
Improving demand planning	74%	23%
Saving costs	70%	21%
Shortening cycles	66%	21%
Network design	62%	8%
New product launch effectiveness	48%	10%
Channel sensing	30%	3%
Revenue management	26%	7%
Other	18%	7%

Top Supply Chain Focal Points

Figure 3.1 The Focus of Supply Chain Executives over the Next Two Years

management process requires a complete reengineering with an outward-in orientation. The process needs to focus on identifying market opportunities and leveraging internal sales and marketing programs to influence customers to purchase the company's products and services. It requires a champion—an organizational leader—to orchestrate the change management requirements of the market-driven value network.

This gap in demand processes is the highest priority area for supply chain leaders to close in the next two years. Figure 3.1 indicates the importance of this priority.

WHAT IS DEMAND MANAGEMENT?

Demand management is the use of forecasting technologies along with demand sensing, shaping, and translation techniques to improve supply chain processes. The journey to become market driven requires rethinking demand holistically: the source of demand signals, and the integration of the demand signal into horizontal processes.

> *For high-tech and electronics companies, the real challenge that you find is the reliability of forecasts. It is the number one issue that they face.*
>
> *—Sanjiv Sidhu, Founder, i2 Technologies;*
> *Current Chairman, o9 Solutions*

This journey starts with outside-in thinking and focuses on identifying the market signals and translating them into the drivers of demand. Market-driven forecasts focus on accurately predicting what customers will buy. This is in sharp contrast with the traditional demand processes that determine what companies will manufacture or ship. The input signals are from the market. There are many possible inputs: weather, events, seasonal response, social sentiment, or competitive pressures.

LEARNING A NEW LANGUAGE TO BUILD MARKET-DRIVEN DEMAND MANAGEMENT PROCESSES

The first step in building market-driven demand capabilities is getting clear on the definitions of a new set of process terms. Although the definitions are simple, the process implications are not. These demand definitions are:

- **Demand sensing:** Shortening the time to sense true market data to understand market shifts in the demand response. This is in contrast to the use of order or shipment data. These more traditional data sources have one- to two-week latency.
- **Demand shaping:** The use of techniques to stimulate market demand. The most common are new product launch, price management, assortment, merchandising, product placement, sales incentives, and marketing programs. These techniques lift demand and are usually worked together in campaigns. They are rarely deployed singularly.
- **Demand translation:** The translation of demand outside-in from the market to each role within the organization. The design of this system recognizes that the requirements for demand visibility for each supply chain leader—distribution, manufacturing, and procurement—are different.
- **Demand orchestration:** The process of making trade-offs market to market based on the right balance of demand risk and opportunity. These trade-off decisions are dependent on the use of advanced analytics to sense and shape demand simultaneously.

	Sell	Deliver	Make	Source
Network Design: Probability of Demand	Channel Design. Cost-to-Serve Analysis	Network Design		Supplier Network Supplier Rationalization
Supply Chain Tactical Planning: Demand Forecast	Category Management	Sales and Operations Planning New Product Launch		Category Management
Supply Chain Policy: Demand Shaping	Contract Management	Corporate Social Responsibility Revenue Management Working Capital Management		Contract Management
Market-Driven Signal Management	Demand/Channel Sensing	Demand Orchestration Demand Translation		Supplier Sensing
Transactional Processing: Order and Shipment Processing	Order Management	Order-to-Cash Procure-to-Pay		Purchase Order Management

Figure 3.2 Demand Signal Management in Market-Driven Value Networks

- **Downstream data:** The use of channel data to sense and shape demand. This can include data for sales at the point of transaction, sales through distributors, inventory in channel trading partners' warehouses, and demand insight data.
- **Demand shifting:** The shifting of demand from one period to another. This includes advanced shipments and moving product into the channel without stimulating actual sales. Demand shifting without shaping demand is a form of supply chain waste.

These concepts are shown in aggregate in Figure 3.2. This definition of demand signal management is quite different from the conventional definition of supply chain forecasting. It requires the active management of the demand signal through the network and planning horizons. This is in sharp contrast to the conventional definition of demand management where the forecast is created and consumed without active management throughout the value network.

WHAT IS MARKET-DRIVEN DEMAND MANAGEMENT?

Demand management is critical to driving out inefficiencies in the supply chain, and it is the most leveragable metric on the supply chain effective frontier. A small improvement in demand planning has a larger impact on improving performance than an equal improvement in other metrics. It is pervasive.

Demand signal is critical. It is needed to coordinate basic operations. Moving goods from the suppliers' raw materials to finished goods in consumers' hands takes time. It synchronizes the processes of sell, deliver, make, and source across multiple trading partners. Predicting future demand helps to determine the right quantities of raw materials to buy, the target amount of finished goods to inventory, the number of products that need to be shipped, the number of people to hire, and the number of plants to build, right down to the number of office supplies (sourcing) that should be purchased.

Most companies do not have the luxury to wait for demand to occur and then react to a customer order. Because of the intricacies of supply chain processes, they must plan to be ready to fulfill channel sales. This includes sensing demand signals, proactively shaping demand, and translating demand into the most effective supply response to meet customer orders.

Market-driven demand management utilizes data from market and channel sources to sense, shape, and translate demand requirements into an actionable demand response bidirectionally from market to market. A true market-driven forecast is an unconstrained view, or a best estimate of market demand based on channel data. Demand shaping is based on campaigns to combine price, new product launches, trade and sales promotions and incentives, advertising, and marketing programs to impact what and how much customers will buy.

Demand Signal

The building of market-driven value networks is a critical part of channel strategy design. When implemented correctly, it exploits (or influences) the strength of an existing brand or segment to propel or pull products through the channels of distribution. It is outside-in. When successful, the data has minimal latency.

This is in sharp contrast with supply-driven demand concepts developed over the past 15 years. These legacy stand-alone product demand processes focused only on historic—not current channel—data. They lacked the ability to flex: to sense and to shape demand. As a result, in these traditional systems, the supply chain was insular to the impact of market dynamics such as price, advertising, sales promotions, marketing events, economic factors, and competition.

The focus in market-driven value networks is to sense and to shape demand to orchestrate the demand response. As shown in Figure 1.3, it happens in stages:

Stage 1: The supply chain drives the efficient response. In this stage, the supply chain focuses on efficiency or asset utilization. The forecasting process is nascent. Companies model demand using basic forecasting technologies based on shipments and order data as inputs. The goal is to forecast future shipments. The data model represents what a manufacturer should make or a retailer should buy.

Stage 2: The supply chain drives the reliable response. At this level of maturity, the supply chain uses multiple signals to improve forecast accuracy including channel data. This modeling becomes more sophisticated and uses multiple indicators (from different data sources) along with enrichment data (e.g., customer demographics and weather data) to model the future forecast. However, the forecast is still a shipment-level demand signal to predict what shipments are required from a warehouse or a manufacturing center.

Stage 3: The supply chain drives the resilient enterprise. With more maturity, the company models channel sales. The forecast is based on what is sold, not what is manufactured or shipped. Demand translation processes are developed in sales and operations planning (S&OP) to translate "ship to" or channel demand to "ship from" or manufacturing requirements.

Stage 4: The supply chain creates the adaptive enterprise. At this stage of development, the company develops mature processes for revenue management and makes trade-offs in channel strategies based on baseline lift factors. The focus is on sensing and shaping demand. This is often referred to as a demand-driven supply chain.

Stage 5: The supply chain drives market-to-market alignment.
In this stage, companies can trade off multiple demand shaping
activities simultaneously in demand orchestration processes. This
is translated bidirectionally into a supply plan balancing demand
and supply uncertainty. For a retailer, this could combine revenue
management, markdown strategies, new product launch, store format impacts, and cross-channel programs. For a manufacturer, this
will trade off the impact of market-mix modeling of advertising,
new product launch, revenue management and product portfolio
management against the raw material risks, and corporate social
responsibility goals in the extended supply chain. This is the definition of the market-driven demand response.

In each stage of the market-driven capability model, the role of
demand changes requiring a redefinition of forecasting processes.
Additionally, at each stage of the demand process, a supply chain
leader can chose to constrain the forecast (reducing volume requirements based on channel or supply-side constraints) to better manage the supply chain.

Demand Challenges

In a May 1916 interview in the *Chicago Tribune*, Henry Ford was quoted
as saying, "History is more or less bunk. It's tradition. We don't want
tradition. We want to live in the present and the only history that is
worth a tinker's damn is the history we made today." Many of the first
generation pioneers in the companies we have interviewed over the
past several months agree.

The historic definition, as defined by the first and second generation of supply chain pioneers, is limited and applicable to only stages
1 and 2 of the supply chain maturity model in Chapter 1 (Figure 1.3).
The basis of the design of these traditional processes is the premise
that an underlying pattern in historical customer shipment data can be
identified using statistics. Any additional unexplained patterns could
be simply addressed as randomness, or an unexplainable variation.
These same processes assumed that the patterns (demand signals)—
in this case, only trend/cycle and/or seasonality—will continue into
the future.

The objective of all mathematical models is to maximize the ability to explain all the underlying patterns in the historical demand and to minimize the unexplained. The overall mathematical formula is:

$$Forecast = Pattern(s) + Unexplained$$

Like a compass, the market-driven demand signal needs to be built as a true north for the organization. To make this happen, companies need to focus on the elimination of bias (consistent overforecasting or underforecasting). It is not easy. The challenges to building market-driven demand management capabilities are many:

- **Incentives**. As long as sales are incented only for volume sold into the channel, and marketing is rewarded for market share, companies will never become market driven. To make progress on demand-driven initiatives, companies must focus on profitable sales growth to customers. The incentives need to be aligned outside-in based on channel metrics. The sales and marketing organizations, based on metrics, will normally contribute input to the demand plan that is the most biased of any organization within the company.
- **Traditional view of supply chain excellence**. For demand-driven initiatives to be successful, they must extend from the customers' customer to the supplier's supplier. The concepts of demand latency, demand sensing, demand shaping, demand translation, and demand orchestration are not widely understood. As a result, they require education and a business champion. Organizations not familiar with the concepts will not understand why the demand management processes need to change.
- **Focus**. In market-driven processes, the focus shifts from inside-out to outside-in. In traditional processes, the process focus is from inside the organization out, as opposed to from the outside (market-driven) in. To manage demand, focus is placed on revenue management as a horizontal process (this is covered in greater detail in Chapter 5).
- **Vertical rewards versus horizontal processes**. In supply-based organizations, the supply chain is incented based on cost reduction; procurement is incented based on the lowest purchased cost; distribution/logistics is rewarded for on-time

shipments with the lowest costs; sales is rewarded for sell-in of volume into the channel; and marketing is rewarded for market share. These incentives do not align to maximize value. To build a market-driven forecast, the forecasting group needs to report to a central organization. The goal of the group should be the reduction of bias and error and the use of the probability of demand.

- **Focus on transactions not relationships**. Today, the connecting processes of the enterprise—selling and purchasing—are focused on transactional efficiency. As a result, the greater value that can happen through relationships—acceleration of time-to-market through innovation, breakthrough thinking in sustainability, and sharing of demand data—never materializes. In a market-driven organization, demand error is part of the top-to-top meeting. Market-driven leaders set price targets based on their ability to forecast.

- **A forecast is not a forecast is not a forecast**. As companies work on demand architectures, they will find that they have multiple forecasts—sales forecast, financial forecast, production forecast, supply chain forecast, and procurement forecast—each with a different data model, granularity, and bias. As a result, tight integration is not a good idea; and the so-called one-number forecast is not realistic. Instead, as companies work through the issues, they will find the need to model market demand in a *ship to* or *channel data model*, and translate this demand to a *ship from data model*. The sales forecast then becomes an input into the corporate forecast, and this corporate forecast becomes the input into the financial forecast. These concepts require education and are often a major change management issue.

- **Data**. Working with data is a challenge for all. In traditional, supply-centric processes, the most common data input is customer orders. The second most common data source comes from customer shipments, or replenishment data. While market data—point-of-sale (POS) data and channel shipments—is growing in frequency and availability, it is not being effectively used today in 95 percent of organizations. Ironically, in the consumer products industries, POS data has been available for 32 years, but fewer than 10 percent of companies use channel data to drive their demand forecasts.

We overforecasted demand with a 34 percent bias believing that it would increase sales. It didn't. As a result, with the downturn in the economy, it added three months to our ability to figure out what was happening.

—Global Director of Demand Planning,
Large Consumer Products Company

■ **Getting channel data**. Traditional demand forecasting and planning processes are focused on planning rather than the use of current market. As industries have consolidated and become more global and leaner, they are more vulnerable to shifts in market conditions. The slightest disruptions in demand have become difficult to manage. To combat this, downstream trading partner data is shared in strong relationships. Companies have to earn the right to see and use channel data. Leaders make forecast sharing part of their top-to-top meetings. They measure bias and error for all trading partners.

■ **Right technology**. Although traditional demand planning systems claim to have 20 or more different statistical methods embedded within the technology to model demand, the team building the market-driven supply chain will quickly find that they are not up to this new task. The technologies were designed to measure patterns based on history, not channel data. As a result, when the historical trend/cycle and/or seasonality patterns are disrupted by a global economic downturn, the supply chain goes on as if nothing had happened because it cannot sense. It is blind to the change.

In market-driven demand forecasting systems, there are four categories of statistical methods: time series, intermittent demand functions, ARIMA, and causal models (e.g., multiple regression, ARIMAX, and unobserved component models). Although all four statistical models are required to accurately predict products sold within a corporate product portfolio, the causal models are designed to sense and to shape demand signals other than trend/cycle and seasonality. The best examples are when price, sales promotions, marketing programs, as well as other related factors, change market demand.[1] In Figure 3.3, we show the conventional demand model and then contrast it with the evolution of the market-driven value network demand model in Figure 3.4.

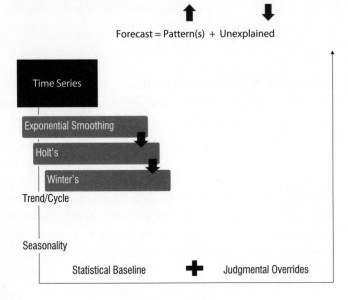

Figure 3.3 Traditional Demand Management Model

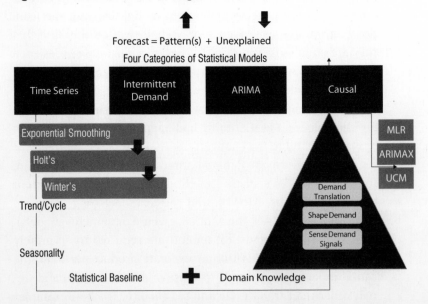

Figure 3.4 New Demand Management Model for Market-Driven Value Networks

Without these techniques to sense market demand, historic systems cannot predict changes in market trend and seasonality. These systems can predict the lift of the trend, but they are blind to determine the start and stop dates. As a result, trend/cycle and seasonality forecasting requires more judgmental or gut-feeling overrides to the statistical baseline forecast in an attempt to explain away the unexplained. Figure 3.4 is a simple illustration of this scenario.

■ **Forecastability**. Given the volatility of demand in the marketplace and the proliferation of products and services, companies are questioning, "How forecastable are our products?" They want to know if the products are becoming easier or more difficult to forecast. As a result, the topic of forecastability is becoming the focal point for many supply chain articles. Companies are realizing that not all of their products are forecastable given data constraints and variability in demand. As a result, companies are asking, "What products are forecastable? What is not forecastable? How is the process of forecasting changing?"

Item segmentation by product forecastability helps companies to achieve greater accuracy in their product forecasting processes. An assessment helps to pinpoint the issues. The framework in Figure 3.5 is a useful way to segment products and apply the concepts to supply chain design.

■ **Overcoming forecast bias**. Forecast bias is consistent over- or underforecasting. The general tendency is for organizations to consistently overforecast. Much of the bias stems from judgmental inputs or gut-feeling adjustments in consensus forecasting. Bias is a major problem for the supply chain.

While forecasters felt that they had good justifications for making adjustments, in an in-depth study Robert Fildes and Paul Goodwin, experts in the demand planning field,[2] found them overly confident that their adjustments would improve forecast accuracy. This study reported three facts:

1. **Large adjustments are more beneficial than small**. In fact, the study showed that large adjustments did tend to be beneficial, but small adjustments did not materially improve forecast accuracy and sometimes made accuracy worse.

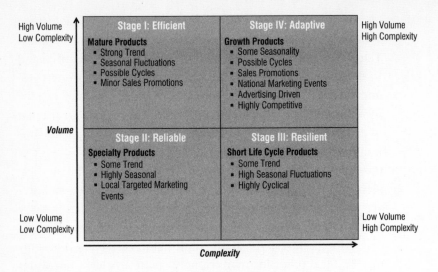

Figure 3.5 Rethinking How Companies Respond to Demand

2. **Negative adjustments are more valuable than positive**. Subsequently, negative (downward) adjustments were more likely to improve forecast accuracy than positive (upward) adjustments. Organizations, based on traditional metrics, are incented for a positive bias.

3. **Recency**. Fildes and Goodwin also found that overoptimism tends to lead to erroneous positive adjustments, while negative adjustments are based on more realistic expectations. Finally, they found a bias toward recency—that is, emphasizing the most recent history while treating the more distant past as bunk. This focus on recency tended to undermine the process of statistical forecasting.

If past history was all there was to the game, the richest people would be librarians.

—Warren Buffett

In this new world of market-driven value networks, companies need to look at the forecast not just as a number but to view it as a range of probabilities. It requires a new approach. Instead of tightly integrating a fixed number to supply, in market-driven value networks, the probability of demand is translated and used to determine supply strategies.

Historically, companies have focused too much on the accuracy of imperfect numbers. A frequent mistake is focusing on the accuracy of a number with high variability. After all, what good is a number with a 50 percent error with 9 significant digits? In market-driven value networks, it is more valuable to know the range of probabilities and the market assumptions than the specific number.

WHAT IS DEMAND SENSING?

Demand sensing is the translation of downstream data with minimal latency to understand what is being sold, who is buying the product (attributes), and how it is impacting demand. Overall, there are four techniques to improve channel sensing:

1. **Focus on market drivers**. For each supply chain, there is a market driver that can be tracked and monitored as an indicator. For a manufacturer of lighting fixtures, it's the number of home starts; while for a manufacturer of asphalt, it's the number of miles of roads to be paved under government contracts.

2. **Use of downstream data (for demand pattern recognition)**. This requires the ability to collect and analyze data across market channels and geographies to understand who is buying which product and in what quantities. In the case of e-commerce, this can be click-through data; and in the case of social data, this can be consumer sentiment patterns. In the case of discrete manufacturing, this can be distributor sell-through data.

3. **Translating market data to supply**. After determining the patterns and trends, the demand signal is translated to supply. This can take the form of distribution targets at the distribution center (replacing traditional demand-consumption logic), manufacturing and inventory targets, and supply requirements.

4. **Measuring the impact of demand-shaping programs**. By definition, this is the company's ability to analytically measure

and determine the impact of demand shaping activities such as price promotions, sales tactics, and marketing events as well as changes in product mix, new product introductions, and other related factors on demand lift. Demand sensing reduces demand latency, or the time to sense market impacts, to measure the effectiveness of the program sooner. It also includes measuring and assessing the financial impact of demand shaping activities related to profit margins and overall revenue growth. Sensing and shaping go hand in hand in demand orchestration.

Traditional demand management processes use structured transactional data (orders and shipments). Unstructured data sources, such as weather patterns and social sentiment data, are increasingly important sources of insight for market-driven value networks. Unfortunately, unstructured data cannot be used in traditional demand architectures.

The minute that you launch the product, you get the market reaction, but it is not being used in the forecast. The use of this sentiment is the next big opportunity.
—Sanjiv Sidhu, Founder, i2 Technologies;
Current Chairman, o9 Solutions

The longer the supply chain, the greater the need for demand-sensing capabilities. With global outsourcing, companies have built long supply chains that translate rather than sense demand. As a result, the use of sensor data, market data, or temporal data (e.g., weather, traffic, etc.) to sense and reduce latency is an opportunity for most companies.

The most successful implementations of demand sensing are in consumer packaged goods and consumer electronics. Following the recent financial downturn, greater adoption is being seen in other industries.

Here are some rules of thumb for demand sensing:

- **Data**. Data requires harmonization, synchronization, and cleansing. It comes in many forms with different frequencies and multiple data definitions. Data structures need to be synchronized at three levels: product hierarchy, calendar, and unit of measure. The synchronization of data from multiple trading partners requires a demand signal repository.

■ **Organization**. The use of downstream or channel data also depends on the organization having the right combination of inspiration (vision), perspiration, and innovation. It is not as simple as stuffing downstream data into traditional supply chain technologies.

■ **Right data model**. To use downstream data, the forecasting model needs to be built to use the data. This requires the modeling of the ship to or channel views and the translation of demand to the ship from or manufacturing views. For 80 percent of companies that have implemented enterprise resource planning systems and advanced planning systems, this is a problem. In short, the technologies have been designed to model what manufacturing should make and not what the channel will sell. This difference is shown in Figures 3.6A and B.

■ **Organizational political impacts**. The use of downstream data gives true visibility to the channel. As a result, it can take time for the sales organization to get comfortable with demand-sensing processes and the use of downstream data. The greater the forecast bias, the larger the political implications and the greater the need to focus on change management.

As described earlier in the chapter, the more sensitive and responsive channel sales are to trends and seasonality, the more important demand sensing is to driving supply chain excellence. The ability to rapidly detect changes in demand gives companies greater flexibility to accommodate those changes, or influence overall demand.

WHAT IS DEMAND SHAPING?

Demand shaping happens when companies use sales and marketing tactics like price, promotion, new product launch, sales incentives,

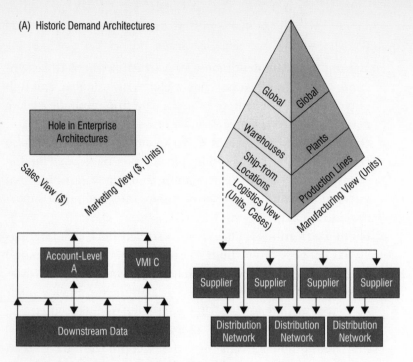

(A) Historic Demand Architectures

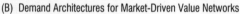

(B) Demand Architectures for Market-Driven Value Networks

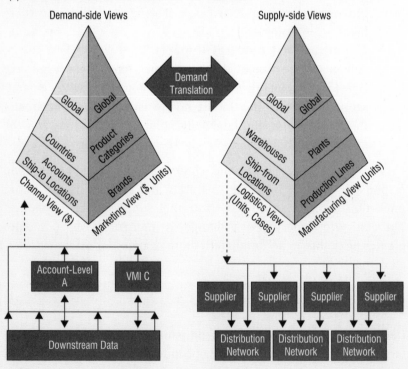

Figure 3.6A and B Data Model for Market-Driven Forecasting Data

or marketing programs to increase market share. The use of these tactics increases demand elasticity. Many times, companies believe that they are shaping demand, but find that they are really just shifting demand (moving demand from one period to another). Demand shaping creates value while demand shifting results in waste.

The first step in the market-driven demand management process is sensing market conditions based on channel signals. The second is shaping demand using advanced analytics. Demand sensing reduces the latency of the demand signal by 70 to 80 percent. Shortening the time to sense true customer acceptance improves the company's ability to understand and see true impacts of demand-shaping activities like price, promotion, sales, and marketing incentives and new product launch to increase demand lift.

Three elements are critical to an effective demand-shaping program:

1. **Data analytics**. Demand shaping is data-driven decision making. It is the ability to increase or decrease the volume and profit of goods sold by changing sales, product and marketing tactics, and strategies. This can be achieved by enabling what-if analysis so companies can understand the impact of changing price, trade promotions, marketing events, advertising, and product mix on demand lift and profitability to make optimal demand shaping decisions. It is an analysis of the elasticity of baseline volume. This usually refers to the shaping of unconstrained demand (i.e., demand shaping independent of supply constraints).

2. **Demand pattern recognition**. Demand pattern recognition uses customer data and channel insights along with multidimensional data (time, geography, channel, brand, product group, and product type) to improve decisions.

3. **Real-time supply visibility**. As demand is shaped, forecast error increases. As a result, it is important to have flexible supply processes to translate the demand impacts to internal and external supply organizations through supply visibility with minimal signal distortion and latency.

CASE STUDY

DELL: A CASE STUDY IN DEMAND SHIFTING

Dell pioneered the direct model for personal computers back in the 1990s, becoming a poster child for supply chain management. Dell's package-to-order philosophy differentiated them from the make-to-stock processes of the other computer makers. Initially, Dell avoided retail channels, instead offering every customer the opportunity to order a unique product built to their specifications. The genius behind Dell's direct model was that every PC that was built was pre-paid. The unique configurations coupled with the short lead times were tough to forecast.

To compensate, Dell shifts demand at the point of sale. For example, if you went online to the Dell website to purchase a Dell Inspiron 15 laptop, you may find a sales promotion pop-up that says, "For today and today only you can purchase a Dell Inspiron 17 laptop with a bigger screen, more processing capacity, bigger hard drive with expanded memory, as well as additional software for a reduced price." Consider a likely scenario of under-forecasted demand for key components for the Dell Inspiron 15 laptop. To align the supply chain, Dell actively shifts demand by offering a sales promotion to move a customer from the Inspiron 15 laptop to the Inspiron 17 laptop. Its goal was not to lose a sale or delay a shipment, but increase profitability.

You know the age-old conflicts between someone wanting to schedule production, and someone else wanting to meet customer demand, all happening while the manufacturing team wants to run one code for ten days without changing.
>   —*Vice President of Customer Service, Consumer Products*

Demand planning has evolved from a shadowy concept to a critical planning function.
>   —*Deborah Goldstein,*
>   *Vice President of Demand Planning, McCormick*

ACHIEVING MARKET-DRIVEN CAPABILITIES

To achieve market-driven capabilities companies need to focus on a four-step process:

1. Sense demand signals through the synchronization of internal and external data.

2. Shape demand using advanced analytics to create a more accurate unconstrained demand forecast.

3. Orchestrate based on cross-functional collaboration with sales, marketing, finance, and operations planning that reflect capacity constraints and market-to-market variability.

4. Create a final constrained demand response.

Using what-if analysis, demand forecasters can shape unconstrained demand based on current sales and marketing activities as well as external factors affecting demand. This includes weather, special events, and economic conditions to optimize volume and revenue while minimizing marketing investment. Figure 3.7 illustrates the four key steps in the market-driven demand management process.

For many, this is a radical shift. Most demand forecasting processes are supply driven with little emphasis on predicting unconstrained demand, let alone shaping demand. In the interviews of 75 supply chain pioneers, when we asked about demand shaping, we found that most companies shift, versus shape, demand to meet supply constraints. Today, the norm is fitting demand to supply, rather than supply to demand.

In contrast, market-driven supply chains sense demand signals and shape future demand based on sales and marketing strategies and tactics, rather than reacting to past supply constraints. It puts more emphasis on downstream activities that directly affect consumer demand, thus creating a more practical view of true unconstrained demand. This design should include an iterative framework that combines analytics and domain knowledge with financial analysis of go-to-market strategies.

To be effective, the process needs discipline. The overall market-driven forecasting process design combines quantitative analysis

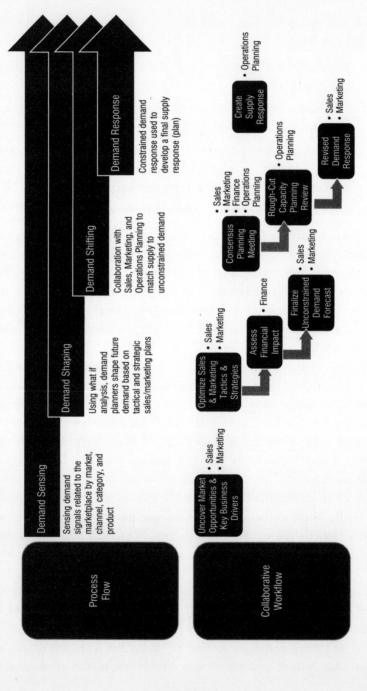

Figure 3.7 Market-Driven Demand Management Process

to measure effectiveness. It allows the demand forecasting process owner to view departmental forecasts from various functional viewpoints, which have different perspectives, to better understand business impacts.

Financial analysis is necessary throughout the market-driven forecasting process to evaluate the profit potential and impact of various sales and marketing strategies and tactics that are designed to drive incremental demand. Finance's role is more of a support function to assess the revenue and profit implications of sales and marketing activities that are used to shape demand. In many cases, the payback, or revenue potential of sales promotions and marketing events, is minimal at best. These activities can cause huge volume swings in demand, which can create havoc throughout the supply chain, shifting resources and adding unnecessary costs. Supply chains with large volume swings must be designed to absorb the impact.

Although the intent of demand shaping is to lure new consumers to the company's brands and products, the large majority of marketing programs only shift demand. Without financial analysis and discipline, this over time can erode brand equity and the overall health of the business

Synchronizing Signals

The financial budget is an initial planning tool to gauge the potential health of the business. In many cases, the financial plan is created six months to a year in advance, making it obsolete after the first demand forecasting cycle update. By the time the first period of the plan is reviewed and updated, more new, and relevant information is available that can be used to assess the variance between the original plan and current market conditions. That same information can be used to influence demand-shaping activities by assessing the profit impact and supporting marketing programs that can close those gaps during the demand shaping activities.

Synchronization of financial budget and channel data is a challenge. Figure 3.8 illustrates the difference between weekly syndicated scanner data for a beverage product as compared with shipments in a market area. Although the data is very close, there are many periods where supply is greater than demand and vice versa, making it difficult to predict true demand using shipment data alone. In the figure, trade (supply) loading due to trade incentives (e.g., off-invoice allowances, trade promotions, and other related trade incentives) is obvious. In addition, there are periods where sales promotions and other related consumer promotion incentives have been implemented to drive incremental demand, as well as selloff of retailer inventories. As a result, the goal should be data synchronization, not tight integration.

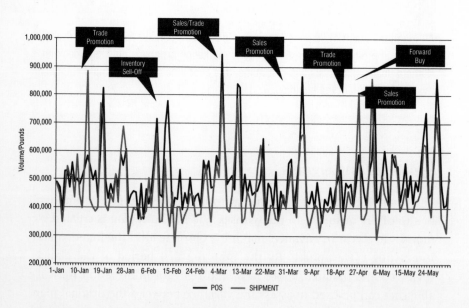

Figure 3.8 Demand versus Supply Response

CASE STUDY

DRIVING BOTTOM-LINE IMPROVEMENTS

The implementation of a new demand management system helped a large U.S. direct store delivery company improve forecasting accuracy by 4 percent and increased service levels by 6 percent. Despite growing volumes, the company was able to hold inventory costs flat. The company also found that based on the new forecast, the sales department was better equipped to plan profitable sales promotions. The project's savings exceeded expectations.

The heavy promotional nature of the products caused demand to wax and wane by store or region. Before using their new market-driven demand management solution, the planners struggled to accurately factor in product seasonality. The sales force was also guessing at how much product needed to be stocked for special promotions designed to drive volume, or even what price point to select to drive enough volume to turn a profit.

"Our existing solutions did a poor job of forecasting demand around promotions," explained the director of demand and supply chain planning.

Data was so scattered in numerous locations. Some of it was sitting in spreadsheets in regional offices and might be sent in once a week, if that. In the division that managed delivery to drugstore chains (a growing business), forecast accuracy was decreasing by the year.

"It was driving a lot of service issues and increasing our carrying costs," explained a senior manager for strategic sourcing.

No Second-Guessing

"When we switched to our new demand management solution, we saw our forecast accuracy improve immediately. We also saw service levels take off in a positive way and our inventories decreased. We exceeded our original projections; the accuracy is driven by a change from a 50,000-foot view of forecasts to a more detailed look. Now we can talk about a particular deal with a retailer and know what kind of lift is generated and then that drives the supply chain. There is no second-guessing," said a demand planner at a food and beverage company.

Creating Synergy between Sales and Demand Planning

The new demand management solution featured an interactive portal where salespeople enter the attributes of a promotion they would like to run and the demand planners provide a variety of scenarios (demand

(Continued)

shaping) to help the sales team decide if the promotion would be profitable. The sales teams now had the capability to measure the impact of in-store merchandising vehicles such as endcap displays to determine the incremental unit volume impact, as well as margin impact within designated market channels (i.e., retail grocery channel).

Using the new demand management solution, the demand planners can make calculations and let salespeople know when there isn't enough specific product in the pipeline near their territory to meet the estimated volume that the promotion will generate, and then work with sales to find a better promotion (demand shifting). They can also help the sales team calculate the lift for a promotion, and whether that sales increase—at that price—will make the promotion profitable.

Critical to this demand-shaping service is the speed to value. The answer needs to be quick. The demand management staff no longer needs from six hours to an entire weekend to gather the data, including tens of thousands of time series calculations. To get an answer, it is now minutes for a response. When it took a long time to gather data, information was released on a rigid schedule, and it was often out of date. With the new system, that is no longer the case.

Achieving Lasting Return on Investment

The company used its demand management solution to build three additional attributes into its forecasts: competitor activities, weather conditions, and promotion cannibalization of existing sales.

"We are trying to understand if our promotions are impacting sales of other products. With more confidence in the forecasts, planners are using the demand data to align the entire organization, affecting what we produce, where we're going to ship, all the way up to our top line financial commitments. This drives all facets of our business. With our new market-driven demand management process and solution, we're able to accomplish our goal of right flavor, right time, right store," said the manufacturer's planner. "It's hard to put a price tag on it, but it is really invaluable in terms of running the business effectively and better serving the customer."

For this company, demand shaping is becoming an essential part of the S&OP process. From a tactical standpoint, demand shaping enhances the demand and supply planning process by improving demand/supply balance. Although most companies use demand forecasting to plan for customer demand, this company now has the opportunity to use demand shaping and shifting to close the gap between unconstrained demand expectations and supply availability.

WHY IS BECOMING MARKET DRIVEN IMPORTANT FOR INDUSTRIAL COMPANIES?

Market-driven strategies are often associated only with consumer product companies. The literature is full of examples of forecasting shelf-level consumer demand and sensing demand using retail POS data. However, demand management is just as important for industrial sectors. The difference is the inputs. For example, an aircraft manufacturing company that has a three-year backlog of planes needs to focus on demand contract management, platform rationalization, back orders, design modifications, and engineering changes.

One problem is the lack of market visionaries in the industrial manufacturing industries. While Procter & Gamble painted the vision of the customer-driven value network for the consumer goods manufacturing sector, there is no industrial company that has waved a similar flag in the discrete manufacturing sectors. Let's look at an example of where market data could change a discrete manufacturing supply chain. The color of an automobile is the singular most important buying criteria for a consumer entering a distributor showroom. Many buyers leave compromising on color because the car that they want is not available. For manufacturing, the selection of color is problematic. It is the first step of assembly and the selection of color drives many other decisions for the car's interior. Automotive manufacturers know that they do not know the product that car dealers want, but they have been slow to collect data on consumer intent (what they wanted versus what they bought). Likewise, the manufacturers have been slow to use e-commerce data from cars sold online to drive features, colors, and styles on the manufacturing line for other channels. The industry has an opportunity to better synchronize demand signals.

Industrial companies tend to be driven by product innovation, not market insights. As the environment for these large organizations becomes more diverse and global, these product-driven industrial sectors are struggling to reduce complexity in their product and supply networks.

A good demand management process will enhance the S&OP analysis by providing a consensus demand forecasting environment that incorporates statistical methodologies, dashboarding capabilities and improves workflow to create a more accurate unconstrained demand forecast. As a result, market insights matter more than ever.

DRIVING THE MARKET-DRIVEN DEMAND MANAGEMENT ADVANTAGE

Market-driven demand management is supported by demand-driven fore-casting principles that have a significant impact on a company, whether the company sells products or services. Companies that have implemented a market-driven forecasting process have experienced four key benefits:

1. **Alignment**. A market-driven forecast is a more effective approach for upstream planning. It better anticipates uncon-strained demand. The benefits of more effective upstream plan-ning include a reduction in out-of-stocks on the shelf at retailers; a significant reduction in customer back orders; a reduction in finished goods inventory carrying costs; and consistently high levels of customer service across all products and services.

2. **Visibility**. Because of improved collaboration, senior manag-ers have a better understanding of what drives profitability, resulting in tighter budget control and more efficient allocation of marketing investment dollars. This results in a better under-standing of product, customer, and market profitability, allow-ing the creation of more focused strategic and tactical plans to allocate resources across brands and products to drive incremen-tal unit volume growth and profitability.

3. **Growth**. As all the stakeholders in the process begin to trust the market-driven forecasting process and enabling solutions, they become more closely aligned, driving quality collaboration among sales, marketing, finance, and operations planning, as well as with external stakeholders. The building of these stron-ger relationships translates into stronger network integration, which helps to minimize the pressures of the market dynamics surrounding the company's brands and products.

4. **Competitive advantage**. The focus is not only on cost savings as a justification for introducing a new world demand manage-ment process and enabling solution. Market-driven value net-works can create a competitive advantage in providing higher

quality demand forecasts to improve customer service over competitors to increase market share for a company's products and services.

Supply chain technology adoption has always been slowed by issues with scalability, data cleanliness, and the sheer volume of data. Today's technology makes this no longer an issue.

A good demand management process will enhance the horizontal processes outlined in Chapter 5. It is the backbone for the S&OP process, providing a consensus demand forecasting environment that incorporates statistical methodologies, dashboarding capability, and workflow to create a more accurate unconstrained demand forecast. It is the baseline forecast for revenue management, and the driving force in network design to determine supplier development practices.

There is a need to hold people accountable in the forecasting process. Accountability is the mortar between the bricks of the market-driven value network. Based on the lessons on bias from Fildes and Goodwin's study, discussed earlier, we know that when people touch the statistical baseline forecast their intentions are good, but their execution does not always add value to the demand forecast. In fact, most people who touch the forecast actually do not add any value. These non-value-added touch points need to be identified and either improved or eliminated. The best approach for a company to take is to implement a new methodology for measuring demand management process performance and accuracy called *forecast value added* (FVA). The term *FVA* was first used by Michael Gilliland in a 2002 article in the journal *Supply Chain Management Review*.[3]

FVA uses standard forecast performance measurements (metrics) to identify value-added or non-value-added activities in the process that contribute to the accuracy or inaccuracy of the demand forecast. The result is a mechanism that reduces non-value-added touch points, thus improving the overall accuracy. Companies that have successfully implemented FVA have experienced significant improvement in overall forecast accuracy and reduced cycle times. If an activity does not improve the accuracy of the statistical baseline forecast, it should be eliminated, or minimized (simplified), to reduce cycle time and resources.

It is also good practice to compare the statistical forecast to a naïve forecast. (The naïve forecast is a simple technique where the forecast equals the volume of goods sold in the prior forecasting period.) Naïve forecasts, in some situations, can be surprisingly difficult to beat, yet it is very important that the organizations ensure that software and a statistical modeler improve on the naïve model. The focus needs to be on continuous improvement. If the software, modeler is not able to do this, it makes sense to implement better software, improve the skills of the modeler, or just use the naïve model as a baseline forecast.

Implementing FVA into the demand management process requires that forecasts be recorded and saved before and after each cycle. Having the capabilities to store forecast history by a stream of activities (e.g., consensus forecast adjustments, managerial overrides, price lift calculations, etc.) is critical to measuring the value-added, or non-value-added, contribution to the overall process. Utilizing the statistical baseline forecast as the default is the key to establishing a benchmark to measure the effectiveness of all the touch points in the process. Unfortunately, few companies capture the appropriate data, or the level of detail on a historical basis, to conduct FVA. This is an opportunity.

Traditional supply chains are operationally disconnected and reactive to demand. Demand volatility and operational complexity require supply chains to become more resilient. Market-driven value networks begin with conscious choices that integrate and synchronize supply with demand channels and product portfolios.

SOCIAL: A NEW FORM OF DEMAND SIGNAL

With the evolution of social technologies (see Figure 3.9), companies can now have a relationship directly with their customers. Most companies are dabbling in the use of social technologies for marketing but have not connected the signals to the supply chain. Instead, Facebook and digital marketing initiatives are currently managed by the marketing department. In the traditional organization, it is marketing for the sake of marketing. The pace of change, as shown in Figure 3.9, and the size of the opportunity are daunting.

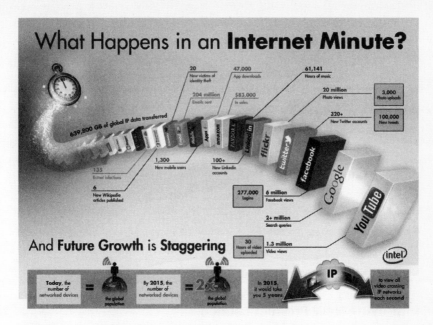

Figure 3.9 The Impact of Social Media on Consumer Behavior *Source:* Intel

Today, too few companies are thinking about the use of social data to improve the demand forecast to become market driven. In interview after interview with pioneers, we have been looking for this change; but so far, it has not happened. What is the difference between a market-driven and marketing-driven approach? It is distinguished by three elements:

1. **It is not about *you*. It is about *them*.** When a company is a marketing-driven organization, the message is all about them. It is about the company's products or the company. The brand managers try to own a closely held message. The goal is to yell the message and get it everywhere. In contrast, when companies are market driven, the goal is to increase customer relevance and create relationships with the shopper, the customer, and the greater market. It is no longer about just the brand or the company; instead, it is about the buyer of the products or services. In this new type of supply chain, the power shifts to the buyer, or end consumer. The goal is to serve the customer.

2. **Open process that is orchestrated cross-functionally**. In the traditional organization, marketing-driven initiatives are tightly controlled within the marketing department. In the market-driven organization, the focus is outside-in and horizontal.

3. **Market-driven companies listen**. These companies also test and learn in real time. They align their supply chains to orchestrate while implementing test-and-learn strategies in the channel. They use data analytics to sense answers to the questions that they do not know to ask. They continuously test and learn. In contrast, a marketing-driven company constructs campaigns, analyzes data, and retests concepts. The campaigns are based on history. They are static. It is hard to listen when you are so busy filling social media sound waves with your message.

Improving New Product Launch

The lifeblood of a corporation is new products. A new product launch is an example of where a marketing-driven approach can yield big dividends. The number one issue for new product launch failure is the lack of good demand insights.

The use of social technologies to listen to consumer sentiment is an opportunity to rectify this situation. This information can be used in cross-functional launch meetings to be more effective. Dell, Newell Rubbermaid, and Whirlpool do this weekly. This could be an easy fix—placement, information, message—and quick sensing allows them to get it right before the product fails.

When companies launch new products, they can now use action buttons to sense the market response to their new product launches. These data can then be used to build forecasting models. For example, if a fan in a company's loyal demographic wants the new product, it is a powerful causal factor to put into a demand forecast. If the majority of consumers hate the product, it is probably time to rethink the product build plan. The value is the speed at which a company can access this insight. Instead of a 7- to 14-day latency to get channel data, the company is able to see the end consumer's response in near real-time (1 to 2 days).

Figure 3.10 Use of "Action Buttons" in a New Product Launch *Source:* GiantNerd.com

Figure 3.10 shows the use of an action button on an e-commerce website. With this type of feature, as the product is shipped to the market, companies can follow the social sentiment closely. It can be used as a causal factor. The action buttons are also a great way to get direct customer feedback. In combination with demand sensing technologies, this helps companies to get a quick read of the market.

Listen and Use Social Sentiment Data

Across the Web, consumers today post ratings and review data about products. This near real-time data is a great opportunity for a company to understand customer sentiment and share the information with retail customers. In the case of Newell Rubbermaid, it enabled its team to leverage immediate feedback from consumers to identify an issue and quickly respond to ensure that the launch was a success. Prior to the use of this type of data, brands faced a 7- to 14-day latency to receive and understand consumer data. In the next case study, we share how Newell Rubbermaid, a leader in the use of social data, was able to identify an issue that could have caused nega-tive word-of-mouth sentiment circumventing leading retailers from returning the product.

CASE STUDY

DEMAND SENSING AND NEWELL RUBBERMAID NEW PRODUCT LAUNCH

Few companies use social sentiment in the supply chain better than Newell Rubbermaid. The company is an S&P 500 company and a global marketer of consumer and commercial products with 2011 sales of approximately $5.9 billion. It is headquartered in Atlanta, Georgia, and has approximately 21,000 employees worldwide.

In April 2008, the company launched Rubbermaid Produce Saver food stor-age containers as an extension to its popular Easy Find Lids line. The product was designed to extend the life of fruits and vegetables by 33 percent com-pared with traditional Rubbermaid containers. Rubbermaid Produce Saver addressed the two factors that age fruits and vegetables quickly—moisture and lack of oxygen—with a vented lid to allow produce to breathe and a tray to elevate food out of moisture in the container. The product launched in three sizes: 2-, 5-, and 14-cup bowls. Sets of four containers retailed at mass retailers and grocery stores ranging in price from $9.97 to $12.99.

The first seven consumer-generated product reviews about Produce Saver on the Rubbermaid.com brand website included two five-star and five one-star reviews. Rubbermaid contacted the five one-star reviewers to find that there was a product usage issue. Consumers were not following instructions to "not wash the produce" before they put it into the container. As a result, the washed produce was rapidly spoiling in the containers, rather than lasting longer. After seeing the consumer comments (see Figure 3.11A), Rubbermaid quickly responded to make sure consumers understood how to use the product by putting additional instruction information on the product page and writing a blog post on how to use Produce Saver for best results (as seen in Figure 3.11B). As consumers used Produce Saver correctly and achieved the desired result—fruits and veggies lasting longer—the result was improved recommendations on the website. Because of early demand sensing and consumer feedback, Newell Rubbermaid was able to take immediate action to help ensure the product launch was a success.

Overall Rating
★★★★★ 1 out of 5

Appearance
Durability
Quality
Ease of Use
Written by: Eliz

Waste of Money

Date: July 11, 2008

I was so disappointed in the Produce Saver. I purchased the 14 c and the 5 c sizes. I filled both with clean, freshly torn romaine lettuce and also filled a regular Tupperware with the same lettuce. After 2 days, the lettuce in the Produce Saver is limp, wet, and starting to turn brown. The lettuce in the regular Tupperware container is crisp and delicious. The Produce Saver has done just the opposite that it claims to do. I would like a refund as I will not use again.

Was this review helpful to you? Yes   No   (Report as inappropriate)

Response from Rubbermaid:

By Product Management Team, July 28, 2008

We are sorry to hear your experience with Produce Saver was not positive. You mentioned that you used Produce Saver to store torn lettuce. This product however is best for un-cut produce that is still in the same form as when you purchased it. Additional information on the best ways to use Produce Saver can be found in the Use & Care Instructions link on this page or at: http://blog.rubbermaid.com/home/2008/07/produce-saver-.html

re this review: 🇫 📧 📑 ⓔ

JUL 25

Produce Saver - "How To" Usage Guide

Posted by Megan Murphy | Comments (0) | TrackBack (0)

I have received a few questions lately on how to correctly use Produce Saver so I thought I would put together a handy "how to" guide based on my own experiences to help answer any questions that may be out there.

First, purchase Produce Saver in the size that will best fit what you are intending to store. For a traditional pack of strawberries, the 5 cup Produce Saver should work nicely. For a large bunch of grapes or a small head of lettuce the 14 cup would be better suited. Finally, for a small container of raspberries or blueberries, the 2 cup should be just about right.

Once you bring produce home from the grocery store or farmer's market **don't wash it before storing**. Moisture will only increase the risk of decay.

Make sure the Crisp Tray™ is in the bottom of the container. Place the produce in the container taking care to not pack the produce in too tightly so it doesn't get bruised or damaged.

Place the lid on the container and store in the refrigerator. Produce Saver containers easily stack on top of one another or with other Rubbermaid food storage containers.

You'll see that excess moisture will settle in the bottom of the container beneath the tray. The vents in the side of the lid will allow produce to breath even with the lid on to protect the produce.

Figure 3.11A and B Listening and Learning in New Product Launch: Produce Saver *Source:* Newell Rubbermaid, SXSW Presentation, 2010

(Continued)

Social media should not be social for the sake of being social. It is not just about the number of fans. The data should not be relegated to the marketing department. The process should not be outsourced to a public-relations firm. Instead, it should be seen as a way to have a new form of relationship with the customer. Leaders recognize it as a new demand signal, realizing that it is a new and valuable input into the market-driven supply chain.

HOW CAN A COMPANY IMPROVE DEMAND MANAGEMENT?

There are several key steps a company can take to begin the transition to a market-driven demand management process:

- Ensure *accountability* and a focus on continuous improvement by using the FVA techniques.
- Make *data sharing* and forecast accuracy part of top-to-top meetings with trading partners. Take ownership of the forecast error in the extended value network.
- Introduce *S&OP processes* based on a strong demand-driven forecasting process that focuses on data and analytics to sense demand signals, and to shape and to translate demand to create a more accurate demand response.
- Increase *granularity of data* analysis to reflect what is sold in the channel. Define the business hierarchy in the model based on profit implications.
- Leverage a demand management technology to automate forecasting workflow to create a more accurate unconstrained demand forecast. The enabling solution should provide a user-friendly interface that allows nonstatistical users (or planners) to systematically run *what-if analyses* to shape demand.
- Evaluate the fit of the data model to use channel data. Investigate integration of *downstream data*, such as retail POS data, to provide a better source of true demand. Synchronize data inputs.
- Embrace new forms of *channel data* to drive innovation.

TO DRIVE CHANGE

- Map available demand signals and design how to use them outside-in.
- Forecast with the goal in mind. Evaluate the fit of the demand models and statistical engines.
- Build demand sensing and shaping capabilities into the process.
- Design supply processes based on the probability of demand.

New types of information, more data granularity with less latency, combined with greater computing power should open up new opportunities. Most of the technologies utilized in traditional demand management processes were first-generation analytics built on established data models based on a predefined set of questions. They are not equal to today's challenge. As a result, many companies embarking on this journey will either need to buy new technologies or reimplement existing systems.

SUMMARY

Demand management is the natural place to start the market-driven value network transformation. To accomplish this goal, focus on:

- Eliminating bias through measurement and accountability.
- Driving continuous improvement processes to improve the demand management process through FVA analysis.
- Implementing a simple, easy-to-use system for sales to calculate the profitability and market share impact of demand shaping programs. Use checks and balances through the finance organization to hold sales accountable for demand shaping profitability.
- Tuning data models frequently (at least once a year) to be sure that the forecasting technology is properly aligned to the ever-changing business requirements.
- Building strong channel relationships to get access to channel data. Use analytics and harmonize the data for usage.

- Embracing new forms of data. Synchronize the inputs.
- Focusing energy on a common plan with role-based views. It is too complex and counterproductive to focus on "one number" or a tightly integrated plan.

NOTES

1. Charles W. Chase Jr., *Demand Driven Forecasting: A Structured Approach to Forecasting* (Hoboken, NJ: John Wiley & Sons, 2009), pp. 21–50.
2. Robert Fildes and Paul Goodwin, "Good and Bad Judgment in Forecasting: Lessons from Four Companies," *Foresight: The International Journal of Applied Forecasting* (Fall 2007): pp. 5–10.
3. Michael Gilliland, "Is Forecasting a Waste of Time?" *Supply Chain Management Review*, July–August, 2002.

CHAPTER **4**

Supply Management Evolution

*The path for supply chain excellence starts with supply.
You cannot achieve supply chain excellence without a
solid foundation of operational reliability.*

—Lora Cecere

The concepts of bricks and supply are inextricably linked. Over the last three decades, the supply chain pioneers have carefully built supply processes from the inside-out. They are honed for efficiency. They are not honed outside-in. The concept of market-driven value networks is a dramatic change.

The strong vertical silos of manufacturing, distribution, and procurement formed the backbone of supply chain management. These processes are more mature than demand, and they are more insular to change. For leaders, the concepts of the market-driven value networks will be a gradual transformation: a continuation of current programs. They will slowly use digital technologies to reduce waste. Their steadfast focus will be on process innovation. They will forge new opportunities to drive value. However, for the laggards, it will not be an evolution. It will be a revolution. Table 4.1 is a holistic overview.

145

Table 4.1 Change Management Issues for Supply in Becoming Market Driven

From:	To:
Marketing driven	Market driven
Sell-in focus	Sell-through focus
Inside-out flows	Outside-in flows
Vertical processes	Horizontal processes
The most efficient supply chain	The most effective supply chain

Many will ask: "Why should supply chain processes change?" For leaders, the answers are clear. The issues for the next decade lie ahead of us. Product complexity has risen. Business continuity, risk mitigation, and corporate social responsibility are new goals. Material scarcity and rising commodity prices are eroding margins. Manufacturing processes are inflexible, transportation is a constraint, and progress on inventory and working capital is stalled. We cannot solve these problems by doing more historic supply chain processes. There are new forms of data, new technologies, and new processes evolving. The solution requires a redesign.

The rate of adoption will be driven by market volatility and the impact of slowing industry sector growth. The greater the margin pressure, the faster companies will adopt the practices of market-driven value networks.

My supply chain is like a tube of toothpaste. We are currently being squeezed at both ends. In fact, until we got our supply chain under control, we were selling product for less than we could make it.
—European Consumer Products
Supply Chain Leader, November 2011

In the evolution, the vertical silos of supply become connected through horizontal processes. The most common horizontal processes are revenue management, sales and operations planning (S&OP), supplier development, and corporate social responsibility (CSR). (This transition is covered in great detail in Chapter 5.) These horizontal processes become connectors for the end-to-end value network. They align the traditional supply processes of source, make, and deliver against a business strategy. When companies successfully build market-driven value networks, demand and supply volatility can be traded off bidirectionally from the customer's customer to the supplier's supplier. When done right, these processes are outside-in and orchestrated from market to market.

Making the transition is easier said than done. It is a stark contrast to the conventional supply processes that drove efficiency in the supply chain for the past 30 years. The journey requires a visionary leader, a guiding coalition, a multiyear road map, and a strong change management program.

CURRENT STATE

Today, market-driven concepts are aspirational. Companies are at the starting line. The concepts are incubating within process improvement initiatives. Organizations have a strong vertical definition of supply processes, they are early in the development of horizontal processes, and they are questioning how to put the processes together to drive greater value. While the questions are percolating in the minds of leaders, they are anything but market driven.

Within a supply chain, the pieces of supply (sourcing, manufacturing, and logistics) are old school. They are steeped in tradition. It is a world where hard hats, safety shoes, and clipboards are the norm. It is a flurry of boxes, pallets, totes, and forklifts. The processes are driven by manufacturing schedules, factory changeovers, shift changes, and quality inspections. Plant managers know when they open the door of a factory if it is going to be a good day by the sound of the equipment. There is a steady rhythm underpinning the day-to-day activities.

In this work environment, real people make real things to ship to real customers every day. It is where the rubber meets the road. It is clear if a delivery is on time or if a shipment met expectations. For people in these organizations, the pace is fast and the challenges are fast and furious. It is a place where good management skills matter. For the rest of the organization, it is largely viewed as boring.

For the external world, the impact of supply processes is pervasive. The processes of supply have long-lasting impacts on the landscapes of cities and rural communities. As factories move to towns, smokestacks redefine city skylines and trucks clog roadways. Traffic patterns follow manufacturing shift changes, and decisions on factory capacity have a direct impact on spending on Main Street.

During 2011, our aggregate commodity costs increased primar-
ily as a result of higher costs of coffee, dairy, grains and oils,
packaging materials, other raw materials, meat, and nuts. Our
commodity costs increased approximately $2.6B in 2011 and
approximately $1.0B in 2010 compared to the prior year.
—Kraft 2011 Annual Report

The community impacts are also everlasting on community infra-structure. Over 85 percent of carbon and water used in a company is used in the supply chain processes. To ensure potable water, clean air, and a safe environment, the community depends on CSR programs and ethical supply chain leadership.

Bricks also matter for economic growth. The transformation—of distribution centers/factories moving in or moving out of a city—can be both good and bad for sleepy cities and rural communities. The increasing pace of network design in the supply chain has accelerated the impact. Changes in supply chain network design, resulting in the relocation/expansion of manufacturing and distribution centers glob-ally, happens four times faster today than five years ago.

What Is Supply?

Within the supply chain, the processes of supply are composed of the subprocesses of source (procurement), make (manufacturing), and deliver (logistics). In general, these processes are more mature than demand, and the back end (supplier relationships) of the chain is more connected than the front end (channel relationships).

The processes of supply are industry specific. Manufacturing, distribution, and procurement processes for a pharmaceutical com-pany are as different as night and day from a discrete manufacturing

The company anticipates that the cost of underlying commodities
will continue to face upward pressure in 2012. We currently expect
the incremental impact of commodity costs primarily in juices and
sweeteners to range between $350 million and $450 million on
our full year 2012 consolidated results.
—Coca-Cola 2011 Annual Report

company making parts for an automotive engine. They are also more resistant to change. The process definitions are:

- **Source:** The sourcing of raw materials and the management of supplier relationships. In recent years, this organization has become externally focused on CSR for sourcing relationships. This role traditionally reports to the procurement manager. Over 60 percent of procurement organizations report to the chief financial officer.
- **Make:** The management of manufacturing processes both within and external to the organization. This usually also includes the processes of quality management and the orchestration of external relationships with contract manufacturers in the value network. This role typically reports to the chief operating officer.
- **Deliver:** The design and execution of inventory, logistics, and distribution processes. This function within an organization also typically includes order management and customer service. In discrete organizations, this can also include warranty, returns, and the management of the service supply chain. They are also tasked to manage relationships with third-party logistics providers and external warehouses. They typically report to either sales or manufacturing.

When the journey for supply chain excellence started 30 years ago, each industry had a different starting point. They also had a different vision and path for their journey. The discrete and make-to-order manufacturers' (aerospace and defense, automotive, and industrial manufacturing) supply chain processes originated in procurement. In contrast, the foundation of process companies' supply chain organizations (chemical, consumer products, and pharmaceutical) was in manufacturing.

Supply processes are steeped in tradition. In stage one of the market-driven value network model (see Figure 1.3), organizations will often use the terms *logistics* and *supply chain* interchangeably. For many, they are still synonymous. In these organizations, there is also little overlap in planning and coordination between supply (procurement), make (manufacturing), and deliver (logistics). Each function operates in isolation with a focus on optimizing itself. For manufacturing, this translates to the lowest cost per unit; for sourcing, this is usually the lowest purchase cost; and for logistics, this is usually the lowest cost to ship a unit. These groups operate as separate teams with different metrics and reporting structures. The overarching goal is efficiency, but the individual functional metrics are conflicting, resulting in internal friction. In interviews, some people liken the relationship to a medieval fiefdom.

Over time, organizations realize that supply excellence needs to be defined by trade-offs in source, make, and deliver. The answer lies in aligning these functions to actualize the business strategy. This realization typically happens in stage 3 of the market-driven value chain maturity model (see Figure 1.3) stimulating the development of S&OP processes.

Building the Global Team

Over the last three decades, changes in the supply processes of manufacturing and distribution have been slow. One of the largest impacts was the expansion into BRIC (Brazil, Russia, India, and China) countries. As supply chains became more global, planning processes were redefined. However, this journey is far from over. Companies still struggle to find the right balance between regional and corporate processes. Each company defines governance of global/local policies in the supply chain differently.

It is a world where data transparency has been both a blessing and a curse. For many, it was a blessing—allowing employees around the world to have the same data in near real-time in a usable form—enabling common data to drive global processes. For some, it was also a curse. Many leaders did not want transparency in their operations.

Using new forms of data, the global pioneers (the second generation of supply chain leaders) redesigned supply chain processes and drove deliberate change. Global process initiatives were designed to improve cycles, decrease waste, and improve agility.

Now, in the most mature companies, these three processes (source, make, and deliver) report to a common leader; but for the majority of companies, they still report separately through different organizations. One of the first companies to have a common reporting structure was Procter & Gamble (P&G). In interviews, the early pioneers attribute the redesign of the organizational structure by a common leader to have helped them better align and leapfrog competition.

It was an enabler to P&G's success. In 2011, P&G redesigned supply processes to add $3 billion in new revenue.

One of the factors that drove supply chain excellence at Procter & Gamble was early recognition of the need to organize all the processes and work within the supply chain, including make, source, and deliver under one functional design. This included the appointment of a single overall supply chain leader as we organized a product supply organization in 1985. This provided an early opportunity to look "end-to-end" across the business and highlight the need for change and trade-offs.
—*Jake Barr, Product Supply Organization, Procter & Gamble*

SUPPLY CHAIN MATTERS

Supply chain management is a complex system with complex processes with increasing complexity. Today, complexity reigns. It is a time of increasing volatility, product personalization, and proliferation of new channels. All of these shifts increase business complexity.

The increase in product proliferation adds costs. Supply organizations have been challenged to improve efficiency (lowest cost per case) in the face of this rising complexity. The focus is how to do more with less.

Companies that are new to supply chain management will confuse complex processes with complex systems. What is the difference? In complex processes, companies focus on understanding the complexity of multiple inputs against a single output. Most companies understand supply chain as a complex process. It is only the most mature that understand and manage it as a complex system. In a complex system, companies focus on understanding the trade-offs among growth, inventory, customer service, demand volatility, supply chain risks, total supply chain costs, and asset utilization. In each company, there is an effective frontier of these trade-offs that is unique for each company.

Supply chain cannot be done effectively on an island.
—*Sanjiv Sidhu, Founder, i2 Technologies*
Current Chairman, o9 Solutions

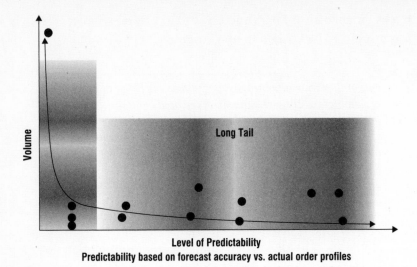

Figure 4.1 The Long Tail of the Supply Chain

One of the issues of complexity is the management of the long tail of the supply chain. This happens when products that have low volume and low order frequency (see Figure 4.1) form a large portion of the product portfolio.

As products proliferate, horizontal processes become more important. If this does not happen, the long tail of the supply chain whips the supply chain into chaos, making it tougher to have visibility to make the right decisions in supply chain execution. Without clarity, employees in the factory are unclear about what to make when or what to ship on which truck to which customers.

No industry knows the impact of the long tail of the supply chain like the consumer products (CPG) industry. In this industry segment, new products abound. Product introduction has accelerated. Today, in CPG, the average company has 5,000 items. Over the last 10 years, this number has increased by 55 percent. Across all CPG companies, 1,600 consumer goods products were introduced into the grocery channel in the United States a year. The tendency is to add, not to rationalize or eliminate products. This has generated more supply chain waste and eroded efficiency gains in supply processes.

We continue to face ongoing challenges in managing and balancing the business need for more differentiation and variety with rising supply chain complexity.
—*Rick Sather, Vice President of Customer Supply Chain, Kimberly Clark*

With product personalization, volume decreases and the predictability of supply declines. As a result, many companies are facing a new world of defining and managing supply processes for long tail supply chains. By definition, the further out the product portfolio is in the tail, the less efficient the supply chain process. It is also less suitable for traditional linear optimization techniques found in the first generation of supply chain planning technologies.

In the period from 2005 to 2010, fewer than 5 percent of companies in any industry had a disciplined process to rationalize product complexity or product profitability. As a result, companies found themselves in a dilemma. Companies look to the supply organization as the bank—savings from cost savings in the supply organization—to finance growth. The expectation is that the supply organization can keep finding ways to save money to help the sales and marketing organizations enter new markets. The fallacy with this approach is that unlike the following World Kitchen case study, there is no disciplined approach to rationalize products or customer profitability. The products and channels proliferate, complexity mounts, and it becomes more difficult to control supply costs. It is a vicious circle that can lead to bankruptcy.

CASE STUDY

SUCCESS IN COMBATING RISING PRODUCT COMPLEXITY

The kitchen is no longer just about utility, it is now a fashion statement. Mixers, cookware, and cutlery now come in multiple shapes and colors to accent the kitchen and make a statement. It was this world that World Kitchen entered with the spinoff from Corning in 1998.

World Kitchen has major manufacturing and distribution operations throughout North America and Asia. Well-known brands include Bakers

(Continued)

Secret, Chicago Cutlery, CorningWare, Corelle, EKco, Pyrex, and Revere. Products are distributed through mass retailers and specialty stores in the United States and Canada.

World Kitchen filed for bankruptcy protection in May 2002, stating that it had accrued unmanageable debt through the buyouts of other housewares companies in 1999. One of the specific issues leading to the bankruptcy and the successful recovery was product complexity. In 2002, World Kitchen implemented a disciplined process for managing its product platform. Marketing owned the process where all products were analyzed quarterly by finance and ranked by volume and profitability. All products were reviewed by the team, but there was an extra focus on products that were low volume and had a small contribution margin. If the marketing team could make the case to keep the low volume/low profit products (e.g., micro segmentation, target market, new product, etc.), the product stayed in the product line. If the marketing team could not make the case, the item was killed.

PROCUREMENT OF RAW MATERIALS

The focus on margins is intense. Increasing personal incomes in emerging economies have increased fertility, reduced mortality, and spurred consumption. Materials are scarce. Demand is growing.

Commodity markets are in turmoil. Material prices have increased sharply since 2000, erasing the prior declines of the twentieth century. In 2011, 58 percent of the Fortune 100 listed the increase in cost of commodities as a risk to earnings in their annual reports. The cost of materials and the associated uncertainty is higher than at any time in the evolution of supply chain practices.

> *In the past three decades, we have had periods where costs have escalated, but it has been a case of one commodity trading off another. It seems that there are now no trade-offs. They all seem to be escalating together, and at a rapid pace.*
> —*Consumer Products VP of Supply Chain*

For many, the situation is dire. Supply chain practices were defined in the early 1990s when crude oil was $10 per barrel. They have changed little despite price increases and increasing fluctuations. Companies are on a rollercoaster ride. No apparel supply chain was ready for the doubling of cotton prices in 2011 followed by a 50 percent drop in 2012. In food and beverage supply chains over the last five years, the demand of world food supplies has outstripped supply. In high-tech and electronics, the dependency on mining and minerals is tenuous. The supplies of cobalt, beryllium, fluorspar, lithium, and tantalum are scarce. In 2011, the British Geological Society published a risk list of minerals. It cited that there were 52 critical minerals and that 27 of these can only be sourced from China.

Unilever estimates that its input costs will increase by around 400 basis points in 2011.

—International Business Times

The rising commodity prices shown in Figure 4.2 were summed up well by a panelist at an event in 2011, when he said, "Today, we are getting squeezed at both ends. So much so, that we are arguing about who is going to pay for the pencils." His point was that when commodity pressures are high, and costs cannot be passed on to channel partners, the organization scrambles to save costs. The discussion on paying for pencils is symbolic of the degree of the issue. The commodity list of pressure points is long: dairy, wheat, corn, cotton, nickel, oil, and so on (see Figure 4.3). In 2010 to 2011, there were few earnings calls of the Fortune 500 that did not mention commodity prices as an issue.

Today, the variability of costs in the procurement of raw materials is the largest source of cost variability for the supply chain.

An opportunity in the face of pending cost increases is the redesign of value networks and the building of stronger supply relationships. Yet, few are ready to seize this opportunity. As documented in a 2011 PricewaterhouseCoopers Report, while 87 percent of major manufacturers understand that material scarcity is a growing issue, the criticality of the issues is only well-understood by 39 percent of their downstream customers.[1]

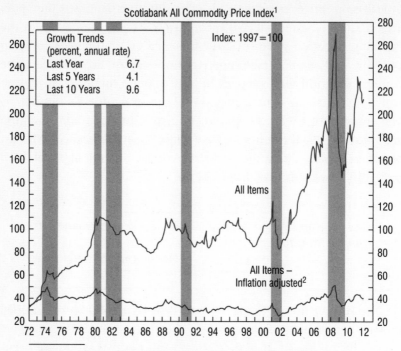

Figure 4.2   Commodity Price Index *Source:* Scotiabank

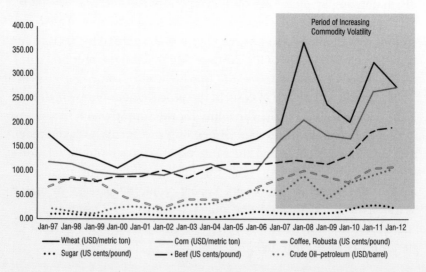

Figure 4.3   Raw Material Price Increases and Volatility *Source:* Index Mundi

Because of the complexity and the importance of sourcing, more and more companies are actively designing their networks and rethinking supplier relationship management. In this process, supplier relationships are segmented and managed based on the importance to the company. The process recognizes that not all suppliers are equal, and it tries to drive value into the more strategic relationships. In these strategic relationships, the focus is on forging value chain processes to reduce costs, spur innovation, and drive improvements in sustainability. These efforts are multiyear. In more tactical or transient relationships, the focus is on cost.

For more mature companies, supplier relationship management is coupled with risk analysis to ensure that the supply chain is resilient to shocks and major disruptions. The execution of sourcing strategies and the mitigation of risk management can make or break earnings as seen in the recent earnings commentaries in the supply chains for consumer televisions and computer hard disk drives. For a greater understanding, contrast the differences in how supply chain leaders and laggards in these two industries fared through the 2011 floods in Thailand, as explained in the case studies that follow.

TELEVISIONS

CASE STUDY

The 2011 floods in Thailand had long-lasting effects. In the fourth quarter of 2011, Panasonic Corp. almost doubled its annual loss forecast to a record ¥780 billion ($10 billion), weaker earnings because of floods in Thailand and slowing demand for televisions.

Samsung and LG are at stage four of the market-driven value network model (see Figure 1.3) while Panasonic is struggling trying to build stage three competencies. While the floods in Thailand made it more difficult for all companies to conduct operations, the lack of strong supply chain practices put the Panasonic team at a disadvantage. The company did not have the flexibility or resiliency in supply chain processes to keep up against stronger competitors in a competitive market.

CASE STUDY

DISK DRIVES TEACH COMPANIES NEW LESSONS ON SUPPLY CHAIN RESILIENCE

The floods in Thailand in 2011 were also a litmus test for high-tech supply chains. Sony, a supply chain laggard at stage two of the market-driven supply chain maturity model, failed. Western Digital at stage three of the market-driven supply chain maturity model held up better than expected. While Seagate, at stage four of the market-driven supply chain maturity model, was the clear winner. As the three companies released earnings to the financial markets, it was a clear signal that bricks matter.

In the third quarter of 2011, Sony's consumer product and services unit sales fell 24 percent year-over-year. Sony reported: "The floods in Thailand were one of the major factors behind the significant decrease in sales and deterioration in operating results for the quarter. Several overall manufacturing facilities incurred direct damage, resulting in a halt in pro-duction and the delayed launch of certain products. Moreover, the supply chain across the entire industry was impacted and the demand decreased as companies we do business with were affected. The decrease in sales and significant deterioration in equity in net income of the affiliated com-panies caused us to report an operating loss for the quarter."

Western Digital did much better. The market expectation was that Western Digital would take a huge hit from the Thailand flooding. With the disaster, Western Digital could not get components from its suppliers, mainly in Thailand. The market surprise was that the company did not take a large hit to earnings. It held its own. Contrast the Western Digital earnings statement to Sony's. CEO John Coyne of Western Digital reported, "We've made substantial progress in our mission to restore our manufacturing capacity in the aftermath of the historic flooding in Thailand. This is reflected in our second quarter financial performance announced earlier today, the continued ramp-up of our Thailand high density disk production capacity, and in the fact that we have now deployed alternate capacity that had been suspended since October 10 made a difference. While much work remains to be done over the next several quarters to reach our pre-flood manufacturing capabilities, the progress is far ahead of our original expectations and is a tribute to the dedicated and effective actions of our employees, contractors and Thai government agencies, the efforts of our supply partners, and the support of our customers."

The report ends with a prediction that hard drive shortages will persist throughout 2012 with gradual improvement.

Seagate, with diversified supply chain operations, did much better than their peer groups in the Thailand flooding. Steve Luczo, CEO, stated: "The disaster in Thailand affected a vast number of individuals and thousands of businesses. Although the industry is continuing to increase output, it is important to note that while many observers tend to believe that mid- to late October was the low point of industry production, we believe the low point was closer to mid-December. Seagate's geographically diversified factory footprint and broad supply chain provided inherent advantages that mitigated the impact of the floods to Seagate's operations.

"Although many of our external component suppliers are still working to recover their businesses and return to full capacity, we have been very impressed with the response and efforts of our suppliers who have worked tirelessly to rebound from the effects of the flooding. There are still clear challenges that lie ahead in our component supply chain. And to help address the gaps in various product lines, Seagate has worked with its customers and suppliers on aggressive qualifications of new parts and factories, allowing us to match precious supply to end demand."

Seagate worked with its suppliers to rebuild the supply chain. The company gave suppliers a break on pricing in exchange for longer-term contracts to drive supply chain stability in the time of crisis. The strategy is paying off in the short and long term. The company was so confident in recovery that it forecasted year-over-year growth of more than 70 percent.[2]

Building the Right Supply Organization

In supply chains, while channel management is regional, procurement is typically global. The aggregation of spend into a global buy allows companies to get better terms and build strategic relationships. As a result, technology and buying practices have aggregated spend into global buying organizations.

In the last 15 years, technology advancements and improved connectivity enabled the procurement organization to aggregate into a global organization with a focus on commodity councils. These commodity councils develop spend strategies, orchestrate risk management programs, and sense supplier health while deploying supplier development activities. An advanced organizational design is shown in Figure 4.4.

As these commodity councils are formed, one of the first places to start is on transactional efficiency. Even today, after 20 years of investment in sourcing technologies, this is still a target-rich environment. These processes are fraught with issues leading to payment and matching issues.

- One in five invoices is incorrect.
- Eighty percent of transactions are manual.
- Only 20 percent of customer orders are handled through business-to-business processes.

Networked enterprises were 50 percent more likely than their peers to have increased sales, higher profit margins, gain market share, and be a market leader.
—McKinsey & Company, "The Rise of the Networked Enterprise, Web 2.0 Finds its Payday," December 2010

In a quick look at history, the reasons become clear. In 1996, e-procurement technologies evolved to automate bidding processes.

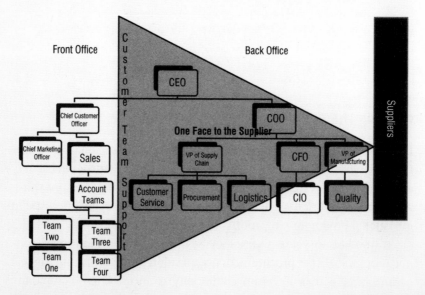

Figure 4.4 Organizational Overview

These technologies brought science to the buying process and allowed greater visibility and automation of spend. The value of these process efforts elevated the procurement organization and made it less focused on day-to-day operations. However, the automation of spend was for indirect procurement, not the automation and orchestration of decisions made on direct materials.

CASE STUDY

GLAXOSMITHKLINE

With 700 staff, the buying team at GlaxoSmithKline (GSK) in 2006 controlled spend of more than £7.4 billion a year, spread across more than 1,000 categories. As a leader in the adoption of indirect procurement technology, the company adopted electronic sourcing. They began with a single online auction and expanded to more than 2,000 events by 2004. The initial electronic sourcing implementation paid for itself with the first three events. Within three years, the company added £1 billion in savings to the bottom line. The savings were equal to the sales of a new blockbuster drug.

The company evolved over the next two years. In 2006, 40 percent of GSK's total spend was tendered using electronic events. To speed adoption of the technology, the pharmaceutical company operates a shared service model run through a center of excellence to support more than 1,400 internal customers using a hosted technology. To do sourcing right, the company also established a 15-person core competency team, each of whom was assigned to support different buyers by sector of business. As a result, GSK has been successful in the deployment of spend analysis and electronic events to the major buying categories of indirect spend, direct materials, capital projects, corporate support for finance, marketing services, and IT and engineering.

MANUFACTURING: THE MAKING OF PRODUCTS

The original supply chain pioneers came from the world of manufacturing. For them, there was no question that bricks mattered. They knew manufacturing well, but few understood procurement and distribution processes. Today, this is changing. The impact is large.

Today's new graduates are entering the world of supply chain without a manufacturing background and companies have outsourced manufacturing processes; as a result, manufacturing is the least understood of the supply processes by the third- and fourth-generation pioneers.

The impacts of manufacturing are far-reaching for countries, communities, and families.[3] For all, bricks matter:

- **Manufacturing jobs have a multiplier effect**. In the United States, one in six private sector jobs is related to manufacturing. Each manufacturing job has an economic multiplier effect. A dollar of sales from a product manufactured supports $1.40 in output from other sectors of the economy.
- **Shift in manufacturing**. The U.S. share of total world manufacturing output fell from 25 percent in 1970 to slightly less than 20 percent in 2009. In contrast, China's share of global manufacturing grew from 1 percent in 1970 to nearly 18 percent in 2009.
- **Growth and importance of China**. The value of U.S. manufacturing to the gross domestic product (GDP) was 13 percent

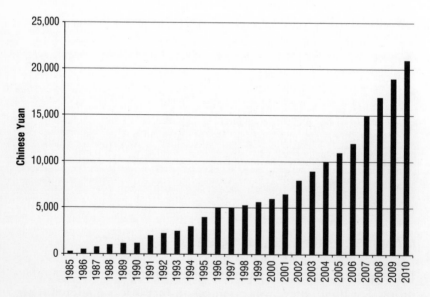

Figure 4.5 Changes in Wages in China *Source:* Data derived from Barclays Capital (data as of December 31, 2010). Drawn by Supply Chain Insights LLC

in 2009. In China, in that same period, manufacturing represented a bigger piece of the economy at 43 percent. Changes in labor rates in China are reversing some of these trends. Chinese wages are reflected in Figure 4.5.

- **Improvement in productivity**. In the period from 1987 to 2008, U.S. manufacturing productivity grew by 103 percent. This was almost double the 56 percent increase in productivity in the rest of the business sector. Since 1986, unit labor costs of U.S. manufacturers have declined by 40 percent relative to average unit labor costs.

As shown in Figure 4.6, the evolution of manufacturing had three distinct phases. In the beginning, it was local. Products were manufactured close to market. Factories were the nexus of the supply chain. Companies organized to improve quality and maximize asset utilization.

As geopolitical walls fell, technology matured, and modes of transport improved, manufacturing became a multinational organizational matrix. Products were manufactured in multiple countries and shipped to multiple markets. These multinational organizations became "mini-corporations."

National Pre-1945	Multinational 1945–2000	Global 2000–Present
• Products manufactured and sold within companies within regions • Imported materials and products exported in trade routes • Vertical integration • Operations handled at headquarters	• Protective trade rules closed trade routes of the past • Products manufactured and sold in regions • Operation of "mini-companies" within regions • Local/regional focus	• Free trade • Optimization of manufacturing beyond country borders into supply networks • Horizontal, globally integrated • Shift from "what to make" to "how to make" • Management of a network

Figure 4.6 Evolution of Manufacturing

The next step was the building of the global manufacturing organization. With the advent of the Internet and advances in logistics, manufacturing became global. Trade routes became more open, and an extended network evolved enabling companies to outsource manufacturing to third parties. Parts and components were sourced from around the world to be assembled and shipped as needed.

In this transition, many learned the hard way that while they could outsource manufacturing, they could not outsource the responsibility for their supply chain. As more and more manufacturing was outsourced, power within the organization shifted from the manufacturing organization to the supply chain team.

Let's take an example. The quintessential Barbie doll is 52 years old. In 1959, the doll was made locally and shipped directly to stores. Over the years, the source of manufacturing has changed. For 23 years, it was made in Japan. Production then shifted to Mexico, and then seven years in Hong Kong and Taiwan. Manufacturing was then changed to be sourced in Korea and the Philippines. Today, the primary manufacturing is in China, Malaysia, and Indonesia, but the component parts to assemble a doll are manufactured in 22 countries and assembled in the market where the doll is sold. In 2012, Barbie is a world traveler.

A high percentage of the manufacturing process is outsourced by the brand owner Mattel. The company's journey is typical of the industry. Mattel announced its global manufacturing principles in 1997 and a global reporting initiative in 2001. Mattel issued its corporate responsibility report in 2004. Barbie may have remained the same, never looking a year older—despite her split with her boyfriend Ken and her fling with the Australian surfer Blaine—but the manufacturing processes behind the scenes shifted dramatically to take advantage of lower-priced labor and access to global markets.

At a technical level, software evolved to help companies manage locally and plan globally while balancing the needs of product specifications to machine design. This software translated product specifications into machine definition, allowing the coordination of global operations. These flows are still evolving and are outlined in Figure 4.7.

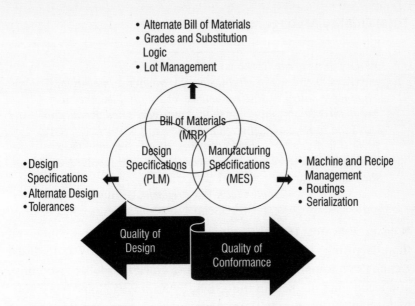

Figure 4.7 Manufacturing Information Technology Overview

TRANSFORMING MANUFACTURING

During the past three decades, manufacturing underwent many transformations. The primary process evolutions were total quality management (TQM), theory of constraints (TOC), Lean and the Toyota production system (TPS), and Six Sigma. It will change even further as companies implement the new processes for digital manufacturing (covered in Chapter 6).

While Six Sigma is a fine-tuning exercise that can be applied to any of the three, the principles of TQM, TOC, and TPS were different techniques that took companies down different paths. It is convergent thinking that is still being rationalized today. Many companies are confused.

In the building of market-driven value networks, each of these manufacturing concepts has a place. However, they need to be rationalized based on the rhythms and cycles of the value network against the business strategy. One size does not fit all. Here we start with the definition and then share a framework on how to apply the concepts.

Total Quality Management

When I think of supply chain excellence, I think of
my recent purchase of a Mini Cooper. I went on the Internet and
I had more than 200 different options for the car. I designed it in
two to three hours and in less than three weeks I had the car that
was built in England delivered to my house in Newark, NJ. It was
perfect. So that to me is supply chain excellence. Imagine. They
had less than a week to produce a car to my design standards and
then ship it.

—Supply Chain Vice President, Consumer Products

William Edwards Deming's philosophy defined TQM systems for manufacturing. The genesis was at the end of World War II. Using Deming's philosophy, the Japanese transformed the global automotive and electronics markets in the 1980s, by achieving global leadership, by focusing on continuous improvement and seeing manufacturing as a system, not as bits and pieces.

Ford failed and then became a great case study for TQM. In the 1980s, Ford Motor Company was manufacturing the same car model with transmissions made in Japan and in the United States. Soon after the car model was introduced, Ford customers were requesting the model with Japanese transmissions and shunning the U.S.-made cars. They were even willing to wait months for the Japanese model. Ford was confused. How could there be a discernible difference to customers when both transmissions were made from the same parts with the same specifications? To answer the question, Ford engineers decided to take apart the two different transmissions. When they did, they found that the American-made car parts were all within specified tolerance levels. On the other hand, the Japanese car parts were virtually identical to each other, and much closer to the nominal specified values for the parts. As a result, the Japanese cars ran more smoothly and customers experienced fewer problems. The reason was Deming's work in Japan.

So, Ford hired Deming. In the period from 1979 to 1982, Ford was in trouble. In 1982, the company incurred $3 billion in losses. After applying Deming's philosophy, by 1986 Ford had become the most profitable American auto company. In a letter to *Autoweek Magazine*,

Donald Peterson, Ford chairman, said, "We are moving toward building a quality culture at Ford and the many changes that have been taking place here have their roots directly in Dr. Deming's teachings."

When they engaged with Deming, the Ford team was surprised that he wanted to talk about more than quality. His focus was in rethinking management systems. Deming said, "I ask people in management what proportion of this problem arises from your production worker. And the answer is always: 'All of it!' That is absolutely wrong! I say that 85 percent of the problem comes from management. There's nobody that comes out of a school of business that knows what management is, or what its deficiencies are. There's no one coming out of a school of business that ever heard of the answers that I'm giving to your questions—or probably even thought of the questions."

Deming's philosophy spawned TQM. TQM is a cross-functional approach to minimize waste and improve quality to meet or exceed quality expectations. Deming proved that when people and organizations focus primarily on costs, that the cost of a product tends to rise and quality declines over time. Instead, he believed that organizations need to focus on the knowledge of variation and reducing deviation.

The principle is that all things in manufacturing processes have a *normal* variation and *special causes* that create defects. The goal is to recognize the difference and to eliminate special causes while controlling the normal variation. Deming taught that making changes in response to normal variation would only make the system perform worse. He believed that the focus needed to be a four-step process—plan, see, check, act—for the entire team. The key principles from Deming's book *Out of Crisis*, published in 1986, are the backbone of TQM processes. The principles are:

- **Constancy of purpose**. The goal is to create constancy of purpose toward improvement of product and service, with the aim to become competitive, to stay in business, and to provide jobs.
- **Adopt the new philosophy**. He believed that we are now in a new economic age. To compete, Deming taught that Western management must awaken to the challenge, learn their responsibilities, and take on leadership for change.

- **It is not about inspection**. Deming taught that inspection does not drive quality. Instead, the focus should be on building quality into the product in the first place.
- **It is not about price. Minimize total cost**. His teachings focused on ending the practice of awarding sourcing contracts based on lowest cost. Instead, he believed that the focus should be on minimizing total cost. To do this, he advocated moving toward a single supplier for any one item, and building long-term relationships focused on loyalty and trust. This is tough today because only 24 percent of companies know their total cost structures.
- **Focus on continuous improvement**. The work is continuous. Improve constantly and change forever the system of production and service, to improve quality and productivity, and thus continually decreasing costs.
- **Train. Train. Train**. Institute training on the job. Training never stops at any stage of the process.
- **Change rewards**. Eliminate work standards (quotas) on the factory floor. Stop the focus on management by objective. Do not align management by numbers and numerical goals. Remove barriers that rob a production worker of their right to have pride of workmanship.
- **All for one and one for all**. Institute a vigorous program of education and self-improvement. Put everybody in the company to work to accomplish the transformation. This change process is everybody's job.

The principles of TQM can help any supply chain process. They should be used widely. Many companies say "TQM," but they are not grounded in "practice" with a common understanding.

Theory of Constraints

The theory of constraints (TOC) is an overall management philosophy introduced by Eliyahu Goldratt in 1984. The principle is that manufacturing and distribution processes have constraints, or limitations. These are termed *bottlenecks*. A constraint in manufacturing is anything that limits a system from achieving higher performance relative to its goal. A company can have many bottlenecks, and the bottlenecks can float based on the mix of products. More than 80 percent of manufacturing processes have constraints.

The underlying premise of TOC processes is that organizations can be measured on three attributes: throughput, operational expense, and inventory. Throughput is the rate at which the system generates money through sales into the channel. Inventory is all the money that the system has invested in purchasing things that it intends to sell. Operational expense is all the costs the system spends in order to turn inventory into throughput.

Before the production goal can be reached, the rate of goal achievement is limited by at least one constraining process. It is only when companies increase the rate of flow through the constraint that companies increase output.

The steps are:

1. **Identify**. Identify the constraint (the resource or policy that prevents the process from obtaining more of the goal).
2. **Maximize**. Decide how to exploit the bottleneck (get the most capacity out of the constrained process).
3. **Align**. Subordinate all other processes to the above decision (align the whole system or organization to support the decision made above).
4. **Resolve**. Elevate the constraint (make other major changes needed to break the constraint).
5. **Manage**. If, as a result of these steps, the constraint has moved, return to step one.

A core principle within TOC is that there are not tens or hundreds of constraints. Instead, there is at least one and, at most, a few in any given process. A constraint can take different forms, and it can shift:

- **Equipment**. The way equipment is used can limit the ability of the system to produce more salable goods/services.
- **People**. Lack of skilled people limits the system.
- **Policy**. A written or unwritten policy can prevent the system from making more (e.g., union contracts or corporate social responsibility standards).

After identification of the constraint, companies design buffers. Buffers are placed before the governing bottleneck, thus ensuring that the constraint is never starved.

Lean

The genesis of Lean is the Toyota production system (TPS). In TPS, value is defined as any action or process that a customer would be willing to pay for. Essentially, Lean is centered on preserving value with less work. For many organizations, TPS has almost become a religion. And, like most religious doctrines, there are many variations of Lean thinking. There are also zealots.

The idea of just-in-time (JIT) production was originated by Kiichiro Toyoda, founder of Toyota. Later, his son, Eiji Toyodo, and employees Taiichi Ohno and Shigeo Shingo read descriptions of U.S. supermarkets and saw the supermarket as a model for what they were trying to accomplish in the factory. Let's look at the concepts. A customer in a supermarket takes the desired amount of goods off the shelf and purchases them. The store restocks the shelf with just enough new products to fill up the shelf space. Similarly, a work-center that needs parts would go to a "store shelf" (the inventory storage point) for the particular part and "buy" (withdraw) the quantity it needs, and the shelf would be restocked by the work-center that produced the part, making only enough to replace the inventory that had been withdrawn. It is about pull, not push. This was a radical shift for the automotive supply chain that had focused on maximizing production and reducing costs without a concern about rising inventories. It is one of the reasons today why Toyota has shorter cycle times, lower inventories, and market dominance in the automotive industry.

> Lean is about flow. There are many streams. Information, product, returns, cash. . . . In lean processes, the fastest flow wins.
> —Director, Operational Excellence, Automotive Company, Presentation at S&OP Conference, February 2012

While low inventory levels are a key outcome of the Toyota Production System, the story does not end there. An important element of the philosophy is to work intelligently and eliminate waste in the entire system. The elimination of waste is termed *Muda*. There are seven commonly accepted sources of *Muda* in the extended Lean supply chain:

1. **Transport**. Moving materials and products when doing so is not required.

2. **Inventory**. The acquisition and maintenance of inventory in all forms. This includes raw materials, work-in-process materials, and finished products.

3. **Motion**. Unnecessary movement of people or equipment. TPS focuses on only what is required to perform the processing of materials into finished goods in manufacturing.

4. **Waiting**. Lost time due to waiting for the next production step.

5. **Overproduction**. Producing items and pooling them ahead of customer demand.

6. **Overprocessing**. Additional work resulting from poor tool or product design.

7. **Defects**. Effort involved in inspecting or fixing defects.

The most dangerous kind of waste is the waste we do not recognize.
—Shigeo Shingo

Lean manufacturing focuses on improving efficiency through optimizing flow. These Lean principles are in direct conflict with the traditional mass-production accrual accounting reward systems. As a result, many Lean efforts falter and struggle. The conventional reward systems are not sufficient. Without strong support and understanding by executive leadership, Lean initiatives can fail.

Lean concepts introduced new terms to the manufacturing world. To implement Lean processes, these terms became part of the supply chain pioneer's new vernacular:

- **Mura**. Leveling out demand to minimize variation.
- **Kaizen**. A focus on continuous improvement.
- **Poka-Yoke**. Steps to making products correctly the first time through error and mistake-proofing. (A common and popular example of mistake-proofing is the design of the VHS videotape player. A videotape will only fully enter a VCR and play if it is placed correctly into the opening.)

Six Sigma

Six Sigma started with Motorola. The goal of this process is to improve the quality of process outputs by identifying and removing the causes of defects. A manufacturing process can be described as a sigma rating—the percentage of defect-free product—produced from a unit operation. It is a scientific/data-driven approach for achieving six standard deviations between the mean and nearest specifications limit. Six Sigma methods can be applied to all aspects of manufacturing, transactional processes, and virtually any form of work or processing. While Deming set companies on the right path with TQM, and TPS/Lean gave manufacturing a focused methodology, Six Sigma discipline fine-tunes the process to reduce variation.

Applying the Concepts to a Market-Driven Value Network

Together, these four processes (TQM, TOC, TPS/Lean, and Six Sigma) redefined manufacturing processes. They grew in importance as the supply chain became more complex. As companies become global, more networked, and dependent on third-party manufacturing relationships, these techniques are the backbone of many change management initiatives to improve supply.

There is nothing so useless as doing efficiently that which should not be done at all.
—Peter F. Drucker, Management Consultant

Each technique is important, but they are not equally important for all supply chains. There needs to be a choice. While all are great concepts to drive manufacturing improvements, the question is, How to put them together? And how do they fit within the road map to build a market-driven value network? Should companies use these techniques to redefine manufacturing to be more responsive to both buy- and sell-side market demands? The answer lies in understanding the rhythms and cycles of the supply chain and using these techniques to design the appropriate supply response.

The principles of TQM and Six Sigma can be applied uniformly to all supply chains. However, the principles of TOC and Lean thinking (TPS) need to be carefully architected and applied to the right situations. For some, this can be a problem. Most companies have multiple supply chains, manufacturing practices, and strong beliefs—almost a religious fervor—about the best fit of these process techniques. They want to broad-brush the application of these concepts without applying the logic for fit.

A Framework to Apply the Logic of Manufacturing Process Improvement Initiatives to Market-Driven Value Networks

Companies do not have one value network. They have many. Each business has its own cycle. They are best defined by the requirements of supply to match channel rhythms and cycles. In applying the principles to market-driven value networks, manufacturing operations can be broken into four types as shown by the quadrants in Figure 4.8.

- **Quadrant I**. In quadrant I, both demand error and volume are high. This is a difficult situation. You might say, "How can

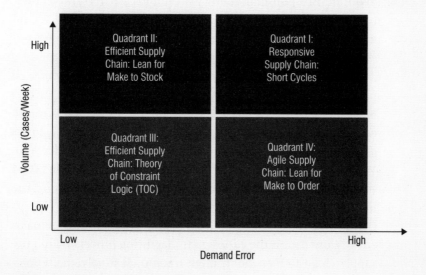

Figure 4.8 Rethinking Manufacturing Strategies

a supply chain have high demand error and high volumes?" And you might ask, "Shouldn't leadership just focus more on demand planning?" The answer is no. These are supply chains with inherent volatility. The response needs to be able to match the volatile nature of the market demand. It needs to be designed to be a responsive supply chain.

The sale of products for these businesses needs to be a quick response to a market need. It is a pull-based signal, so it cannot effectively be a push-based supply chain. (A push-based supply chain is one where product is pushed into the channel as an anticipatory move to satisfy demand.)

The triggers are many. They can be weather or the reaction to an event. Examples include the sale of cold medicine during a flu epidemic, a hot-selling fashion product that flies off the shelf, snow removal equipment during a blizzard, or bathing suits during a hot spell at the beach. It can also be event driven. Examples include a new product launch or products sold under extreme demand shaping programs (e.g., low price or aggressive promotion tactics).

Marketing programs can introduce demand volatility and transform a supply chain that is usually in quadrant II to a quadrant I response. Inventory pre-builds are necessary, cross-functional coordination is an imperative, and supply chain excellence is defined by quick cycles and excellence in demand sensing.

In this quadrant, companies need to build flexibility into all operations and focus on cross-functional orchestration. Success is all about reducing cycles. The right tactics include the use of postponement inventory strategies, the location of factories close to markets, and shortening the time to sense true demand. While some of the manufacturing theories are applicable (TQM or Six Sigma), this would not be the right supply chain for the implementation of Lean process thinking.

■ **Quadrant II**. In this scenario, volume is high and demand error is low. This is the easiest manufacturing process within the supply chain to manage through traditional supply chain practices. It is the perfect scenario to apply Lean process thinking.

It is also the best scenario to work with suppliers to build JIT relationships. These supply chains can easily deliver the most efficient response.

These are also the easiest supply chains to outsource to a third party. However, not all industries have viewed this opportunity the same. For high-tech leaders that defined the best use of their manufacturing capacity to be focused on the launch of new products (with less of a focus on internal asset utilization), they quickly outsourced products in this quadrant to third-party manufacturers. For consumer products leaders with a myopic focus on internal asset utilization, they keep the production of products in quadrant II for internal production, and outsource products in quadrants I and IV. As a result, consumer products companies reduce manufacturing costs but increase total costs of the supply chain.

- **Quadrant III**. In this quadrant, volume is low and demand error is low. Efficiency in this supply chain can be achieved through advanced planning systems (APS) that utilize the TOC logic. Through the use of the software, these lower volume items can be combined with higher volume product cycles to reduce the impact of constraints and decrease the impact of cycle stock on inventory carrying costs.
- **Quadrant IV**. In this supply chain, products have high demand volatility and low volumes. In this situation, the first question that should be asked is: "Should these products be made at all?"

This is the long tail of the supply chain (see Figure 4.1). The design of the response needs to be an agile one. An agile supply chain is designed to produce products at the same cost, quality, and customer service with a given level of demand variability (e.g., as demand changes, the supply chain response needs to have the ability to produce products at the same quality, cost, and customer service levels). The design needs to be make-to-order manufacturing. This is the perfect application of Lean thinking for make-to-order production processes. The response can be improved through the use of common components, rationalized product platforms, and standardized recipes.

Design with the Goal in Mind

Supply chains need to be defined with the goal in mind. Although companies will often talk about wanting to drive an efficient, agile, and responsive supply chain, the type of output needs to be defined based on the principles of the market-driven value network. There are trade-offs among efficiency, agility, and responsiveness, and the manufacturing principles and processes applied need to be aligned with the desired outcome. No company can achieve all three.

The use of manufacturing processes to drive supply chain excellence is not a new thought, but in this chapter we share two case studies: Xiameter and Seagate. Xiameter built a new business around the efficient supply chain to maximize asset utilization in a commodity business while Seagate transformed its manufacturing operations over the course of 15 years to drive a market-driven value network. Both are valid business strategies when they are designed outside-in and have alignment of sell, deliver, make, and source to the business strategy.

CASE STUDY

XIAMETER: A NEW BUSINESS MODEL

Dow Corning is a 70-year-old company. The company is the global leader in silicones: silicon-based technology and innovation. The 9,000-person company is jointly owned by Dow Chemical and Corning, Inc. It is global with more than 50 percent of the company's sales outside of North America.

In the 1990s, Dow Corning had a problem. Sales were stagnating. Competitive landscapes were changing. Globalization was changing the landscape and new technologies were ushering in new opportunities with business models. Executives knew that they needed to do something different. So, the company took a look at customer segmentation, and asked itself, "What do our customers want?" In this process, the company found that there were multiple needs within its customers. There were four distinct buyers within a customer each with unique needs. The manufacturing processes needed to adapt to meet these requirements:

- **True innovation**. Buyers within research and development (R&D) in their customer base wanted to work collaboratively to develop new products. The goal was codevelopment.

- **Small tweaks to existing products**. Within some industries, companies wanted to partner to make small tweaks to existing products to better fit their needs. This goal was customization.
- **Improve operations**. The manufacturing buyer within the customers wanted to buy products to improve the operations and to reduce the costs of equipment. These were standard products with higher levels of service.
- **Lowest cost**. Another set of buyers within the customers wanted silicon materials, but they also wanted the best pricing. These customers wanted commodity products priced with no frills at the lowest cost.

As a result of this exercise, Dow Corning saw an opportunity. At the time, the company had one model: high customer service accompanied by deep technical expertise. Services were tightly bundled. They were creating value through the services. As a result of the customer exercise, the company decided to unbundle the services and build an offering directly targeted to the customer seeking the lowest cost. This was the launch of the Xiameter brand.

The CEO sponsored the formation of a new business. A new team was put into place and a new company was formed. The new business was an e-commerce self-service model. The challenge was how to get the two distinctive business models to coexist within the same company and service different needs within the same customer. The secret was administration of business rules.

Leadership was the key element for success. A traditional chemical company is risk adverse. The new business was launched in 2002 and customers were given a choice. Buyers within customers that were looking for standard products with standard lead times at the lowest costs were able to now buy products from Xiameter. This new business model allowed Dow Corning to increase asset utilization. The use of strict business rules helped to manage the conflicts between the two business models. Payback was less than three months.

Xiameter is not about growth. It is about improving operational efficiency and providing better service to a niche of customers. The company introduced a new business model in quadrant III of Figure 4.8. There are times when products are unavailable, but customers know that this is part of the business model. To make it work, customers order products in minimums (full pallets) and the organization has to stay disciplined with a focus on sticking to the business rules.

SEAGATE A DEMAND-DRIVEN LEADER

Founded in 1979, Seagate is today a leading provider of storage devices. The road has been bumpy, but it holds great lessons in why the design of manufacturing operations matters to corporate viability.

Background

In the period from 1985 to 1991, Seagate focused on delivering on the promise of low-cost or efficient manufacturing. The company relocated manufacturing to Singapore to take advantage of lower labor costs. With the high value of the Japanese yen, Seagate was able to undercut the prices of Fujitsu, Hitachi, NEC, Toshiba, and others, and dominate the hard disk market. Beginning in 1985 Seagate experienced a phenomenal rise in sales, hitting $1 billion in revenue by 1987, with a record $115 million in profits. As the market grew, Seagate was able to maintain its dominant share by keeping its prices down. It had reduced the costs of storing data by 95 percent since it first went into business.

However, Seagate's concentration on efficient production, while allowing technological innovation to take a backseat, made it vulnerable to the boom and bust cycles of the rapidly changing high-technology industry. In 1987, the market changed. The company was not resilient. Computer manufacturers started demanding the smaller 3.5-inch drives earlier than anticipated. Seagate could not adapt; as a consequence, Seagate's profits declined by 39 percent. Profitability remained low through 1988. Seagate had an edge on its competitors in its ability to provide consistently lower priced products, due to vertical integration of its disk drive components, but the supply chain was not flexible. The company's emphasis on high volume manufacturing over product innovation led to the resignation of the CEO under pressure from the board.

The focus then shifted to new products. In this period, Seagate enjoyed the highest level of sales for high-capacity, mid-size, and small disk drives. By 1997, Seagate had evolved beyond its position as the world's largest disk drive and components manufacturer into a leading provider of technology and products that enabled people to store, access, and manage information.

Redefinition of Manufacturing to Fuel Growth

In the early years, there were many ups and downs. In 2000, the company was taken private to re-enter the market in 2002. Over 15 years, the Seagate supply chain was redefined to improve agility for a high-volume business with high-demand volatility. There were four stages.

In the period from 1995 to 1998, the focus was on efficient operations. The company built products to forecast. The high-demand volatility drove up inventory levels.

In the second period from 1998 to 2000, the company focused on building a hybrid model. It implemented vendor-managed inventory models with customers and stocked customer hubs to drive a pull-based replenishment signal. While criticized for building too high customer inventory

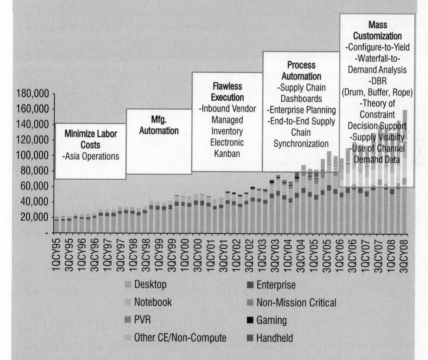

Figure 4.9 Supply Chain Building Blocks for Seagate *Source:* Re-created from Seagate Presentation at 1998 SCOR Conference
Note: % Growth/Qtr is compounded

(*Continued*)

signals, this earlier and quicker demand signal helped the company to better sense demand for high-volume products with unpredictable demand. To expedite time-to-market for new products, the company implemented a new product launch process. As shown in Figure 4.9, this multiyear transformation happened over the three years from 1995 to 1998.

In the third phase, the company implemented a build-to-demand model using the theory of constraints and designed a strategic buffer program. In the fourth phase, the company combined TPS lean thinking at the factory floor along with TOC thinking in planning to synchronize the supply chain. The added flexibility enabled mass customization to embrace a divergent product mix. By 2008, the company successfully shipped 100 million drives per year consuming 90 million parts per day with four weeks of supply to hundreds of customer hubs. Over the period, there was a 114 percent inventory turn improvement, a 37 percent reduction in manufacturing cycle times, a 50 percent reduction in global inventory, and a 500 percent productivity improvement. Today, it remains a supply chain leader. The design of manufacturing and supplier systems helped the company to launch new products and withstand the shocks of the past recession and the 2011 floods in Thailand.

Manufacturing Summary

Over the last 30 years, there has been more progressive thinking on the evolution of manufacturing processes than on any other area of supply chain management. Improvements propelled growth and enabled the building of the global supply chains.

Today, companies stand at a fork in the road. The improvements made through traditional manufacturing programs have driven success; however, as products proliferate and demand becomes more volatile, these traditional techniques have hit a roadblock. It calls for a redesign. Why? It is because traditional manufacturing processes are not built outside-in with a market-driven goal in mind. As a result, they are on the back foot, delivering a late response. They are out of sync with channel fluctuations.

Because they have been built solely to respond to a customer order, not channel demand as it happens, demand latency and demand translation is long. (The translation of channel demand into a signal for manufacturing in conventional supply chain practices is 28 weeks.) As demand volatility increases and products proliferate, the rationalization of manufacturing practices based on an outside-in view through the definition of market-driven value networks is needed to better align costs and working capital with increasing expectations for customer service and corporate social responsibility.

LOGISTICS

In the 1980s, better math combined with computing power shifted the term *logistics* from the dark halls of the departments of defense and warfare to be a recognized requirement for distribution-centric industries. The growth and development of supply processes was driven through vertical, and often isolated, silos. In the progression of practices, logistics was one of the most insulated. It is resistant to change and one of the slowest processes to mature.

Logistics is the management of the flow of goods from origin to destination to meet the needs of customers. It is both inbound (to a factory or distribution center) and outbound (to a customer or into the channel). Supply chain execution technologies suites composed of available-to-promise, order management, transportation management, warehouse management, supply chain visibility, and global trade and logistics have accelerated logistics maturity.

In the first two decades, not much changed. Logistics capacity was readily available; the question was cost. In the last five years, there have been major shifts in logistics that have dramatically changed the processes. Today, logistics is more constrained, costly, and important.

It has also been outsourced. Over the last decade, logistics has progressively been outsourced with 32 percent of volume on average moving through third-party logistics (3PL) facilities in North America. Rates are higher in China and Europe, where 3PL relationships represent 80 to 90 percent of freight movement. Logistics effectiveness has been accelerated by the evolution of mobility, geo-location tracking, and bar coding/radio frequency identification technology.

The degree of process maturity varies by industry. It is the most mature in process companies such as chemical and pharmaceutical industries; in consumer-driven companies such as apparel, food/beverage, consumer packaged goods and retail; and in fast-moving goods such as high-tech and electronics. It is not as significant a factor of supply chain excellence for industrial conglomerates or discrete manufacturers.

Logistics is a fragmented ecosystem. It takes a village of government, shippers, carriers, and logistics providers to get an order from origin to destination. The planning needs to be viewed in aggregate across the modes—air, rail, barge, truckload, and less than truckload—with a focus on multimode planning and building strong relationships.

There is currently tension, as outlined in Figure 4.10, between small, frequent shipments and the corporate goals of social responsibility. The ability to effectively work with carriers on multiple-mode capabilities with improved lane visibility can greatly improve the ability to get loads delivered on time and on cost.

A Yale University management professor once commented on Fred Smith's paper proposing a new business for a reliable overnight delivery service: "The concept is interesting and well-formed, but in order to earn better than a C in this class, the idea must be feasible." The rest is history. The idea became the basis of a new business launched in 1971 and named Federal Express (more commonly known as FedEx). Today it is a $39 billion company with 275,000 employees worldwide. Fred Smith, the founder, earned a salary of $1.45 billion in 2011.

As transportation has become more constrained, fuel costs have escalated and corporate social responsibility initiatives have increased in importance. Customer service expectations have also increased. For example, retailers want consumer product manufacturers to ship smaller quantities more frequently at a lower cost and with a lower carbon footprint. This is just not possible. As a result, there is increased tension among trading partners. To make this happen, companies have to work together to combine, or pool, shipments to a retailer.

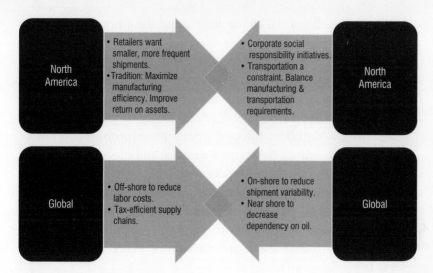

Figure 4.10   The Logistics Dilemma

Connectivity and the Pace of Change

Communication is at the heart of logistics. In the mid-1880s, smoke signals gave way to the telegram. Sixty years ago, the telegram gave way to the fax and over the course of the last 20 years, the fax gave way to the Internet as the primary method of communication. This capability fueled the launch of air-parcel shipments (FedEx and DHL). In the late 1990s, these processes drove the need for track-and-trace systems for parcel tracking.

Over the past two decades, advances in technology have shortened logistics cycles and improved data latency by 30 to 50 percent. Today, loads are tendered and received electronically and are optimized in minutes not hours, shipment visibility is transmitted in near real-time, and load over/short and damage reports are transmitted upon receipt. As a result, logistics cycles have been decreased by one to two days for load tendering, shipment authorization, and delivery receipts.

Challenges

Customer service expectations have increased and delivery windows are also now more precise. In the last two decades, dock appointments at Walmart warehouse receiving have gone from hour windows to 15-minute increments.

Cycles have shortened and variability has increased. Time to ship on all lanes—ship, air, and truck—is more variable. Rail hub congestion, roadway conditions, governmental regulations, slow steaming of ocean fleets, and the shortage of overall capacity all drive variability.

Logistics has also been affected by the introduction of corporate sustainability scorecards, the increase in compliance fees, and the tightening of definition for the perfect order. Although each change may seem benign in isolation, the combination of them has greatly changed logistics practices. As we look holistically, we see that the industry has become more complex (outsourcing and regulations), with more options (freight modes) and more compliance (scorecards, penalties, expectations).

Despite the obstacles progress has been made. Transportation is currently 5.4 percent of the U.S. gross domestic product. In contrast, it was 7.3 percent in 1981. Although the processes have become more efficient, as outlined in Figure 4.11, transportation obstacles in the race for Supply Chain 2020 will be many.

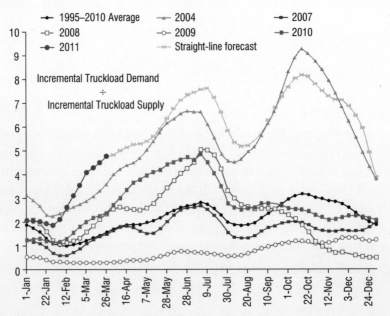

Figure 4.11 Freight Demand *Source:* JP Morgan

> *We got serious about logistics when the costs to deliver the product to the channel exceeded the costs to manufacture the product. This happened in 2005.*
>
> —Keith Harrison, Global Product Supply Officer, Procter & Gamble, 2001–2011

Freight demand has increased and it is now a constraint. An overview of this conundrum is outlined in Figure 4.12. In the traditional supply chain, there is an assumption that supply chains can keep on trucking—that there will always be a truck, ship, or train available at the time of shipment. However, this is changing. Supply chain planning applications in the period from 1985 to 2005 evolved based on the assumption that manufacturing was a constraint and transportation was abundant. Transportation now plays a more important role in the cost of goods and meeting customer service goals.[4]

While companies gather at logistics events and carefully detail the issues, the gravity of the situation of transportation capacity is a risk to the supply chain. It comes in many forms—driver shortages,

- Domestic demand is outweighing supply causing capacity constraints
- International supply and demand are in balance

The U.S. heavy-freight market is large and is forecast to grow at 10% CAGR through 2013 during the cycle

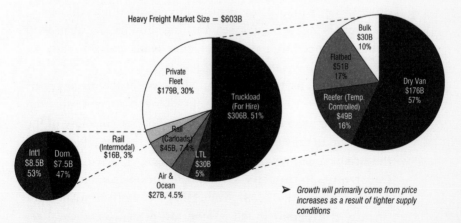

Figure 4.12 State of the Logistics Transportation Industry *Source:* FTR Associates, Transport Fundamentals, ATA, Baird, Council of Supply Chain Management

regulation, and rising fuel costs—but many carry on as if there are no issues. The impacts of tight capacity are not well-recognized by the greater supply chain community.[5] It can no longer be carelessly considered abundant.

Consider these facts for just the United States:

- **Rising volume**. In 2011, truck tonnage rose 5.9 percent over the previous year—the largest annual increase since 1998. Trucking represents 67.2 percent of tonnage shipped for distributors and manufacturers.

- **Recession recovery slow and painful**. In 2010, shipping volumes were about half of prerecovery levels, but air and truck carriers were at capacity. The Great Recession had a devastating impact on logistics capacity with 16 percent of truckload capacity removed from the U.S. system since 2006. This slowed in 2011 with only 665 carriers filing for bankruptcy protection.

- **Transportation costs increasing in importance**. In 2005, due to the rising costs of oil, the cost for distribution exceeded the cost of manufacturing for most consumer goods manufacturers. The traditional supply chain is designed based on the principles of 1985 when the cost of oil was $10 per barrel.

- **Constraints with drivers**. There is expected to be a shortage of 400,000 drivers by the end of 2013. There are few young drivers: fewer than 25 percent of drivers are under the age of 35. There is also an equally concerning shortage of equipment. Companies need to make contingency plans and get ready for the day that they cannot get a truck.

- **Impacts are costly**. In October 2002, two of the biggest ports were closed for 11 days because of striking workers. Costs from that episode were estimated at $65 million for each day of the shutdown. In the end, almost all ships that had been blocked by the strike landed within the next month.

- **Constraints in capacity**. Over 2,000 trucking companies went out of business in 2008. Availability of over-the-road truck capacity is expected to fall another 40 percent between 2009 and the end of 2012. Increasing regulation and government intervention will make this a stewpot that will boil over in the back-to-school and winter holiday seasons.

Transportation and logistics can also be used to redefine business models. They are key components of a channel strategy. As more and more countries face aging populations, there will be greater population density in larger cities. This increased density at the nucleus of city centers allows the redefinition of the channel and transformation of delivery options. We can see some of these changes currently happening in Asia. Home plus in Korea is an example of this.

CASE STUDY

HOME PLUS KOREA

South Korea has more than 10 million smartphone users in a population of fewer than 50 million people, it has a dense metropolitan area supported by subways, and its people are time constrained. In Seoul, South Korea, Tesco, a £3.54 billion retailer, launched a format Home plus that has become the second largest retail chain in Korea. In 2011, the company launched Home plus's e-commerce initiative. The stores are located in Seoul's subway stations. The subway station has pictures of a store shelf. These pictures show shelves stocked with food and other consumer goods customers resembling an actual store. As they wait for a train, shoppers can point their smartphones at the quick response codes, click, and add items to their online shopping basket. The goods are delivered to their home while they are in transit. The Home plus online store is now the number one e-commerce site for groceries in South Korea.

Inventory

In the past decade, as shown in Figures 4.13 and 4.14, progress on inventory has stalled.[6] Inventory levels across all industries, with the exception of high-tech and electronics, have flattened. Initially, through the use of technology, companies replaced inventory with information, lowering inventory levels by 10 days on average across supply chains. Gradually, with the building of global supply chains, these have increased.

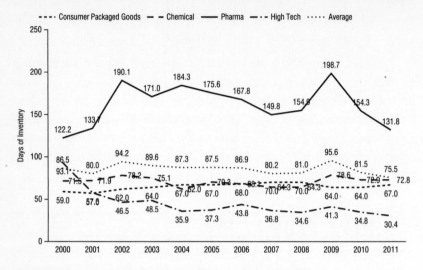

Figure 4.13 Changes in Days of Inventory by Industry 2002–2011

Today, technology is helping companies to maintain inventory levels in the face of increasing complexity in the number of products, changes in channels, and increasing demand volatility.

> *Advanced planning solutions were designed to manage constraints, but not variability. Inventory optimization technologies are designed to help companies reduce variability in their supply chain.*
> —*Sean Willems, Founder, Optiant; Current Chief Technical Officer, Logility*

The economic downturn in the period from December 2007 through July 2009 shook the core of most companies. As demand declined, inventories grew. Supply chain organizations cruising forward in neutral were suddenly jerked into hyperdrive to answer questions about demand, cash flow, product portfolios, and markets in a way that had never happened before. Supply chains grew in

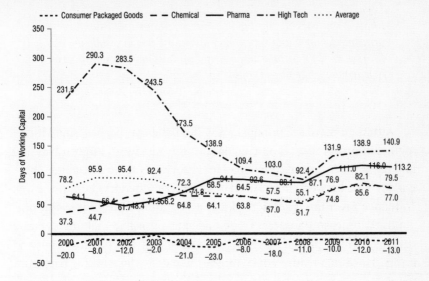

Figure 4.14 Changes in Days of Working Capital by Industry 2002–2011

importance. Supply chain discussions suddenly became boardroom debates. As aggregate volume declined 23 percent and fundamental demand patterns shifted, the importance of supply chain management in the boardroom increased and organizational structures shifted to give greater prominence to decisions for the end-to-end value chain.

In response, companies tightened their belts and slowed manufacturing. In the recession, for 6 percent of the Fortune 1000 companies, their days of working capital grew. Facing new market obstacles in collections, payables, and inventory management, companies scrambled for cash.

As inventory levels climbed during the first part of 2009, tension grew in supply chain discussions, and horizontal processes (discussed in Chapter 5) grew in importance. This was the most problematic— even desperate—for some companies that defined high-asset utilization as supply chain excellence. Those companies that rewarded high-asset utilization took five times longer to sense the downturn and align their supply chains.

> *I have been working hard to help our executives understand the
> principles of form and function of inventory, but it is difficult
> because most financial groups do not understand and don't want
> to learn the principles of supply chain.*
> —*Reader of Supplychainshaman.com*

Although there are no longer any big-bang approaches, small incremental improvements can be made through a focus on forecast bias and looking at the form and function of inventory. It is about discipline. There is a direct tie between forecast accuracy and required levels of inventory. To reduce inventory variations, focus on continuous improvement programs that measure forecast value-added analysis and map the demand streams (which product stream is contributing the greatest bias and error). Then, as a team, reduce forecast variability by working backward to reduce bias and error. An example of the impact of bias improvements on inventory from a real food and beverage company in the Fortune 1000 during the economic downturn is shown in Figure 4.15.

Form and Function of Inventory

In the building of market-driven value networks, an important shift for leadership teams is to move from a focus on inventory levels to look at the form and function of inventory. Today, most companies focus on the level of inventory—how much inventory is the right amount—for their supply chain. The shift to look not only at the amount but also at the type of inventory requires a deepening of processes and technology. These shifts are outlined in Table 4.2.

Table 4.2 Form and Function of Inventory

Form of Inventory	Function of Inventory
Raw material	Cycle stock: Inventory required to cycle through the production schedule.
Semifinished product	Forward coverage of events: Promotions, new product launch, etc.
Finished product	Safety stock: Inventory buffer for demand and supply volatility.
Finished product in the channel	Seasonal stock: Inventory requirements to cover seasonal variation.
	SLOB: Slow and obsolete inventory.

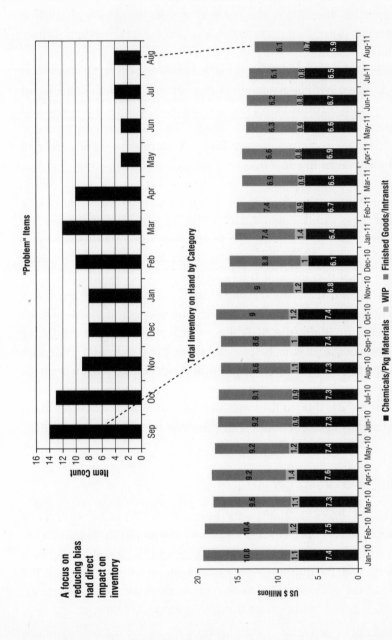

Figure 4.15 Small Focus on Forecast Bias Can Impact Inventory Levels

191

The form of inventory is the state in which it is stored. Inventory can be stored as a raw material, a semifinished good, or as a finished good (or final assembly). The further back in the supply chain that inventory is stored (e.g., raw materials), the greater the supply chain flexibility. A technique used to improve flexibility is postponement. In postponement strategies, a good is stored in a semifinished form and is finished with late-stage manufacturing only when demand for a specific item is confirmed. The function of inventory is the role that the inventory plays in the supply chain. There are many forms: cycle stock, seasonal inventory, pre-builds of inventory for events. They all must be managed in concert.

An area of opportunity for most companies is cycle stock. While most companies talk of safety stock (the decision to hold inventory to buffer supply and demand variability), cycle stock—the inventory that is necessary to cycle through products or from manufacturing to distribution cycles—is often a missed opportunity. Many times decisions are made that increase the need for cycle stock without thinking through the impact. For example, a manufacturer of jams and jellies built a new factory to respond to an increase of demand. In the process of building the plant, the R&D team decided to change the hold, or dwell, time of the product before shipment. The impact of the decision to change the manufacturing hold time from one day to two weeks increased inventory cycle stock by 40 percent, but the supply chain team had not considered the impact on total inventory. To better manage the supply chain, train all teams to think holistically end to end.

Dealing with Volatility

Demand and supply variability is increasing. In the 1990s, companies had two supply chain buffers, or shock absorbers, to protect the supply chain. The first buffer was manufacturing capacity and the second buffer was inventory. With the outsourcing of manufacturing and the elimination of this buffer, the practices of inventory management are more important.

In the supply chain, variability comes in many forms:

- **Value**. Variability stemming from demand shaping activities including price, trade incentives, new products, services, freshness, responsiveness.

- **Variety**. Production variability stemming from product configurations, items, platforms, components, brands, processing technologies.
- **Velocity**. Changes in supply chain cycles for lead times, order-to-delivery cycles, inventory turns, time-to-market for products.
- **Volatility**. Changes in demand and supply volatility including product market demand, inventory levels, schedule changes, manufacturing reliability, and production yields.
- **Volume**. Increases and decreases in planned production in manufacturing facilities, warehouses, distribution centers/points, product flow.

Map your source of variability, reduce what you can through continuous improvement, and design the supply chain to absorb what you cannot eliminate.

SUMMARY

The processes of supply—source, make, and deliver—have all undergone significant changes over the past three decades. Leaders such as Dow Chemical, Procter & Gamble, Samsung, and Seagate have focused on making the transition by addressing these basic principles:

- **Are we shaping or just shifting demand?** Demand shaping increases market share. It happens when companies use techniques—price, promotion, new product launch, sales incentives, or marketing—to increase market share, or share of wallet. The use of these techniques increases demand elasticity. Demand shifting, or shifting demand through advance shipments, stuffing the channel or pre-shipping at the end of the quarter, increases supply chain waste. The greatest impact is on supply.
- **Get to know your own DNA**. Just as deoxyribonucleic acid (DNA) forms human cells with twisted strands of polymers forming a double helix, each item has its own DNA. You can only master the supply chain when you know each item's DNA. The twisted pairs or long polymers in the DNA cell makeup are replaced by demand and supply strands (representing the rhythms and cycles of demand and supply) in the supply chain. The processes of supply can only be effectively designed outside-in with a goal in mind (e.g., supply chain strategy).

- **It is easier to run downhill than uphill**. This statement was made by a supply chain director who was also a marathon runner. His belief is that each promotion or seasonal event is like preparing for a race, and that if you start from a point of strength, with the right information and the right inventory, it is easier to run downhill (or decrease volume) than to run uphill (or increase volume). This requires planning.

- **Go slow to go fast**. One of the most important lessons that we hope companies can learn from this chapter is that supply chain transitions take multiple years. Seagate built agility in their supply chain over 15 years of concentrated redefinition of manufacturing processes. Procter & Gamble reorganized supply processes to report to one leader three decades ago. Many companies limit potential by focusing on a quick implementation.

Focus, vision, and design go hand in hand. There is no substitute for leadership and wisdom. In Chapter 5, we will focus on building horizontal processes, and in Chapter 6, we will focus on building a three-year road map.

While knowledge and insights can be dealt with through systems and process, how does one capture wisdom? Supply chain leaders at winning companies demonstrate wisdom.
—Consulting Partner response after reading the first draft of Bricks Matter

---

TO DRIVE CHANGE

- Understand the impact of business complexity on cost and supply chain drivers. Implement cross-functional processes to evaluate product and customer complexity.
- Identify the rhythms and cycles of the supply chain and align manufacturing strategies.
- Build strong financial supply chain processes to know total supply chain costs. Help the internal organizations within supply make trade-offs to reduce total costs, not optimize the costs within the silo.
- Invest in network design technology and build a team to design the supply network based on market scenarios. Get good at what-if analysis.

NOTES

1. PricewaterhouseCoopers, "Minerals and Metals Scarcity in Manufacturing: The Ticking Time Bomb," December 2011, http://www.pwc.se/sv_SE/se/metal-mining/assets/minerals-and-metals-scarcity-in-manufacturing-the-ticking-time-bomb.pdf.

2. Larry Dignan, "Hardware Makers Slog through Hard Disk Drive Shortages," *Between the Lines*, ZDNet, February 2012, http://www.zdnet.com/blog/btl/hardware-makers-slog-through-hard-disk-drive-shortages/68615.

3. *The Facts on Modern Manufacturing*, 8th ed., National Association of Manufacturers, October 2009.

4. American Trucking Association, Trucking Index, 2005.

5. Council of Supply Chain Management Professionals, *State of Logistics Report*, 2005–2011.

6. Working Capital Studies, 1998–2011, *CFO Magazine*.

CHAPTER **5**

Building
Horizontal
Connectors

*Companies need to have strong operations in vertical
processes before they can move horizontally to
build processes to sense and respond.*

—Lora Cecere

F
ailure gave birth to supply chain horizontal processes. Today's
leaders in horizontal process evolution—Cisco Systems, Coca-
Cola, IBM, Intel, Hewlett-Packard, Samsung, and Walmart—all
learned the need for horizontal processes the hard way. Each stubbed
its big toe and stumbled before learning that bricks matter.

Each supply chain leader learned that strong horizontal supply
chain processes are a prerequisite to drive success in building market-
driven value networks. They need to be built brick by brick. This chapter is about their journey. Let's start with the most pivotal case studies:

- **Cisco stumbles and then builds strong supply chain
processes**. The dotcom era was a speculative market bubble
from 1995 to 2000 (with a height on March 10, 2000). During

the mid- to late 1990s, due to their market capitalizations, Cisco Systems, Dell, Intel, and Microsoft were known as "the Four Horsemen of the NASDAQ." In this period, a combination of rapidly increasing stock prices, market confidence on future profits, and speculation in individual stocks along with widely available capital created a "Wild, Wild West" environment where many investors were willing to overlook traditional metrics in favor of confidence in future technological advancements. Caught in this e-commerce hype, Cisco Systems did not foresee the bubble getting ready to burst. As the company spiraled in the up draft of the market, it built inventory. The company did not see the market downturn. As a result, the company was forced to write off $2.3 billion in inventory charges in April 2001. The company stumbled, and its stock value fell 6 percent.

What was the answer for Cisco? The company built strong horizontal processes to connect sales and operations planning (S&OP) to contract manufacturing. Based on this process evolution, it was one of the first companies to sense the economic downturn of December 2008. It weathered the storm of the recession with no write-offs.

I need more T-shaped managers to manage my T-shaped processes.
—VP of Supply Chain,
European Logistics Conference 2012

■ **Samsung dodges a bullet and learns the value of inventory**. In 1995, soaring worldwide demand, coupled with tight capacity, pushed prices of four-megabit dynamic random access memory devices (DRAMs) upward. As a consequence, DRAM manufacturers overinvested in new fabrication capacity. Recognizing an impending price collapse in December 1995, the president of Samsung's semiconductor business informed the manufacturing department of the urgent need to reduce cycle time. The huge work-in-process inventory was expected to lose its value rapidly. A project team was formed and a new process was born. It was termed *SLIM* (an acronym for *s*hort *c*ycle time and *l*ow *i*nventory in *m*anufacturing). Between 1996 and 1999, Samsung implemented SLIM in all semiconductor manufacturing facilities. It reduced manufacturing cycle times to fabricate DRAMs from more than 80 days to fewer than 30. SLIM enabled Samsung to capture an additional $1 billion in sales.

This process innovation was a wake-up call for the Samsung management team. The leadership team at Samsung became innovators in inventory management and supply chain processes championing horizontal process evolution of S&OP, revenue management, and supplier development to never have to write off inventory.

■ **A fire changes an industry. Nokia moves ahead of Ericsson**. In March 2000, a lightning bolt struck a high-voltage electricity line in New Mexico. As power fluctuated across the state, a fire broke out in a fabrication line of the Royal Philips Electronics radio frequency chip manufacturing plant in Albuquerque. The plant was a primary supplier for Nokia and its archrival, Ericsson. The two companies accounted for 40 percent of the plant's shipments.[1]

Plant personnel reacted quickly and extinguished the fire within 10 minutes. However, smoke and water had contaminated the clean room environment where millions of chips were stored for shipment. Some 4,000 miles away, at a Nokia plant outside Helsinki, a production planner who was following a well-defined process for inbound materials failed to get a routine signal from Philips. He contacted the top component purchasing manager.

In Albuquerque, Philips engineers and managers grappled with the aftermath of the fire. They realized that cleanup would take at least a week. A few hundred miles away, executives at Ericsson also got a call from Philips. Until this call, Ericsson's planners and managers had not sensed a problem.

Recognizing that Philips's problem could affect the production of several million mobile phones, Nokia took three key steps. The company mobilized to help Philips. The company changed its network, rearranging manufacturing plans in factories as far away as Shanghai. One team focused on the redesign of chips to be produced in alternate factories while another team searched and found two alternate suppliers.

Because of Nokia's initial sensing of the problem and its rapid and effective response in the third quarter of 2000, its profits rose 42 percent and the company expanded its share of the global market to 30 percent. Its quarterly statements and annual report for 2000 did not even mention the fire.

In contrast, on July 20, 2000, Ericsson reported that the fire and component shortages had caused a second-quarter operating loss of $200 million in its mobile phone division. Annual earnings were lowered by between $333 million and $445 million. Six months later, it reported divisional annual losses of $1.68 billion, a 3 percent share loss, and corporate operating losses of $167 million. It also announced the outsourcing of cell phone manufacturing to Flextronics and the elimination of several thousand jobs. The company finally returned to health in 2004 but as a much smaller company. Compared to 2000, its revenues had fallen 52 percent, its total assets had fallen about 30 percent, and the number of employees had fallen 52 percent; net income and operating income were almost, but not quite, the same.

The face of the mobile phone industry had changed forever, all because of a fire that had been contained in 10 minutes. The gravity of the situation spawned a focus on supplier development within the industry.

■ **Things don't always go better with Coca-Cola**. At the time of writing this book, when you visit the Coca-Cola website, you see a commitment: "We believe that our first responsibility is to manage our own water resources in our operations wisely. Our nearly 900 bottling plants around the world rely on water as it is the most important ingredient in our beverages. Water is also used for beverage manufacturing processes such as rinsing, cleaning, heating, and cooling. In 2008, on average we used 2.43 liters of water to produce a 1-liter beverage. One liter goes into the beverage itself, and 1.43 liters are used for manufacturing processes such as rinsing, cleaning, and cooling. We are nearly halfway to our 2012 goal of 2.17 liters per liter, which will be a 20 percent improvement." However, in March 2004, the story in India was quite different.

The $16 million Coca-Cola bottling plant was shut down by local officials in Kerala citing a drastic decline in both the quantity and quality of water available to farmers.[2]

Was the water decline due to drought or overuse? There was, and continues to be, a raging debate in the Indian court systems. It has dragged on for years. As a result, the brand image was tarnished. As the case moved through the Indian court systems, the Coca-Cola Company became laser-focused on building corporate social responsibility systems to avoid a similar issue in another market.

Stories like these gave birth to the evolution of horizontal supply chain processes to drive operational excellence. Building them requires vision, tenacity, and the ability to bridge the gaps of corporate functional processes. This world was driven by the leaders that could fill in the process holes and build new processes in the world of gray. Brick by brick, these horizontal processes bridge the gap between the customer's customer and the supplier's supplier.

Supply chain management is a career for people that can handle the gray areas. It requires a different kind of person because a black and white orientation and rules-based logic will not be as successful. In the world of supply chain, you have to make your own rules and challenge the system.
—*Denise Layfield, VP of Supply Chain, McCormick*

THE BUILDING OF HORIZONTAL SUPPLY CHAIN PROCESSES

As the great stumbled, the path forward was horizontal processes. The most common are revenue management, sales and operations planning, supplier development, and corporate social responsibility. These horizontal processes bridge the links of the supply chain to give it structure, purpose, and connectivity.

In the evolution of supply chain management, the first horizontal processes were transactional. They were billing systems created to automate the order-to-cash and procure-to-pay processes. These systems of record were implemented using standard out of the box functionality in enterprise resource planning. However, for these new horizontal processes, there is no standard out of the box system for implementation.

A Brief Look at History

From 1990 to 1998, in the early phase of supply chain evolution, the supply chain pioneers' focus was on the development of vertical processes. It was a zealous focus on optimizing vertical silo processes of make, source, and deliver. As a result, there was little cross-functional overlap; and as a consequence, there was no way to orchestrate trade-offs in supply chain execution. In the last five years, the focus on planning processes has shifted from vertical to horizontal. In addition, from an inside-out (within the organization) to an outside-in (from the external markets in to the organization) focus. Both of these shifts are fundamental to the building of market-driven value networks.

A driver was total cost management. In 2005, fewer than 5 percent of companies surveyed knew their total costs. Today, it is 24 percent. This is a small improvement as well as a major problem. Why? Historically, the supply chain has been the de facto bank. When companies want money, they turn to the supply chain; but the lack of understanding of total costs leads to bad decision making.

When it comes to building market-driven value networks, the toughest group to convince is the finance guys. You have to get top management and the top board convinced on why it matters. The metrics and incentives are so different. There is a massive hole in the market for people that understand it.
        —Principle and Founder of a European Consulting Firm

Using functional excellence and continuous improvement programs, supply chain teams have stepped up to the plate to generate cash to fuel company growth. When companies need money, the supply chain has been the traditional source of cash. However, after years of harvesting the low-hanging fruit, generating these savings is getting tougher. Yes, companies can still wring pennies from functional excellence programs, but they want and need bigger savings. They want more bang for their buck. To gain these advantages, they need a new approach. They need to turn the supply chain over, lay it horizontally, build new processes, and ask a different set of questions.

This allows companies to wring savings from the gaps between the processes and, by analyzing the trade-offs among functions, to get the best costs. Horizontal planning processes help companies to accomplish this goal.

The supply chain costs represent 18 percent of total sales, and every percent that we shave off is $22M in savings to the company. It is just hard to forget about that.

—Supply Chain Director,
Food and Beverage Company

In the building of horizontal processes, goal alignment is critical. The design needs to overcome the limitations of traditional metrics. For example, when sales is rewarded on volume, marketing on market share, finance on minimal budget variance, manufacturing on asset utilization, and sourcing on the lowest cost of materials, can companies ever align on value? Or can they build strong horizontal processes? The answer is no. Fewer than 5 percent of companies surveyed for this book have sufficient alignment to build strong horizontal supply chains. Most have a traditional organization where vertical silos have individual goals that do not add up to the whole. The dilemma of traditional organizational goal alignment is outlined in Figure 5.1.

In the last five years, the shift from vertical to horizontal process excellence has escalated. The ends of the supply chain are fragile. The organizations at the end of the supply chain—either sales or procurement—are fueled by transactional goals.

One of the issues is the lack of analytics. An order is not an order. Orders vary by demand type (e.g., replenishment or turn orders, orders to satisfy the needs of a promotion, orders to satisfy the needs of market demand for a new product launch, etc.). The cost of an order can vary based on cumulative net profit. However, in a supply chain today, there is no visibility to make these differences actionable. A typical company has a profile such as the one shown in Figure 5.2.

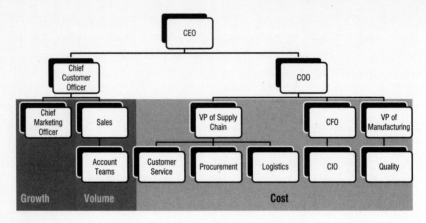

Figure 5.1 The Lack of Goal Alignment in the Typical Organization

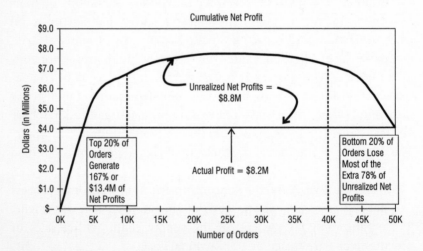

Figure 5.2 Visualization of Profitable Orders *Source:* Acorn Systems

Leadership alone is not sufficient. It requires a redefinition of incentives. To do this, support is needed from the chief operating officer or the chief executive officer to drive change. If not, the horizontal connectors that are essential to the building of market-driven value networks do not happen.

The challenge is connecting what we do and how we connect to the other functions. There are a few that are there already. There are many that are not ready. We need to have strength in numbers. We know that cost reduction is up front and center. It is the right of entry. We will always have a pull for cost reduction and the supply chain will always be a bank. There needs to be a defined path to getting both savings and value. It needs to be an and. *We need support by leadership to get there.*

—*Vice President, Pharmaceuticals*

In building the horizontal processes, metric definition is step one. Alignment is step two. After aligning on common and cross-functional metrics, companies need to ask the hard questions to gain greater value in the building of market-driven value networks. These questions help companies to understand what drives value in the value chain and when they should build value networks. The value networks are then built through strong horizontal connectors. Key questions include:

- How many value chains are there? What are the value drivers? What determines value in each?
- What does global mean? What should be global and what should be regional in source, make, deliver, and sell processes?
- How do we plan globally to execute regionally?
- What does customer service mean? What is the best design to support value-based outcomes with customers?
- How do we best sense, shape, and orchestrate demand and supply? And how to minimize the bullwhip effect?
- What is the role of horizontal planning processes in driving and accelerating value in the value network? In the supply chain?

REVENUE MANAGEMENT

When companies shape demand (the combination of price, promotion, marketing, sales incentives, and new product launch), dollars are spent to stimulate purchase behavior and increase sales lift. Most often, these demand levers are not pulled singly or separately; instead, they are used together. As a result, data analysis is difficult.

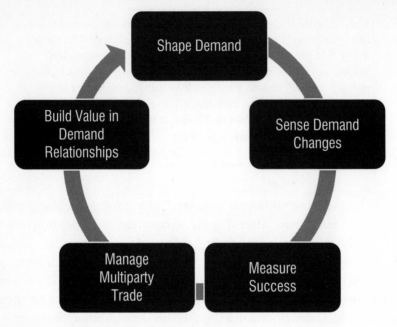

Figure 5.3 Definition of Revenue Management

There is tension. Sales groups are incented to sell. Sales organizations are incented on volume-based metrics. Marketing wants to stimulate demand to build market share.

The definition of revenue management is outlined in Figure 5.3. The process starts with the demand shaping initiative. Through revenue management, the company manages the flow of spend through multiple parties throughout the value network. For the most advanced companies, it is in a closed-loop cycle using advanced analytics to evaluate spend effectiveness.

The organization wants to be profitable. So, how do they drive profitable volume? What should be easy becomes complex quickly. Companies struggle to answer simple questions such as:

- How effective was the trade promotion spending campaign? Which trade promotion tactic was the most effective?
- Was it assortment planning or merchandising that made the difference in store profitability?
- What was the most effective pricing strategy by market last year? What tactics should be deployed this year?

- What is the most effective combination of price, promotion, advertising, or sales strategy for the new product launch?
- How effective was the rebate? How did it affect returns?

The processes of revenue management are designed to answer these questions. Revenue management is the analysis of demand shaping programs to evaluate the effectiveness to improve volume profitably. In the early stages of maturity in the market-driven value network model, companies measure volume as a metric for revenue management. For some, spend effectiveness and return on investment (ROI) are largely unknown. Demand shaping activities are seldom measured and there is little accountability for incremental lift or ROI of demand-shaping activities. In the words of one executive interviewed, "We don't have the tools or processes to measure the impact of our pricing programs. In many ways, it is just another cost, although we do not count it in the cost of goods sold."

As companies mature, multiple technologies are deployed to analyze the effectiveness of demand-shaping programs and the impact of revenue management on profitability. This includes the capabilities to analyze multiple demand levers simultaneously. The process then becomes a closed loop. In addition, market data—not history—is used to measure program effectiveness. The models are complicated. It is not easy. Failures line the path. Data modeling, effective technology deployment, training, and change management are obstacles. For example, the average company in consumer products has deployed three different technologies for price and promotion with many still searching for a new solution.

Because the demand-shaping levers vary by industry, the techniques and focus of these processes also vary. For example, the most important demand-shaping lever for consumer products is trade promotion management. The most important aspect of aerospace and defense is program management in new product launch. For high-tech and electronics manufacturers, the driver for channel success is an effective rebate program for a new product launch. For retail companies, it is price management in combination with assortment planning.

- **Consumer products**. In consumer packaged goods, one of the largest expense items on the balance sheet is trade promotion expenditure. While it is impossible to calculate an overall industry average—there is no standard definition and financial reporting varies by company—no one would disagree that the spend is substantial. However, based on five years of market studies, only 52 percent of trade promotions are evaluated. A large number (estimated between 40 and 68 percent) of trade promotions are not executed properly at the store.

The processes of trade promotion management are complex with workflows involving four groups: sales, marketing, finance, and supply chain. These teams work on an annual planning schedule where funds are allocated by brand/region and then executed by the sales teams.

In the early stages of supply chain maturity, companies design programs based on historic information. The average time to measure effectiveness is six weeks. Despite these obstacles, trade promotion management remains the number one demand-shaping lever of consumer products and food and beverage companies.

As retailers gained channel power, the management of trade programs has grown more complex. To better manage retail trade relations, consumer companies were forced to create individual account teams that now act like general managers of trade serving a specific retailer. The average consumer products company has 22 account teams in modern trade areas of North America and Europe (e.g., specific account teams for retailers like Kroger, Sainsbury's, Target, Tesco, and Walmart). These account teams are given autonomy to create their own programs. The processes get quite complicated as companies create new processes to plan globally and execute locally and assess effectiveness. The evolution of account teams adds to the process complexity of measuring trade promotion programs in consumer products industries.

Reducing data latency becomes a priority. Companies want quicker turnaround to understand what an effective program in the channel is. The shift is to near real-time sensing and the use of current market data. In addition, the shift to the adoption of digital technologies (as outlined in Figure 5.4) makes programs more volatile, demand more unpredictable, and programs more difficult to analyze. Coupon redemption from Internet sources in 2010 was six times higher than printed media coupon

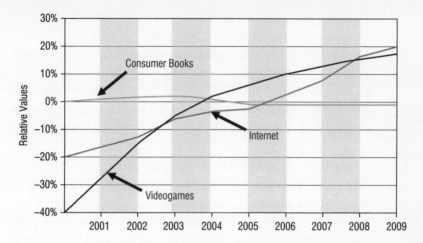

Figure 5.4 Consumer Shifts in the Use of Digital Technologies *Source:* U.S. Census

redemption. In 2012, 40 percent of food purchases were influenced by digital technologies.[3] In Figure 5.4, we show these marked shifts.

The rise of the digital path to purchase programs in consumer value networks will escalate the use of analytics and demand sensing techniques through 2015. A digital path to purchase program uses digital technologies to influence purchase at the four moments of truth in the shopping experience: the list, the basket, the transaction, and the usage. This shift will increase demand-shaping volatility. The convergence of social, digital, mobile, and e-commerce technologies to shape demand over the next five years will redefine trade promotion management.

■ **High-tech and electronics**. In high-tech and electronics, managing sales against contracts is a gap. More than 45 percent of companies use off-invoice rebate programs. Yet, only half of those respondents (56 percent) track historical and current contract compliance. With the short life cycles of consumer electronics, consumer preferences are always shifting. The use of technologies to sense demand-shaping effectiveness increases in importance. Only 30 percent of companies are satisfied with their current processes.

Over the course of the last 30 years, the price of consumer electronics products has declined as the life cycle of the product has shortened. For the supply chain, it is a double whammy. Margins are thinner, and market timing is more critical, increasing the importance of revenue management. Consider the facts. In 1982, a personal computer sold for $3,000 built from components that cost a dealer $600 with a typical gross margin of $1,000. By late 1998, the average selling price of a personal computer in the United States dropped below $1,000. In 2010, it dropped even further with an average selling price of $615. The personal computer market is now a $250 billion industry with cutthroat pricing. The market for digital cameras and cell phones is similar. Today, the life cycle (launch to the decline of sales) of a digital camera is four months with an average selling price of $154. In 2007, it was six months with an average selling price of $555.

Market sensing and data analytics have grown in importance as companies try to better manage profitability with shorter life cycles and thinner margins. The current focus is the use of user-generated content through ratings and reviews to sense consumer demand changes and quickly translate consumer shifts into pricing actions.

■ **Retail**. More than 90 percent of retailers want to improve price management. The personalization of assortment by store cluster increases the need for price management. To be successful, demand insights are more granular, data intensive, and complex. As companies mature, it is not price alone. The focus is on the combination of price, merchandising, and promotion by trip type. An example of trip type placement of trade promotions is shown in Figure 5.5. By analyzing this "heat map," the retailer is able to tailor the placement of promotions and assortments based on buyer shopping patterns.

In the most mature companies, revenue management is a subprocess or a piece of cost-to-serve analysis. *Cost to serve* is defined as a process that calculates the profitability of products, customers, and

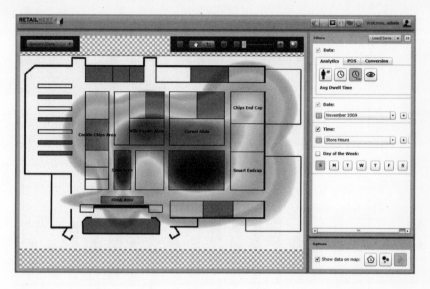

Figure 5.5 Merchandising Objectives Tailored by Analyzing Trip Missions in the Store *Source:* RetailNext

routes to market providing a fact-based focus for decision making on service mix, demand-shaping levers, and operational changes for each customer. It is the application of activity-based costing to the customer interaction to improve the profitability of the relationship. Today, fewer than 5 percent of companies calculate cost-to-serve. The rest have no visibility of how demand shaping ties to the profitability of a relationship, an order, or an industry segment. In the words of one supply chain pioneer, "We were actually losing money from top to bottom throughout the organization. By optimizing literally every department we are now delivering double-digit profit margins. We have lowered our cost of goods, freight, and optimized promotional spend." The average time for ROI of cost-to-serve projects is less than nine months. The barrier is getting to financial data.

The benefit of cost-to-serve analysis is twofold: identification of the cost elements of a relationship and the visualization of orders that are not profitable. The relative costs per customer can vary greatly as shown in Figure 5.6.

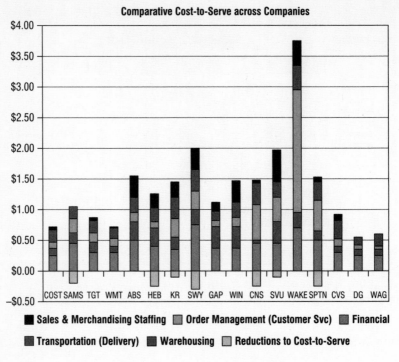

Figure 5.6 Relative Costs of Supply Chain Activities by Customer

> *An important change that we made early in the supply chain pro-*
> *cess was the implementation of customer profitability and measur-*
> *ing price and trade promotion. We started the program in 1992,*
> *and it has been the most important change to drive improvement*
> *that we have made in our supply chain processes.*
> — *Randy Benz, Retired Vice President and*
> *Chief Information Officer, Energizer*

SALES AND OPERATIONS PLANNING

For manufacturers and retailers, supply chain is business. The S&OP process aligns the organization to the business strategy. However, as shown in Figure 5.7, one of the issues is clarity of business strategy and the understanding of supply chain processes by the executive teams.

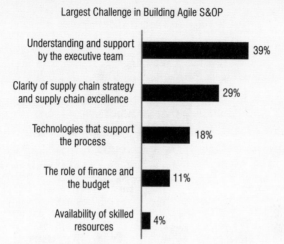

Figure 5.7 Challenges in Building S&OP Processes

As companies have become more global and face rising complexity, volatility, and uncertainty, the importance of S&OP has increased. In 2011, examples of this complexity included:

- 90 percent of supply chains are grappling with skyrocketing costs and supply volatility.
- 87 percent are struggling with the integration of business planning and supply chain planning technologies.
- 85 percent of supply chains experienced a disruption.
- 51 percent of companies have multiple S&OP processes. The average is five.
- 36 percent of companies' S&OP processes are stalled or are moving slowly.
- Industry progress on inventory reduction and supply chain working capital is stalled.

S&OP is defined by the Association of Operations Management as "a process to develop tactical plans that provide management the ability to strategically direct its businesses to achieve competitive advantage on a continuous basis by integrating customer-focused marketing plans for new and existing products with the management of the

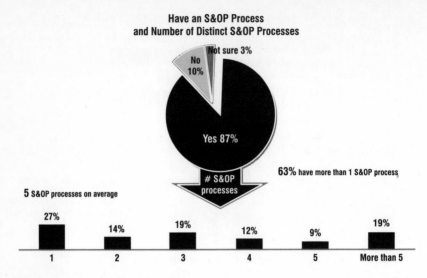

Figure 5.8   S&OP Process Overview

supply chain." For manufacturers, it has become more important to power growth, improve resiliency, and drive efficiency improvements.[4] The complexity of these systems is outlined in Figure 5.8.

> *Why am I focused on the supply chain? The answer is simple. It is a barometer of my business. All the problems show up first in the supply chain.*
> —*Michael Dell, Founder, Chairman, and CEO, Dell*

Evolution of S&OP to Become Market Driven

The term *S&OP* is 30 years old. However, as supply chain processes have matured, this term has been redefined. Today, companies are at one of five stages of maturity. Each stage offers increasing opportunity and ROI.

Each stage of S&OP process maturity has a different process goal. More than 75 percent of companies lack goal clarity, which undermines S&OP success. Frequently, cross-functional teams form with a different, often unexpressed, goal in mind. These teams will align to deliver an S&OP process, but each member will have a different definition of the term. In these cases, the team will struggle for months—or years—to gain alignment.

The most mature companies in the selection of S&OP processes can easily answer five questions:

1. What is your S&OP goal?
2. How do you achieve balance between demand and supply?
3. How do you make decisions?
4. How does your organization measure success?
5. How do you tie S&OP planning to execution?

Stage 1

Goal: Deliver a feasible plan. The original S&OP processes originated with a goal of developing a feasible plan. Early evolution of the advanced planning solution market enabled organizations to develop a forecast, visualize operational requirements, and align metrics. The introduction of theory of constraints in 1984 and the evolution of the concepts into manufacturing planning applications enhanced this capability. It allowed organizations to identify constraints and build a feasible, or realistic, plan. Note that these models are industry-specific. A conglomerate composed of process, discrete, and apparel manufacturing may find that it needs multiple systems to model operations. Likewise, the building of a one-size-fits-all model by the enterprise resource planning expansionists has delivered generic models that do not fit any company well. These stages are depicted in Figure 5.9.

Stage 2

Goal: Match demand with supply. As organizations mature, teams need a solution with more advanced capabilities to model the

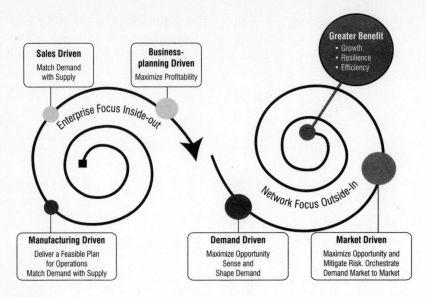

Figure 5.9 Stages of Sales and Operations Maturity

trade-offs of volume and product mix. These trade-offs are complex. Through the use of technologies, companies are able to better visualize and balance customer service and to assess strategies and inventory plans to best match demand with supply. To meet this requirement, companies have invested in what-if modeling environments. Over the last 10 years, these processes were augmented by inventory management specialist capabilities to evaluate multitier inventory analysis. Typical benefits to be gained from a process in stage 2 of S&OP maturity are outlined in Figure 5.10.

Stage 3

Goal: Drive the most profitable response. While stage 1 is supply driven and stage 2 is sales and marketing driven, stage 3 is business-planning driven. This is commonly dubbed integrated business planning (IBP). At this stage, it is critical to have a clear supply chain strategy and well-defined definition of supply chain excellence. For most, this is a gating factor for success.

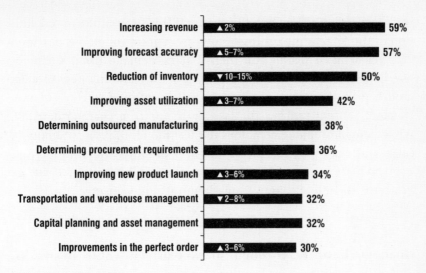

Figure 5.10   Benefits Received from S&OP Processes (Stage 2 Maturity)

To accomplish this modeling, the demand and supply hierarchies must be decoupled to enable volume/mix what-if trade-offs iteratively between process steps. This S&OP maturity stage requires the addition of two new capabilities: demand translation and supply orchestration. The process of modeling demand volume/mix trade-offs between demand and supply is demand translation. In supply orchestration, trade-offs are determined and translated into buying strategies in commodity markets to determine the most effective formulation or platform design to schedule for manufacturing.

One of the issues in this stage of S&OP is unit conversion. The average company will have five to seven definitions of *volume* that require translation. In addition, to properly determine trade-offs the analysis needs to be calculated in volume not currency.

Stage 4

Goal: Build demand-driven supply chain capabilities. At this stage of S&OP, the process is designed from the outside-in. It is focused on product sell-through in the channel, whereas the earlier steps were focused on selling into the channel. This step requires a redefinition of the forecasting processes to sense market conditions based on channel demand signals and then shaping demand using technologies like price optimization; trade promotion planning; new product launch plan alignment; and social, digital, and mobile convergence. Demand sensing reduces the latency to see true channel demand, while demand shaping combines the techniques of price, promotion, sales, and marketing incentives and new product launch to increase demand lift. Examples of companies working at this stage of S&OP are Procter & Gamble, DuPont, Dow Chemical, and Samsung.

Stage 5

Goal: Orchestrate through market-driven value networks. The horizontal processes in stages 3 and 4 are foundational to build market-driven value networks. This technology portfolio helps companies to sense and shape demand and supply bidirectionally between sell- and buy-side markets. This process of bidirectional trade-offs between demand and a commodity market is termed *demand orchestration*. This capability allows companies to win in this new world of changing opportunities and supply constraints. It is especially relevant with the tightening of commodity markets.

Why Does It Matter?

Each step in advancement of the S&OP process delivers incremental, positive business results. In the Great Recession, companies with strong market-driven S&OP processes sensed and aligned to the economic impacts five times faster than laggard companies. They were also able to obtain better year-over-year results in days of working capital.

The results are substantial. Companies reaching stage 2 of supply chain maturity in sales and operations planning are able to drive an average improvement of 2 percent increase in growth and a 3 to 7 percent improvement in asset utilization. Other benefits include reductions in inventory and improvements in new product launch success. S&OP allows companies to make the right trade-offs in metrics based on the supply chain strategy.

One of the reasons that S&OP is so important is the benefit that it has across a range of metrics. While many supply chain processes will improve one to two metrics, the benefits of improving S&OP maturity are pervasive: touching many metrics and raising the bar of total performance.

> *The word* supply chain *is so different for everyone in the company.*
> —*Director of Planning, Consumer Products*

What Does a Good S&OP Process Look Like?

A good S&OP process is a meeting that executives cannot wait to attend. It is balanced and aligned to action. It is seen as the best way to maximize opportunity and mitigate risk.

As companies align and mature their "S" and "OP" definitions, the organization will balance the elements of market drivers and competition against the form and function of inventory, network, and commodity strategies. Only 20 percent of companies have balance in S&OP processes. In these organizations, there is metrics alignment, clear direction on business strategy, and reporting to a line-of-business manager responsible for profitability. The five metrics that are recommended to drive alignment are customer service, forecast error, inventory/working capital, profitability, and revenue. The greatest issues with balance occur when the process reports to either sales or manufacturing leadership and the metrics are not cross-functional. A visualization of the trade-offs is shown in Figure 5.11.

Key elements to consider in the design of the S&OP process include:

■ **The right time horizon**. The number one issue for most companies in setting up an S&OP process is determining the right time horizon. It should not be confused as a short-term process. It is not a process of days or weeks. Instead, the S&OP process is a form of tactical planning. It balances the needs of demand and

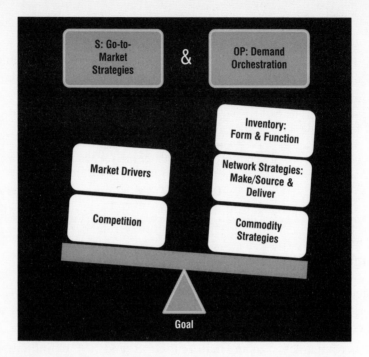

Figure 5.11 Achieving Balance in S&OP

supply processes in a longer-term horizon of 12 to 18 months allowing companies to balance opportunity and risk.

While the duration can vary by industry, it is never days or weeks, and it is never real-time. Instead, it is a longer-focused planning process that is aligned with the timing of critical decisions. As such, it should focus on the decision points that can be affected or changed within the planning horizon. Consequently, it is shorter in high-tech and electronics (typically 12 months) and longer in pharmaceuticals (36 to 60 months). The typical consumer products and chemical company is 18 months while automotive is 24 months.

The time horizon in the S&OP process is the time horizon for planning. If it is too short, companies lose the opportunity to impact important decisions. If it is too long, then companies can spend a lot of time on data that has little meaning. If it does not have the right focus on critical time horizons for decision making, companies will not get the right visibility. In the design of the S&OP process, it is critical to take all of these factors into account to pick the right time horizon to model decisions.

- **The right balance of the urgent and the important**. A common mistake is to focus the S&OP process on short-term results. Companies that are just getting started in S&OP processes will often make the mistake of confusing the urgent with the important. Short-term planning, or operational planning, is a reactive response. If the organization only focuses on short-term planning, it will lose the greater value proposition for growth and inventory planning that can be harnessed through tactical processes as outlined in this chapter.
- **The right level of granularity**. In short, if companies do not get tactical planning right, they will struggle to align cross-functionally. Strategic planning is at too high of a level and the levels of planning below it do not align the functional silos. Getting it right is paramount to drive balance.

Because of the market confusion on tactical planning, company after company feels that it needs a unique name for S&OP. Letter-perfect means correct to the last detail. We believe that the term *S&OP* is letter-perfect; but over time as the goal has shifted, the practices have become imperfect. The embellishment of the standard S&OP acronym is a current fad. The list of names—SIOP, DDS&OP, DDBS, IDDSP, IBM, and IBP—goes on and on. The danger is that as it is renamed and embellished within S&OP initiatives, we run the risk of losing the essence and the meaning of planning and the goal of this important process. The letters, when understood, stand strong on their own, as shown in Table 5.1.

S: The S in S&OP is about selling strategies and market drivers. Effective processes focus on go-to-market strategies. It is often confused to be about sales.

&: The *and* in the S&OP process represents the cross-functional coordination/alignment required to meet the strategic goal of the process. For example, if the goal is to be demand driven, the focus is

Table 5.1 S&OP Letter Definitions

Letter	Common Practice	Market-driven Practice
S	Ask sales	Focus on market drivers: How do we best shape demand?
&	Direct integration to supply	Design of the value chain to optimize trade-offs, minimize risk, balance cycles, and orchestrate demand
OP	Manufacturing plan	Trade-offs among make, source, and deliver

on outside-in market sensing. The demand plan is an input into the financial plan and the organization is tasked with determining:

- **The best working capital plan:** Determining the right form and function of inventory versus constraining inventory or focusing on just inventory levels.
- **Trade-offs:** The alignment of the value chain to balance growth initiatives with the trade-offs among sustainability, corporate social responsibility, tax efficiency, speed to market, and costs.
- **Network design:** Based on demand and supply variability, and market conditions, what is the best network design to minimize risks and maximize the market opportunities?

At Cisco Systems, the supply chain organization is called the customer value chain management organization (CVCM) for a reason. (The company did not want it to be just about supply. Instead, it is about value and delivering the right customer response.) The company runs a risk management engine of 4,300 inputs with more than 1,000 simulations by 10 planners each month. To do this, companies need to start with the goal in mind and work backward.

- **OP:** OP needs to drive decisions about operations in the network. It is not just about the factory or the enterprise. It is about the network: making the right trade-offs in the network across the processes of deliver, make, and source. When done right, S&OP planning is also tied to execution. An example is Celanese. The teams have worked multiple years to be able to align plant strategies with demand variability using software that optimizes the manufacturing rhythm wheel (product sequencing) for each of the plants based on demand variability and cost inputs.

To achieve this level of maturity, companies need to overcome many barriers including:

- **Ownership and reporting relationships**. Balance can only be achieved if the organization has shared metrics and if the organization reports to a profit-center manager. When this happens, companies can more easily align to a common goal. Organizational structure matters and will limit maturity. Organizations with reporting structures to sales or commercial organizations will never get out of stage 2, and organizations with reporting structures aligned to manufacturing will have difficulty moving past stage 1 of the maturity model.

- **The role of the forecast**. The forecast model changes throughout the stages of the S&OP process. It becomes more disciplined, granular, and market driven. As the organization matures, the organization deals more easily with uncertainty. It comes to realize that it is not the number in the forecast, but the probability of the number that matters.

- **The role of the budget**. The integration of the financial plan into the tactical operational plan is the number one change management issue for companies in tactical planning processes. One reason is that *budget* is a loaded term. By definition, the financial budget is a static document in a dynamic world. For this reason, tight integration between financial and operational processes is never recommended. It can be an input but not a constraint to the process. Training of the financial teams is critical to get past this obstacle.

- **Planning skills and capabilities**. What-if functionality in predictive analytics is evolving, and it is a critical skill set for an effective S&OP process. In a recent survey of 80 supply chain executives, when asked, "Has the need for what-if analysis increased in importance in 2010?" more than 60 percent of the respondents said yes. When asked, "Do you have what you need in what-if analysis?" the answer from the group was mixed: 45 percent of the respondents were just beginning to use what-if analysis and 42 percent said that there was a significant gap in what was available in the market with only 13 percent stating that they have what they need to perform their jobs today.

- **The hoax of one number forecasting**. A forecast is a hierarchy of numbers based on primary keys or attributes. In modern forecasting tools, there are multiple views, and representations of the forecast in multiple units of measure. There are also multiple forecasts in the organization (e.g., sales forecast, financial forecast, material forecast). Each forecasting process is built with a goal in mind, and as a result, the underlying context of the data is different. Multiple forecasts can be synchronized using a common set of assumptions, but the goal of tight integration or having one number hamstrings an organization. As a result, the promise of one number is too simplistic. Instead, the goal should be for a common plan.

Automating S&OP

With the advances in computing power, demand and supply modeling have improved, along with advances in optimization for inventory and financial modeling. The complexity of global supply chains requires putting together the pieces to encompass the needs of both global and regional modeling; and the synchronization and visualization of multiple S&OP processes. As a result, there is a dilemma: so many pieces, so much opportunity, and so many requirements.

A useful technique is to define the technology based on the maturity model with each step having both a different goal and set of applications. A common mistake that companies make is to tightly integrate applications. Instead, planning is iterative. Technologies are combined to enable what-if analysis to determine the best plan. Only 8 percent of companies today believe that they have what they need to do what-if analysis correctly.

I think for a good S&OP process, you need to have a cultural change. It needs to be understood that S&OP is not a supply chain program. It may be orchestrated by supply chain but it needs to be led by the business unit lead.

—Álvaro Cuba, Vice President,
Kraft Foods Canada

Organizational Considerations

Due to mergers and acquisitions, and the growth in emerging econ-omies, supply chain organizations have grown. In some cases, the increase has been more than 200 percent. This growth has resulted in more users in more time zones with an increase in organizational complexity that has changed the need for collaborative workflow, sce-narios, and what-if management and visualization.

The reporting structures have also changed. In 2003, fewer than 10 percent of companies had a well-defined S&OP organization. In 2012, three out of five projects for supply chain planning software were driven by a person with the S&OP-specific title, and industry conferences dedicated to S&OP abound. As a result, yesterday's S&OP technology may not be up to the task. Organizational size and com-plexity are major considerations.

SONOCO PRODUCTS

CASE STUDY

Sonoco Products and Owens Illinois compete for market share in the delivery of packaging materials to the food manufacturing industry. Sonoco Products, a $4.5 billion company, is located in the south-ern portion of the United States, and manufactures packaging film. The company has been on a six-year journey to become more market driven with a strong focus on S&OP. Owens Illinois (OI), a $6.3 billion company, manufactures glass containers, with headquarters in the Midwest. It has been more focused on transactional efficiency, procure-ment, and IT standardization. As seen in Figure 5.12, OI has had more inventory than its peer group for the past six years. In contrast, Sonoco Products has driven growth (with 65 percent less spending in research and development than OI), and managed inventories at better than peer group averages over the course of its S&OP transition. One of the keys to success for Sonoco Products has been the early identification of oppor-tunities to sell available manufacturing capacity in the channel through

(Continued)

closer coordination with its upstream customers. In the words of Keith Holliday, director of supply chain at Sonoco Products, "S&OP has been a strong contributor to the company's ability to drive growth while controlling inventories below peer group levels."

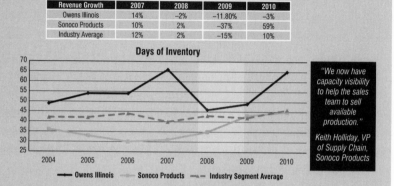

Revenue Growth	2007	2008	2009	2010
Owens Illinois	14%	−2%	−11.80%	−3%
Sonoco Products	10%	2%	−37%	59%
Industry Average	12%	2%	−15%	10%

"We now have capacity visibility to help the sales team to sell available production."

Keith Holliday, VP of Supply Chain, Sonoco Products

Figure 5.12 Comparison of Sonoco Products versus Owens Illinois and the Role of S&OP *Source:* Sonoco and Owens Illinois balance sheets, 2004–2010

SUPPLIER DEVELOPMENT

Supplier development programs matured the fastest in discrete industries. The Nokia/Ericsson story was a catalyst for high-tech and discrete manufacture adoption. A supplier development program is an orchestrated initiative using the supply chain strategy to define supplier relationships. It includes one or more of these key elements:

- **Supplier sensing**. Active sensing of the health of the supplier relationship and setting up programs that improve supplier health. This includes financial terms, order policies, transportation and freight requirements, and adherence to CSR programs.
- **Quality management**. Providing experienced professionals to help suppliers navigate the differences between quality of design and quality of conformance to ensure the receipt of quality materials.
- **Supply chain process design**. The design of warehousing, transportation, and data information sharing systems to reduce demand latency and streamline material flows.

- **Open innovation networks**. The alignment of programs to drive open innovation. In these programs, suppliers are incented to share new ideas and collaborate with research and development teams to work together to accelerate innovation.
- **Corporate social responsibility**. In this program, suppliers are included in CSR goals, and programs for measuring, monitoring, and reporting CSR improvements are put into place. This often includes fair labor monitoring in apparel and specialty retail, water and energy monitoring in food and beverage supply chains, and carbon and emission monitoring in chemical and process value networks.

In the initial phase of supply chain maturity, supplier development programs focus on the lowest purchase cost. In these early phases, the procurement team operates as an isolated silo and buys with a singular cost focus.

I started in a company where everything was decentralized. We were like cowboys roaming the earth. I think we realized that we were a jack-of-all-trades and masters of none.

The default was local; if I could not afford local, I would default to regional and then make it global. The key is the coordination. Two things that hurt: information technology evolved slower than the need and center-led, distributed management. So, we hired people that were experts and identified functions in all of the regions. We defined the role of global would only be to the extent that we could add value. If not, we distributed it . . . even for global procurement.

—Marty Kisliuk, Director, Global Operations and Business Development at FMC Corporation, Agricultural Products Group

---

Over time, the supplier development program transitions to focus on total cost and the building of value. This includes the design of programs to work with suppliers to accelerate open innovation, reach CSR goals, and build strategic relationships to use assets and key relationships to penetrate new markets. It takes different forms in different supply chains.

- **Dell**. Dell traces its origins to 1984. When Dell set up its supplier program, it was famous for beating up its suppliers. In the history of supply chain, there has never been a company more successful in improving the velocity of working capital as Dell. This success was largely due to the high-velocity, low-cost distribution supplier network to support built-to-order manufacturing.

  In 1998, the company had two days of working capital and in 2010 it operated with a negative 31 days of working capital. It successfully built supplier and information systems to fund the supply chain. To do this, the company pared down its supplier companies from 204 to 47 and moved to a just-in-time (JIT) inventory program with suppliers warehousing their components only 15 minutes from the Dell factory. This JIT inventory system decreased inventory costs and led to a 6 percent profit advantage in components.

  Through the use of an integrated supplier network, Dell's inventory turnover time was reduced by 57 percent and production space expanded due to the decreased storage area needed for inventory. Without these relationships, Dell would not have been able to support a 50-plus percent growth rate for three consecutive years that led to $12 billion in annual sales by 1997.

- **Lockheed Martin**. This aerospace and defense giant has a 1-800 number that rings at the desk of a senior engineer. Who is calling? Typically, it is a supplier looking for clarity on a part specification, a drawing, a delivery, or just general information. The person on the other end of the phone at Lockheed is not a third-party call center or an outsourced service desk. The job is too critical. Instead, it is an experienced engineer who is rewarded by this senior position. Most of the work is on the interpretation of quality of design to quality of compliance. Specification and material usage clarification, staffed by experts at Lockheed, is 24 hours a day, 7 days a week.

- **Johnson & Johnson (J&J)**. To help identify potentially weak suppliers, J&J shares its supplier list regularly with Alix Partners and asks for help in identifying supplier issues. Alix Partners specializes in debt restructuring. Over the course of many years, J&J used the data and has built strong skills in identifying at-risk companies.

When an issue is found, the J&J team is dispatched to the location to see how it can help the supplier. This team evaluates the supply chain's design to see how small improvements can help improve supplier viability.

■ **Intel**. In the economic downturn of 2008, Intel dispatched supplier development teams to understand the financial viability of suppliers. The company gave its teams the ability to design the supply chain to improve supplier viability. It was a good thing. The company found nine suppliers on the edge of failure and was able to make quick changes to avoid part shortages and ensure up time of its manufacturing facilities.

■ **Land Rover**. The company faced a potential long-term shutdown in the production of its bestselling Discovery SUV. A key supplier, UPF-Thompson, which made the Discovery's chassis, was on the verge of insolvency. Land Rover had no alternative supplier. Scrambling into action, Land Rover resolved the situation by agreeing to buy UPF-Thompson for approximately £16 million in order to guarantee future deliveries of the chassis.

The action or outcome may vary, but the best results start with early sensing.

Supply chain discussions started as holistic, but over time they have morphed into a discussion of trucks and sheds becoming more centered on the physical movement of goods. We lost our way . . . the procurement professional should not just "buy." Instead, they need to know how materials fit into the total supply chain to drive value. Too few know how to do this.
—European Consulting Partner

Starting a Supplier Development Program

Companies ask how to get started. One of the first steps should be supplier rationalization. Not all supplier relationships are equal and there is no one program that should fit all.

Supply chain is finally being viewed by hospitals as strategic.
There has always been a supply chain role since the beginning of
time, but it was seen as a transactional role. Now the supply chain
group's focus is one of clinical integration.
                                    —Rosaline Parson, Chief Operating Officer,
                                            Healthcare Purchasing Alliance LLC

Supplier rationalization and supplier relationship management is a key component to supplier development. In this work, the supplier base is stratified using a framework. The framework should tie to the goal and the programs should be built based on the outcome. It should consider the importance of the relationship, the competitive market conditions, commodity market risk and price fluctuations, and the role of the supplier in driving value.

One of the leaders in supplier relationship management is Unilever. To support the global Unilever regional teams, the organization built a common way to segregate suppliers based on three dimensions: strategic positioning, scope positioning, and relationship attractiveness. The segmentation scoring then classified the suppliers into one of three categories: integrated suppliers, collaborative suppliers, and transactional suppliers. The scoring mechanism is featured in Figure 5.13.

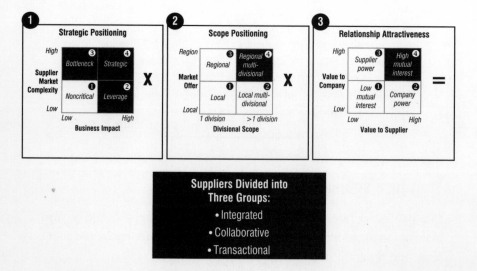

Figure 5.13 Supplier Relationship Management

We use Unilever as an example in this book because it is one of the few case studies where we see the delineation of regional/global presence and the discussion of relative power in the extended network. This more holistic approach leads to better segmentation.

Corporate Social Responsibility and Sustainability

Today, 89 percent of the Fortune 500 manufacturers have a sustainability or CSR report as part of their corporate communication efforts. The first CSR report was published by Dow Chemical in 1996. Over the last decade, the processes have evolved.

The quest is to better understand how carbon and environmental impacts change value networks. The recognition of the importance did not happen easily. There were a number of stumbles:

- **Nike: A Rolling Stone**. In 1994, *Rolling Stone*, the *New York Times*, *Foreign Affairs*, and the *New Republic* reported that Nike was using child labor to manufacture products. The company tried to sidestep the issue, claiming it could not be held responsible for the practices of suppliers. However, in June 1996, when *Life* magazine published pictures of a child in Pakistan assembling Nike soccer balls, a company-sponsored audit of a Vietnamese factory was obtained. When it was leaked by the Transnational Resource and Action Center (now known as CorpWatch), Nike's chairman and CEO Phil Knight issued a mea culpa.

  "The Nike product has become synonymous with slave wages, forced overtime, and arbitrary abuse," Knight said at a 1998 press conference at the National Press Club. At this conference, he declared that he would implement a more rigorous social auditing regime and extend U.S. operating rules and processes to its overseas contractors. Since then, Nike has been diligent about CSR standards.

- **Sweet ending?** In March 2010, the environmental group Greenpeace linked candy giant Nestlé to oil palm–related deforestation and the deaths of orangutans. Angered over the video, Nestlé retaliated by having it banned from YouTube and replaced with this statement: "This video is no longer available due to a copyright claim by Société des Produits Nestlé S.A." This reaction caused a public relations circus. The outrage

spread far and wide through social media resulting in a boy-
cott of Nestlé products. Greenpeace used this outrage to push
that Nestlé was responsible for illegal deforestation in Indonesia
through one of its palm oil suppliers, Sinar Mas. While a palm
oil plantation may sound green to the normal consumer, studies show that these plantations result in a drastic reduction in
biodiversity and increase carbon emissions due to deforestation.

Nestlé canceled its contract with Sinar Mas, but the damage
was done to its brand. At the April 2010 Nestlé Annual General
Meeting, Nestlé Chairman Peter Brabeck-Letmathe announced
a partnership with The Forest Trust (TFT). Together with TFT,
Nestlé published Responsible Sourcing Guidelines.

- **Sweat shops not good for business**. In 1996, the National
  Labor Committee, a human rights group, reported that sweat-
  shop labor was used to make clothing for the Kathie Lee line, sold
  at Walmart. Kathie Lee Gifford was a well-known television
  celebrity. Her first reaction was to challenge the labor committee. In a tearful and angry reaction on her show *Live! with Regis
  and Kathie Lee*, she claimed that the accusations were false.

  After one of Kathie Lee's factory workers paraded around the
  U.S. Capitol to testify about her experience working in the factory,
  Kathie Lee and her husband Frank Gifford retraced their steps
  and tried to make amends. As sales of their products plunged,
  they brought paychecks to the Hill in an attempt to show the U.S.
  Congress that they were paying the workers a fair wage. They
  pledged to eliminate child labor through activism in Washington;
  however the damage was done. The brand was tarnished.

- **Apple**. When the *New York Times* reported health and safety
  issues at Foxconn, one of Apple's contract manufacturers in
  2012, Tim Cook, CEO of Apple, retaliated. He should have
  taken a lesson from Kathie Lee's playbook when he said.

As a company and as individuals, we are defined by our
values. Unfortunately, some people are questioning Apple's
values today, and I'd like to address this with you directly.
We care about every worker in our worldwide supply
chain. Any accident is deeply troubling, and any issue with
working conditions is cause for concern. Any suggestion
that we don't care is patently false and offensive to us.

As you know better than anyone, accusations like these are contrary to our values. It's not who we are. For the many hundreds of you who are based at our suppliers' manufacturing sites around the world, or spend long stretches working there away from your families, I know you are as outraged by this as I am. For the people who aren't as close to the supply chain, you have a right to know the facts.

Every year we inspect more factories, raising the bar for our partners and going deeper into the supply chain. As we reported earlier this month, we've made a great deal of progress and improved conditions for hundreds of thousands of workers. We know of no one in our industry doing as much as we are, in as many places, touching as many people.

We are focused on educating workers about their rights, so they are empowered to speak up when they see unsafe conditions or unfair treatment. As you know, more than a million people have been trained by our program.

We will continue to dig deeper, and we will undoubtedly find more issues. What we will not do—and never have done—is stand still or turn a blind eye to problems in our supply chain. On this you have my word.

Shortly after Cook issued this statement, a story aired on *Nightline*'s special edition television series on February 21, 2012. The story downplayed the 4 deaths and 77 injuries from metal explosions. It also spoke about the 9 suicides with 19 attempts to jump from the Foxconn building. No matter how many words Mr. Cook utters, the world will never forget the pictures of the suicide nets at Foxconn. It will be an ever-lasting symbol of corporate CSR programs gone wrong.

Social responsibility is about more than green. Its impact is more pervasive. Companies in the first stages of supply chain maturity will adopt corporate sustainability initiatives; but under the covers within the company, it will be only about cost reduction. At this stage, CSR becomes synonymous with reducing costs. In these first stages of maturity, manufacturing and operations executives quickly get on board to save water, energy, and material waste.

It quickly becomes more about value. CSR can be a powerful strategy. As companies mature, they depend on third-party audits and sensing mechanisms to build an extended supply chain that meets their

Table 5.2 Corporate Social Responsibility Rankings

Company Name	Rank	Carbon Dioxide Productivity	Leadership Diversity	Percentage Tax Paid	Country
Novo Nordisk A/S	1	$68,585	18%	80.45%	Denmark
Natura Cosmeticos SA	2	$284,661	0%	73.90%	Brazil
Statoil ASA	3	$6,508	40%	100.00%	Norway
Novozymes A/S	4	$4,229	19%	91.87%	Denmark
ASML Holding NV	5	$70,094	15%	80.54%	Netherlands
BG Group plc	6	$3,308	7%	99.83%	United Kingdom
Vivendi SA	7	$129,114	33%	68.67%	France
Umicore SA/NV	8	$24,360	20%	74.67%	Belgium
Norsk Hydro ASA	9	$4,520	33%	100.00%	Norway
Atlas Copco AB	10	$83,790	36%	100.00%	Sweden

corporate social responsibility objectives. The most mature companies use CSR programs to build competitive advantage and new business models. Table 5.2 details the current top listing of the Global 100 Most Sustainable corporations in the world. Launched in 2005, the Global 100 is announced each year at the World Economic Forum in Davos.

In this process, companies quickly learn that although they can outsource their supply chain, they cannot outsource the risk or responsibility associated with the extended supply chain from the customer's customer to the supplier's supplier. It needs to happen by building the value network brick by brick.

■ **Adidas.** In January 2012, the Adidas Group has made it for the eighth consecutive time into the ranking of the Global 100 Most Sustainable Corporations in the World. The company established workplace standards for subcontractors in 2005 and has worked through supplier development programs and labor auditing to execute a fair program. In 2011, the company extended its network and includes 1,230 independent factories in 69 countries. The standards include guidelines for working hours, fair wages, freedom of association, and child labor. The focus of the program is self-governance where Adidas acts as both an inspector and an advisor.

- **Hewlett-Packard (HP)**. A leader in corporate social responsibility is Hewlett-Packard. HP was founded in 1939 and is headquartered in Palo Alto, California. Fiscal year 2011 revenues were $127 billion. The company operates in 187 countries and has championed CSR strategies as an important corporate initiative since 2005. HP reached its carbon reduction goals one year early—cutting it by 25 percent compared with 2005 levels—and is now looking for more cuts. In 2010, the company recycled 1.95 billion pounds (884,000 tons) of electronic products and supplies. In total, more than 2.36 billion pounds (1.07 million tons) of electronic products and supplies have been recovered and either reused (electronic products) or recycled (electronic products and supplies) by HP since 1987. The company has focused on reuse, recycling 410 million pounds (186,000 tons) in 2010.

- **Walmart**. This retail giant has used CSR strategies to change its image. This $258 billion company was founded in 1962 and currently operates 8,500 stores in 15 countries under 55 different brand names. Over the last 15 years, the company has undergone much scrutiny on CSR impact. A professor of economics from Iowa State published in *Farm Foundation* in 1997 that small towns can lose almost half of their retail trade within 10 years of a Walmart store opening. In contrast, a study commissioned by Walmart in *Global Insights* published that the average family reduced its food costs by 9.1 percent due to Walmart's ability to sell groceries at a lower cost.

  Over the years, Walmart has been battling this argument along with legal issues on labor and sexual discrimination lawsuits. It has not been pretty. The company's image had been tarnished. However, Walmart felt that it had a unique opportunity to change all of that. In November 2006, the company released a standard for packaging scorecards for supplier self-assessment to deliver against its commitment to reduce packaging across its global supply chain by 5 percent by 2013. It did not stop there. Walmart followed with a sustainability index in 2009. In the rollout of the index, the company asked suppliers to self-assess themselves on 15 hard-hitting questions on corporate social responsibility. While this has not yet been firmly linked to the buying behavior of the Walmart merchandisers, it has driven a change in supplier behavior and the consumer's impression of the Walmart brand.

I hate to admit it, but it's true—it's getting harder and harder to hate Walmart. Details are surfacing about the gigantic retailer's initiative to create a sustainability index. One that would meticulously measure the environmental impact of every single item it stocks. Needless to say, the idea alone raises plenty of questions. But if it's successful, the index could literally change the face of retail forever. Apologies if that language was a tad grandiose, but it's actually pretty accurate.
—*Brian Martin, Treehugger.com blog, July 14, 2009*

■ **IBM Global Asset Recovery**. International Business Machines Corporation manufactures and sells computer hardware and software. It is the second-largest publicly traded technology company in the world based on market capitalization. After 20 years of taking machines off lease, the Global Asset Recovery Group (GARS) was established in November 2004 to formally remanufacture (disassemble and reutilize materials) computers, hardware, and accessories. Designed as a value-added service and part of IBM Global Financing (IGF), it is responsible for leasing equipment to IBM's large customers and clients. When these leases expire, equipment, including non-IBM equipment, is returned to GARS for end-of-life management and dispositioning.

GARS, a global operation, handles more than 20,000 machines per week or approximately 73.4 million pounds per year. If the total demanufacturing weight of products processed was loaded into railway coal hopper cars, the total length of the train would extend 2.1 miles.

The goal is to recycle and reuse as many materials as possible. In 2011, IBM landfilled or incinerated less than 1 percent of its waste stream. Parts can be harvested either for IBM internal reuse or made available for wider resale at these locations. In 2011, the team sold more than 30 million parts. The GARS staff as well as the employees of the de-manufacturing plants know which IBM components are on a save list, so operators can pull out specific parts and send them for testing or cleaning. GARS also knows if there are industry-standard parts (not proprietary to IBM), such as some memory components, that can go for resale through outside channels.

The issues on the future of the supply chain cannot be disputed. They will grow worse, not better. Companies that embrace this as permanent change and work with it as an input to their supply chain business strategy will drive long-term value.

- **Water**. One of eight people in the world today has no access to potable water. Due to the increasing complexity of the global economy and the interrelated nature of supply chains, the stress on the world's water supplies is expected, within the next 15 to 20 years, to trigger a global food crisis with projected shortfalls of up to 30 percent in world cereal production. Water will become the new currency of the future supply chain.[5]
- **Food**. The world produces enough food to feed everyone. World agriculture produces 17 percent more calories per person today than it did 30 years ago, despite a 70 percent population increase. This is enough to provide everyone in the world with at least 2,720 kilocalories (kcal) per person per day. However, one-third of food is wasted in the supply chain. This is a major opportunity for food and beverage manufacturers; as we will see in Chapter 6, it will require the redesign of the supply chain to use big data techniques.[6]
- **Carbon**. A carbon footprint is a measure of the impact of activities on the environment from the burning of fossil fuels. It is measured in tons or kilograms of carbon dioxide equivalents. As part of the CSR initiatives, supply chain leaders should measure carbon usage and prepare for carbon taxation.
- **Electronic waste**. Waste from the disposal of consumer electronics is estimated at 50 million tons per year. Government

agencies in the United States and Europe estimate that less than 20 percent of the waste is recycled. In the United States, 70 percent of heavy metals in landfills currently come from discarded electronics.

For consumer electronics companies, there is a risk to future sales. The landfill issues could rise as much as 500 percent and will be a barrier to driving new sales. As a result, waste and disposal needs to be adopted as the fourth moment of truth in the supply chain. Companies need to take ownership of disposal and design systems for demanufacturing and remanufacturing into the value network. CSR initiatives are here to stay.

The future is going to be [about] much more than cost reduction. The movement to growth and sustainability will create change. The secret will be to hold on to it and continue to drive forward.
—*Vice President of Transportation, Pharmaceutical Company*

The supply chain leader sees CSR as an opportunity, while the supply chain laggard complains about the burden of corporate social responsibility initiatives for its supply chain. For all, it is an opportunity to build value networks brick by brick.

TO DRIVE CHANGE

- Build strong horizontal processes from the outside-in.
- Work holistically to align these programs.
- Charter a group to think end to end and process redefinition.

Rules of Thumb

In building effective horizontal processes, follow these rules of thumb:

- **Horizontal processes take time to build**. Rome was not built in a day, and horizontal process excellence is not either. Companies that are excellent in these processes have built these capabilities over the course of three to five years. Look forward in the design and focus on value.

- **Don't start them all at once**. Design with the end in mind. Start with the most important horizontal processes. Build these one at a time as supply chain building blocks against a master plan.
- **Build a guiding coalition**. Typically, horizontal processes are born through failure. Failures at Cisco and Samsung spurred action to build strong S&OP processes, supplier failure at Ericsson drove the development of supplier relationship management excellence in the high-tech and electronics industry, and failure on corporate social responsibility at Nike and Coca-Cola drove the strongest CSR processes. Sidestep failure by building a guiding coalition to drive horizontal processes to drive growth and business strategy.
- **Report to the chief operating officer**. Horizontal processes will not be successful reporting to a single function. They require leadership. To maximize success, charter the development of cross-functional processes through the supply chain center of excellence reporting to the chief operating officer.
- **Carefully define governance**. In each horizontal process, carefully define the role of the central group and the role of the regions remembering that the definition of *global* is different for each supply chain and for each function (e.g., for consumer value chains, procurement is global while sales is regional). Learn from others with similar supply chains. There are patterns that are characterized by industry. For example, in asset-intensive industries (e.g., chemicals, mining, and paper), the need for strong global control will be higher, and the regions will need to align to the global strategy. However, in regional supply chains operating under a global brand (e.g., retail), the regions will have the power and the global supply chain organization will set standards and design processes.
- **Need for supply chain strategy**. The importance of supply chain strategy in the design and building phases of supply chain horizontal processes becomes clear very quickly. Don't start without it.
- **Supply chain center of excellence**. The supply chain center of excellence orchestrates the horizontal processes and

enables process development for the definition of supply chain metrics, establishing metric targets and the building of best practices.

- **Align metrics**. Recognize that the most effective supply chain is not necessarily the most efficient. Align financial metrics to support the supply chain strategy. One of the greatest issues that Procter & Gamble had in the implementation of customer-driven value networks was getting alignment with the financial organization.

- **Reduce demand latency**. Demand and supply sensing are essential capabilities to deliver success in horizontal processes. Build outside-in sensing capabilities and focus efforts to capture and use market data with minimal latency.

- **Train**. Supply chains are complex systems composed of complex processes with growing complexity. To understand the true dynamics of the supply chain in horizontal processes, invest in simulation activities so that cross-functional groups can understand the trade-offs of this complex system that is called a supply chain.

- **Take ownership of the data**. As part of the building of horizontal processes, take ownership for the data. Design metadata and data standards, and invest in systems for data harmonization, pattern recognition, and the use of both structured and unstructured data.

We cannot make things cheap enough to beat the competition. I have learned that there is a lot of information and a lot of data, but that the only way that we have been able to serve our customers is to force people to reconsider the mechanics. Let's use the tools to test employees' creative ideas and simulate them. A supply chain can never stop delivering costs and compliance and adherence to cadence. It must be reliable, but it has to step up to the opportunity to drive unique value.

—Marty Kisliuk, Director, Global Operations and Business Development at FMC Corporation, Agricultural Products Group

---

SUMMARY

Of all the areas of supply chain processes, the area requiring the greatest redesign in the journey to be market driven is the area of demand. To make this transition, focus on:

- **Define**. Define the right set of horizontal processes and build a three-year road map based on the company's definition of supply chain excellence.
- **Sense**. Reduce demand latency through the use of channel data. Use this redefinition to build outside-in processes to sense and shape demand.
- **Focus**. Build the forecast with the goal in mind against a master plan. For many this means a shift from forecasting what is to be manufactured to forecasting what is going to be sold in the channel.
- **Redefinition**. Charter ownership of horizontal process through the Supply Chain Center of Excellence.
- **Realistic**. Align goals and metrics cross-functionally. Using what-if analysis, ensure that they are realistic based on demand variability.

NOTES

1. Amit S. Mukherjee, "The Fire That Changed an Industry: A Case Study on Thriving in a Networked World," *Financial Times*, October 1, 2008.
2. "Cola and Water in India: Episode 2," *Corporate Social Responsibility and Environmental Management* (14): 298–304.
3. Pete Blackshaw, "Rise of Social Commerce Presentation," Altimeter Group, November 1, 2010.
4. "2011 Sales and Operations Planning Practices and Challenges," Association for Operations Management and Institute of Business Forecasting, 2011: 64.
5. M. Burnett and R. Welford, "Good for Goose, Bad for Flock," World Economic Forum, 2012.
6. Jenny Gustavsson, Christel Cederberg, Ulf Sonesson, Robert van Otterdijk, and Alexandre Meybeck, "Global Food Losses and Food Waste," Food and Agricultural Organization of the United Nations, Rural Infrastructure and Agro-Industries Division, 2011, http://www.fao.org/docrep/014/mb060e/mb060e00.pdf.

CHAPTER 6

Supply Chain 2020

We leave the supply chain in the hands of new supply chain teams welcoming the fourth generation of supply chain pioneers.

—Lora Cecere

As we close the book on the first three decades of supply chain management, the race for Supply Chain 2020 lies ahead. What will the next decade hold? Companies want to connect through value networks market to market. The pace of change is faster. Frustration with current technologies is growing.

Effective operations, and the building of market-driven value networks, are becoming more important. For manufacturers and distributors, supply chain is business. It is central to the business operating strategy. The supply chain is the foundation for growth in either conquering global markets or introducing new product innovation to market. The road ahead is not easy. Organizations are large and cumbersome. Supply chains are complex. They are like a large ship lumbering through the night sea on a steady course at full speed ahead.

It is hard to turn a large ship. The captain of a ship navigates the seas using both art and science. Navigating the uncertainty of winds and tides makes it art. Technology combined with physics lends to science. This is analogous to today's supply chain organization. Supply chain teams today are focused on functional excellence, integration, and optimization. It is siloed with tremendous momentum to maintain status quo. Turning it and driving an organizational change transformation requires both art and science. It requires a steady hand on the rudder with a focus on both strategy and execution. It is a leadership challenge.

In this chapter, we focus on readiness for this race. We share insights: how to tackle the organizational change management issues and how to train teams to excel. To help jump-start the efforts to build a road map, we also share insights from the pioneers on future trends and tipping points.

> When I review projects with my team, I always hear that we are achieving outstanding results; but when I look at our progress, I feel that we are running in place. The organization is making too little progress toward our goals. I feel that the issue is that we are not taking a holistic approach against a multiyear road map.
> —Senior Vice President of Supply Chain, High-tech and Electronics Manufacturer

LEADING THE JOURNEY TO DRIVE MARKET-DRIVEN VALUE NETWORKS

So, why change the status quo? Why run the race for Supply Chain 2020? The reasons are many. Industry growth has slowed, progress on inventory management has stalled, commodity prices are escalating, materials are scarce, and social responsibility is becoming more critical. Power has shifted to the end buyer and the expectations for product and service delivery are high. Supply and demand volatility is the highest in four decades. Supply chain excellence has never mattered more.

The inertia to continue historic supply chain practices is high. During the first 30 years of supply chain management, pioneers built strong, functional silos. They focused on projects and aligned metrics internally, but they made little progress in building the extended supply chain. Accomplishing this goal requires a new approach. These new processes will be based on new forms—social, mobile, unstructured data, maps and geo-location information, and trading partner requirements—of data. They are designed outside-in.

Progress over the next decade will be a stark contrast to the work of the early pioneers. It will move much faster. The clock speed of the supply chain is changing. The shifts will be more extreme. It is a revolution not an evolution. So, how do companies get there from here?

> *We were hit with the realization that the current operating model just wasn't going to work. Many things happened all at once. We had the economic downturn. We had pricing actions and categories contracting. Commodity prices were increasing. It created an environment where we needed to rethink the operating model. We now have an incentive to change.*
>
> —*Tim Weidenhaft, Demand and Inventory Planning and Strategic Modeling, General Mills*

Changing the course is a major shift. The change management hurdles are high. It is a multiyear journey. The challenges are many. They include:

- **Knowledge**. At a leadership level, there is a gap in understanding how the end-to-end supply chain business process really works. This gap has two dimensions: the understanding of supply chain as a complex system and its potential as a business differentiator. Over the last five years of supply chain research, the knowledge of supply chain principles by the executive teams is rated as the number one change management issue for driving supply chain excellence.[1]
- **Reward systems**. Businesses and supply chains are functionally organized and rewarded. This functional orientation limits organizational progress toward building horizontal systems and shaping demand.
- **Goal alignment**. There is a belief that supply chain best practices are known and can be widely adopted. As a result, there

is a steady momentum for status quo. Companies are getting more efficient in the delivery of order-to-cash and procure-to-pay processes but not building the end-to-end supply chain. Leaders see what they understand. Many lack an understanding of supply chain excellence and, as a result, have not had the courage to challenge what they do not understand.

■ **Courage**. It takes courage to question the status quo and break down the functional silos. Leaders need to be resolute and turn the organization on its ear—a move from a vertical to a horizontal orientation—to drive substantial change. This includes building horizontal processes, driving cross-functional career paths, building corporate goals that reflect the supply chain effective frontier, and an unwavering focus on the customer.

■ **Removing silos**. Continuous improvement, change management, and technology projects are managed today in isolated silos. Leaders question the value from technology investments and how to maximize value, yet they do not know how to break the cycle. One of the main issues is a project-based approach driven from a strong functional orientation. To reverse this, companies need to build a road map and align cross-functionally to deliver an operating strategy. Functional silos are the *bricks* to break down.

The first step in turning the ship is plotting the course. It requires defining the multiyear strategy. This has three elements: defining supply chain excellence, redefining supply chain practices, and building a guiding coalition against a three-year road map. The next step is shaping organizational behaviors and values. After taking these two steps, companies can then chart the course for the future.

Supply chains are handicapped by a functional, project-based approach. Changing this is a leadership imperative.
—*Roddy Martin, Senior Vice President, CCI*

Leadership guidelines:

- Reduce barriers within the organization to work horizontally market to market. Each profit center is a barrier.
- Do not confuse marketing driven with market driven or sales driven with demand driven.
- The customer order is not representative of market demand. It is the result of sales policies and negotiated terms. Focus on channel demand.
- The more steps back in the supply chain, the greater the demand latency and the larger the change management issues to overcome in becoming market driven.
- If given the choice between speed and reliability, choose reliability.
- The average organization has five to seven supply chains. Most companies forget about the service supply chains.
- New forms of unstructured data are growing that enable quicker insights and less data latency. Traditional supply chain processes were based only on structured data.

Define Supply Chain Excellence

Supply chain excellence has evolved. The definition has morphed from the efficient supply chain to a market-driven value network. Today, the concept of a market-driven value network is largely aspirational. It is a new goal. As supply risks and costs have grown, companies realize that a demand-driven approach is not sufficient. The focus needs to be about more than the channel. Instead, the supply chain needs to be driven through strong horizontal processes bidirectionally from market to market. Accomplishing the goal requires a redefinition of both buy-side and sell-side processes, and the use of new forms of analytics to sense, shape, and orchestrate bidirectionally market to market.

While 57 percent of companies have market-driven value networks as a goal (see Figure 6.1), fewer than 5 percent of companies have made substantial progress against the target. The building of the end-to-end supply chain from the customers' customer to the suppliers' supplier now lies in the hands of the executive leadership teams guiding the third and fourth generations of supply chain pioneers.

Figure 6.1 Definition of Supply Chain Excellence

As outlined in Figure 6.1, for today's supply chain leaders, the definition of supply chain excellence is all over the map. As a result, an important first step for the leadership team is to make a strong statement and define it for the organization. It needs to be a deliberate statement to detail "what it is and what it is not." The task then is to build a guiding coalition to achieve it. Defining supply chain excellence is job number one for the executive team.

This book is designed to help. Each of the prior chapters is written to help the leader plot the course. Key points to guide the journey are highlighted in Table 6.1.

Question Conventional Supply Chain "Best Practices"

The next step is to make it actionable. As the first generation of supply chain pioneers retire, and new leadership teams form, a barrier for the organizational leaders is challenging the status quo.

Companies will need to summon courage to question what is believed to be supply chain best practices. It is time. Nearly 60 percent of all corporate quality and process improvement initiatives have failed to meet their stated objectives.[2] The satisfaction rate with current supply chain technologies has never been lower. The failure rates are too high. Yet, companies continue in the same patterns. We do not have "best practices." Instead, we have "evolving practices" that must be shaped and molded by the leadership team.

Table 6.1 Key Points from Prior Chapters to Consider in Developing the Road Map

Leadership Questions	Key Concepts from *Bricks Matter*					
	Chapter 1	Chapter 2	Chapter 3	Chapter 4	Chapter 5	Chapter 6
How do companies think differently to drive market-driven differentiation?	Think of the supply chain as a complex system. How do you make the right trade-offs? Focus on the bricks. How well have you defined the supply chain strategy around each element of the brick framework? How do you ensure balance in making the trade-offs to the operating strategy?	Think of the supply chain as a value network. How do you forge the right network relationships? How do you align trading partner aspirations and capabilities to forge value-based outcomes? How do you reward trading partner relationships? How does this need to change?	Think of the supply chain outside-in. How does the outside-in focus supply chain change processes? What steps do you take to reduce the time to sense demand? What are the important demand signals today and tomorrow? How effectively do you use them?	Think of the supply chain leaders as stewards of limited resources. Define a plan. What resources are limited? What does this mean for social responsibility?	Put your supply chain on its ear. Focus on building horizontal processes. What horizontal processes are important for your supply chain?	How do you build a guiding coalition around a three-year strategy to drive market-driven differentiation? How do you strike the right balance between strength, balance, and flexibility?

(Continued)

249

Table 6.1 (Continued)

Leadership Questions	Chapter 1	Chapter 2	Chapter 3	Chapter 4	Chapter 5	Chapter 6
			Key Concepts from _Bricks Matter_			
What are the change management issues to be tackled?	Defining supply chain excellence. Moving from cost to value. Redesigning for value-based outcomes.	Defining the role and importance of a value network. Redefining the expectations for a relationship in a value network. Aligning sales and sourcing incentives to better partner in relationships.	Understanding that the forecast is always wrong and learning to adapt: how to embrace demand error. Moving the forecast based on an enterprise view to a channel view. Learning to listen and use customer feedback cross-functionally. Implementing a program to drive continuous improvement in demand management processes: • Forecast value-added analysis • Product forecastability analysis	Define the role of manufacturing in market-driven differentiation. Help the teams with how to make the right trade-offs between source, make, and deliver. How are decisions made? What is the role of the global organization and regional teams?	What is the role of the budget and finance in driving market-driven differentiation? How should teams make decisions? What is the right governance in horizontal processes across organizational silos and regions?	Moving from a project-based and functional orientation to a holistic supply chain road map.

What are the hurdles?	Build the right team. Invest in talent development and the shortage of supply chain talent. Train employees to understand the supply chain as a complex system.	Redefine the role of sales and the role of procurement to focus on value. Move from a laser focus on cost to reward value.	Identify and use channel data. Building continuous improvement processes for demand management using forecast value add analysis. Understanding that we cannot get too perfect with imperfect data.	Traditional functional metrics are not sufficient. Learn how to make trade-offs cross-functionally. Redefining the role of functional excellence in driving supply chain performance.	Redefining the role of the finance team and what the integration of the budget into horizontal processes means. Build process connectors between new product launch, supplier development and S&OP.	Value process innovation. Build not only strength, but also balance and agility in horizontal decision-making processes.
Symptoms?	Project of the month. Ever-changing focus. Many projects. Lots of initiatives. Overall performance is stalled. Financial performance is unpredictable.	Transactional relationships that are focused only on costs. The supply chain is slow to respond to market shifts. The company is always reacting.	Lack of bias and error forecast measurement. Lack of trust of the demand management system output. Slow to sense changes and acceptance of new products.	Manufacturing operating as a silo. Procurement working as a silo. Transportation as a silo. Working in isolation.	Programs for horizontal processes stall. They cannot get momentum due to political in-fighting. Social responsibility surprises. PR issues and damage to the brand.	A functional, project-based approach that goes nowhere. Performance is not equal to peers. Surprise write-offs.

Executive leaders must focus concurrently on three time horizons:

1. *Make the present business effective*
2. *Identify and realize the potential of the business*
3. *Make the present business into a different business for a different future.*

—*Peter F. Drucker, Management Consultant*

Redefine Technologies

In the development of this Supply Chain 2020 strategy, along with the questioning of best practices, the leadership teams will struggle to rationalize current technology investments. While the investments of the last decade promised a lower total cost of ownership, greater visibility, and the transference of best practices, progress against these goals is questionable. A lot of money has been spent, but supply chain excellence remains elusive. As leadership teams review their projects and future spending, three things will quickly become obvious:

- **Growing gaps**. As companies try to put new forms of data into existing systems, they will quickly find that it is like putting a square peg in a round hole. They will be forced to acknowledge that their IT investments of the last decade are becoming obsolete.

   As shown in Figure 6.2, the largest gaps are currently in supply chain planning and enterprise resource planning systems. The solutions least affected are warehouse management and transportation execution. Closing these gaps will require reimplementation of existing systems or new technologies. The investments in supply chain execution will require the least overhaul. The new solution will be a combination of cloud services, outsourcing, and new forms of analytics.

   In the race for Supply Chain 2020, the goals of system standardization will be less important. The supply chain leader will exercise power in the buying decision, and system selection will be more heavily based on industry expertise and value-added services than on system standardization.

Current Level of IT Importance vs. Satisfaction

■ Importance (6–7) ■ Satisfaction (6–7) ☐ Gap (Sat–Impt)

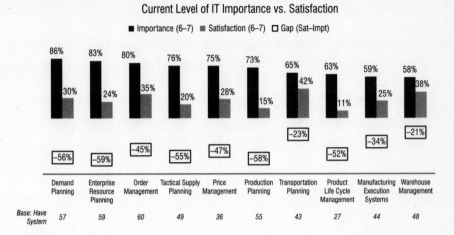

	Demand Planning	Enterprise Resource Planning	Order Management	Tactical Supply Planning	Price Management	Production Planning	Transportation Planning	Product Life Cycle Management	Manufacturing Execution Systems	Warehouse Management
Base: Have System	57	59	60	49	36	55	43	27	44	48

Figure 6.2 Gap in Supply Chain Information Technology Systems

- **The future**. As companies try to drive early-mover advantage, they will quickly find that the plausible solutions are only with new start-up technology companies. Because of myriad issues with package application development over the past 10 years, companies will find that the list of traditional and large players will only fit the needs of the mainstream and laggard adopters. They will also find that most consulting partners lack an understanding of market-driven supply chain processes.

- **Deployment options abound**. Over the course of the last decade, as computing power rapidly increased, the options to deploy technology exploded. Today, companies can buy software as a service solutions, hosted solutions, and services through business process outsourcing. Companies are no longer dependent on their own IT resources or local consultants. As we get ready for Supply Chain 2020, these alternate methods of technology deployment become increasingly important.

New technologies offer promise. New forms of data are growing at a rapid pace. Analytics are evolving to yield better insights. Excitement is growing in the market. However, yesterday's architectures cannot use these new forms of data, and the technology providers for supply chain management are caught in old paradigms. Processes and technologies have not adapted to be outside-in.

As companies move forward in the definition of new processes, they will quickly realize that their supply chain systems are obsolete. Existing technology providers will fight this awakening. It will be uncomfortable. Solving the problem is a revolution that cannot be tackled as an evolution. To build the effective market-driven value network, the supply chain will require a redesign.

Build a Clear Supply Chain Strategy

Companies lumber along. They attack problems through projects and functional initiatives. It is not comprehensive. It lacks a systems understanding. The greatest progress is made when companies work a comprehensive three-year road map that is tied to a supply chain strategy. When this happens through active leadership, complexity is rationalized against value, and relationships are redefined to reduce latency and improve market sensing.

This type of transformation is needed now more than ever. The force of the winds of change is unprecedented. Supply chains are fragile. Materials are scarce. Commodity price volatility is the highest in 100 years. Services are eclipsing products in driving differentiation and market value. The pace of change in global markets is accelerating. Compliance for safe and secure supply chains is increasing. Pressure is mounting for more stringent corporate social responsibility programs. The need to redesign for product safety has never been higher. Yet, 95 percent of companies do not have a clear supply chain strategy, and they have not had the courage to question the status quo.

As companies build their strategy, they will discover an uncomfortable reality. They will learn that a supply chain is not a supply chain is not a supply chain. Effective ones are designed and built. However, most companies have inherited their supply chains. Fixing this situation will not be as easy as a "Ctrl-copy and Ctrl-paste" of a competitor's supply chain definitions. It requires thinking through the definitions in the first five chapters of this book and defining a three-year road map.

The path forward has large pitfalls and potholes. Active leadership is required to ensure that the organization can avoid the traps. In the market, there are myriad definitions for a supply chain, and a bevy of charlatans that pose as supply chain experts. As a result, it is imperative that the leadership team define a course of action and set its own rudder for change. It requires redefining supply chain excellence using a new lens. In questioning the status quo, they need to question their own biases and ask new questions to drive new answers. Here are five areas to start:

- **Outside-in processes**. How could the redefinition of the supply chain from inside-out to outside-in add value? And, if so, how does this redefine the processes? And, how do we use this shift to drive added value in customer and supplier relationships?
- **Digital and mobile changes everything**. As we absorb the impact of the digital world, how does the shift from near real-time to real-time data affect the design of processes? Are there new opportunities to drive value through new forms of process innovation? How does digital manufacturing transform the supply chain? Redefine the business opportunity?
- **Building value-network effectiveness**. In the extended supply chain, what should be the role of the corporate and regional teams? In our organization, what does global mean? What is the right structure for governance?
- **Improving the effective frontier. Making the right trade-offs**. How many supply chains does the organization have? What defines supply chain excellence for each? What is the effective frontier? How can the company organize to make the right trade-offs? What is needed to raise the potential of the company's effective frontier for their supply chain?
- **Building the right horizontal connectors**. How can the organization build strong horizontal processes to sense, translate, and shape demand while sensing and translating supply risk? What is the best way to connect research and development (R&D) launch plans to horizontal processes? How do horizontal processes best support the business strategy? Who should lead them? Is there a need for a formal commercialization process and turnover?

The three little pigs were smart. As the winds whipped against their shutters, they ran from the house of straw and the house of sticks. The pigs then ran to the house of bricks and built a fire in the fireplace. Today, the fires are burning in organizations. They are calling for a redesign of the supply chains.

It is more than the automation of your father's old-fashioned supply chain processes. To get there requires a new form of leadership.

BUILDING A GUIDING COALITION

The journey forward to Supply Chain 2020 starts with leadership. It will be propelled by teams. The largest hurdle in building teams is achieving a shared understanding of the supply chain. The principle that a supply chain is a system with finite trade-offs bounded by an effective frontier is a stumbling block. Seventy-five percent of supply chain leaders cite the lack of supply chain understanding by executive teams as a barrier in driving supply chain excellence.[3] Smart leaders will retool and learn the concepts. They will use the current winds of change in the market to build a guiding coalition.

Successful transformation is driven through the power of a volunteer army made up of leaders from across the enterprise who band together to knock down all the barriers to successful strategy implementation.

—*John Kotter,* Leading Change

A guiding coalition for Supply Chain 2020 needs to be composed of both managers and leaders who work together as a team. There needs to be the right balance of each. They need to be trained. It is important that they are credible in leading the change efforts.

As the speed of the supply chain metronome increases, the managers steer the process road map while the leaders drive the change in organizational structure, rewards, and metrics. A guiding coalition with good managers but poor leaders is likely to produce plans but not vision. A guiding coalition that has all leaders and no managers is unlikely to create the short-term wins necessary to sustain a change initiative. For this to be effective, the guiding coalition has to have a clear vision of what drives supply chain excellence and why the race for Supply Chain 2020 matters.

History tells us that success will happen when there is alignment around a well-understood goal. In Chapter 2, we discussed how this was defined by A. G. Lafley, past CEO of Procter & Gamble, as the alignment of the organization against the customer's moments of truth. In Chapter 4, we discussed Ford's journey for quality. Each of these efforts was driven by clear alignment and the need to be more competitive.

While today's executives grumble about the lack of team spirit, collaboration, and alignment, they fail to take responsibility to drive clear definition, goals, and direction. Many are blinded by what they do not know. Some cannot see the greater whole or articulate a vision. They are often caught in their own paradigm—a past set of experiences within a specific function such as manufacturing or procurement— and cannot see the supply chain end to end. For some, it is ignorance. They have never been exposed to the principles. The teaching of supply chain management as a college discipline is new. As a result, there is a standoff among the competing interests. It is like the poem of the six men of Indostan feeling the elephant.

It was six men of Indostan
To learning much inclined,
Who went to see the Elephant
(Though all of them were blind),
That each by observation
Might satisfy his mind.

The First approached the Elephant,
And happening to fall
Against his broad and sturdy side,
At once began to bawl:
"God bless me! But the Elephant
Is very like a wall!"

The Second, feeling of the tusk,
Cried, "Ho! What have we here
So very round and smooth and sharp?
To me 'tis mighty clear
This wonder of an Elephant
Is very like a spear!"

The Third approached the animal,
And happening to take
The squirming trunk within his hands,
Thus boldly up and spake:
"I see," quoth he, "the Elephant
Is very like a snake!"

The Fourth reached out his eager hand,
And felt about the knee.
"What most this wondrous beast is like
Is mighty plain," quoth he,
"'Tis clear enough the Elephant
Is very like a tree!"

The Fifth, who chanced to touch the ear,
Said: "E'en the blindest man
Can tell what this resembles most;
Deny the fact who can,
This marvel of an Elephant
Is very like a fan!"

The Sixth no sooner had begun
About the beast to grope,
Then, seizing on the swinging tail
That fell within his scope,
"I see," quoth he, "the Elephant
Is very like a rope!"

And so these men of Indostan
Disputed loud and long,
Each in his own opinion
Exceeding stiff and strong,
Though each was partly in the right,
And all were in the wrong!

MORAL.

So oft in theologic wars,
The disputants, I ween,
Rail on in utter ignorance
Of what each other mean,
And prate about an Elephant
Not one of them has seen!

—*John Godfrey Saxe*

The first- and second-generation pioneers were much like these blind men of Indostan. They defined supply chain processes based on their experiences. However, they were blind. Each only saw his own function and set of experiences. These were adopted and passed on as best practices. As we have discussed in this book, much has changed. It is now time to question the status quo. Many of these process definitions are inadequate.

Drive Organizational Cohesion

In the race for Supply Chain 2020, there is not enough time for consensus. This is often the elephant in the room. Instead, there needs to be a guiding coalition. While the term *collaboration* is bandied about, work teams can only collaborate when there is goal clarity. It happens when there is a clear win-win value proposition and teams have a common goal. The supply chain team needs clarity of role and purpose. The challenge for leadership teams is defining the supply chain strategy in a way that all functions see the entire elephant, not only different parts.

There is much work to do. Traditional metrics drive competition of functions, not cooperation. They can be the cement that holds the walls between functions. As a result, they need to be broken down. Channel relationships need to be designed and continually refined to be focused on value, not just volume or cost. Incentives need to be aligned.

As the issues bubble up in the boardroom, now is the time to realize that bricks matter. Companies can only be successful in the long term if they design for value, clearly communicate the goal, and understand the potential of their own supply chain (effective frontier). There has never been a better time to build a guiding coalition to redefine the supply chain as a value network or to map the supply chain outside-in as a set of processes stretching from the customer's customer to the supplier's supplier. Now is the time to design for value-based outcomes.

Currently, the second and third generations of supply chain pioneers are tackling these challenges in small steps. Unfortunately for many, it is a project approach. It is a series of small projects embedded within functions without a long-term road map. As a result, for most, it is inadequate. Horizontal processes are evolving slowly. Value networks are in their infancy. Organizational incentives have not been aligned. The current level of satisfaction with supply chain applications is low. Companies want to seize the opportunity to use process innovation to fuel new business models. They are struggling. It is a time for executive leadership to drive the necessary step change.

As companies answer these questions and build their supply chain strategies, it is time to look forward. We can learn from history, but need to forge the path forward to drive differentiation. Before we can run the race, we must train. This training requires behavioral modification in three areas: building supply chain agility, learning how to listen and learn, and valuing process innovation.

RUNNING THE RACE

To run the race for Supply Chain 2020, companies need to train. Like an athlete training for a competition, the teams need to be agile, to listen to coaching, and to make the right investments. Most organizations need to work on these three behaviors to have the right stuff to win the race.

Building Agility

The first step is a readiness assessment. The supply chain needs to have strength, agility, and balance. Most do not.

The focus of the supply chain pioneers over the past 30 years has been on improving strength. In interviews, the supply chain professionals often express the need for greater flexibility or agility and the need to gain balance.

Balance is easier to accomplish than agility. Through the understanding of how to make trade-offs at the supply chain's effective frontier and implementing horizontal processes outlined in Chapter 5, companies can achieve better balance. Today, 80 percent of supply chains believe that they are out of balance. In sales and operations planning (S&OP), 48 percent are too heavily weighted toward operations and 32 percent are too heavily weighted toward sales. Balance and alignment comes from executive leadership, but agility has to be a conscious design element in the supply chain strategy.

An effective supply chain is built for purpose. It is designed with the goal in mind. As companies have implemented global systems, improved the cost structures, and implemented lean programs, the supply chain has become less agile. Today, for many, it is brittle. It is stronger in the middle than at the ends.

Historically, agility has not been a design element of most corporate strategies. (Achieving agility often requires a cost trade-off.) As a result, in the face of supply and demand volatility, the company is less resilient. In the research for this book, three things quickly became obvious:

- **Inconsistent definitions**. There is no standard industry definition for *agility*. Although companies frequently use the term and quickly acknowledge the need, they do not have a clear definition. As a result, the term needs to be defined by each organization. Its meaning cannot be assumed. Without it, the organization will thrash about, finding it difficult to design the supply chain and drive alignment on agility. In Figure 6.3, we share how 116 supply chain executives recently defined agility.[4] For a market-driven supply chain definition, the best definition of agility is the design of the supply chain to have the same cost, quality, and customer service given the level of demand and supply volatility.

  Many companies, early in their understanding of supply chain management, will erroneously define agility as a shorter

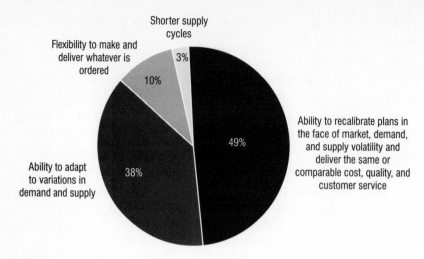

Flexibility to make and deliver whatever is ordered

Shorter supply cycles

10%

3%

49%

Ability to recalibrate plans in the face of market, demand, and supply volatility and deliver the same or comparable cost, quality, and customer service

Ability to adapt to variations in demand and supply

38%

Figure 6.3 What Is Agility?

cycle time. Speed is important, but only if you are improving the speed to do the right things faster. All too often, companies will speed up ineffective processes, increasing waste and reducing reliability. In designing a supply chain, if given a choice between speed and reliability, choose reliability.

■ **Agility is growing in importance**. Today, there is a growing gap in agility. In interviews for this book, this gap is frequently cited as an issue by the second-generation supply chain pioneers. In Figure 6.4, 89 percent of companies see agility as important, but only 27 percent of companies rate themselves as agile. Companies with mature S&OP processes are three times more likely to rate themselves as more agile than those that are less mature. (See Chapter 5 to understand the difference between stage 2 maturities and stage 4 maturities in S&OP processes.)

■ **For many, the gap is growing**. Many supply chains today are brittle and fragile. The programs driven by the first-generation pioneers—tight integration of the supply chain, Lean process improvement programs, e-procurement, and electronic bidding—made the supply chain stronger; however, there was an unconscious trade-off of agility.

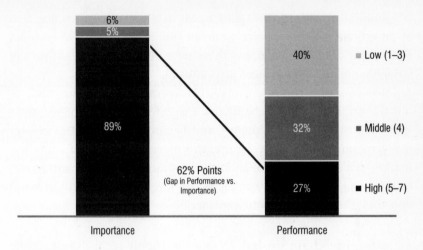

Figure 6.4 Agility Importance versus Performance

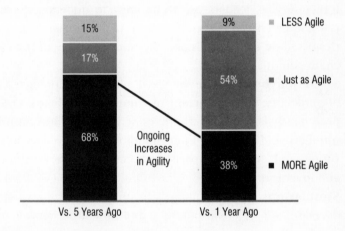

Figure 6.5 Agility Today versus Past Performance

For companies with more advanced maturity in supply chain management, 68 percent say that their supply chains are more agile than five years ago, and 38 percent state that the supply chain is more agile than a year ago. The details of the study results are shown in Figure 6.5. The largest contributing factors are strong horizontal processes, the use of predictive analytics, and a focus outside-in.

Building organizational agility needs to be a conscious choice. Just as an athlete makes a choice to do flexibility exercises and to build agility, the supply chain needs to be designed with the right mix of strength, agility, and balance.

No two supply chains are alike. The average company has not one but five to seven supply chains. As a result, the design for the right trade-offs of strength, flexibility, and balance can vary. The greater the demand and supply volatility, the more important to apply the market-driven definition of agility (the ability to drive the same cost, quality, and customer service given the level of supply and demand volatility). To increase agility, consider:

- **Supply chain design**. Design the supply chain based on the expected level of demand and supply variability. Since there is an inverse relationship between variability and cost or customer service, leaders use technology to understand what is possible given the trade-offs. These teams set goals and metrics based on the analysis and the understanding of the supply chain potential.

- **S&OP playbooks**. Base the S&OP plan on the predicted level of variability. Ninety percent of companies with strong S&OP processes believe that it improves agility. Focus less on precise numbers and more on understanding how the variability of supply and demand impacts costs, customer service, quality, and inventory.

- **Simulations**. Train employees to understand how variability decreases supply chain potential and how little improvements in reliability can add up to great improvements in supply chain effectiveness. This can be simulated to help teams understand the impact (building an event simulator or game environment). While companies have seen a number of corporate initiatives come and go, a steadfast focus on improving the reliability of operations is the foundation for great results.

- **Drills**. Practice the simulation of supply chain disasters. While the calamity that will strike your supply chain may not be the same one that you train for, the understanding of how to make decisions in the face of adversity will be invaluable. A clear understanding of roles and responsibilities is an important component of improving agility and working through volatility.

Learning to Listen

Companies yell their message into the market and supply chains respond. Customers are tired of the yelling. They want to be served. They want products that they want when they want them. They want differentiated services that add value.

Not only can the organization not hear what customers want, the supply chain response is also not a smart response. Instead, it is typically a slow, calculated response based on historic, not market, data.

As supply chains focus on the design of outside-in processes, and sensing demand and customer sentiment, processes will evolve to listen to the customer holistically and cross-functionally to better serve the channel. Today, this is aspirational; but within two years, it will become a reality for early adopters. The fastest adoption will happen in high-tech and electronics, media and entertainment, and consumer durables.

To make this transition, leadership teams need to move from a marketing-driven approach (where the message is yelled) to a market-driven approach where customer sentiment is welcomed and used in the supply chain by cross-functional teams. Listening becomes the foundation of horizontal processes. The first step is unlocking the data that is often tightly controlled by marketing.

Listening can now happen in many forms. Whether it is the use of Twitter for customer service, Facebook to improve product loyalty, active usage of rating and review information, or mobile commerce to drive purchases, we have a new opportunity to listen to the customer for the first time. It will not be easy. Organizations are not trained to listen. The first response is often denial. There is no place within enterprise architectures to put these new forms of data. It sounds easier than it is.

Frank Eliason, in his book *@YourService*, shares his view of this journey.

Dear customer,

I saw your Tweet about how upset you were with your experience with our product. I didn't see it live, but someone forwarded it to me via e-mail on my BlackBerry. I guess what was delivered didn't meet your expectations. Hey, it happens to everyone. But, you sure did let us know in your own way, didn't you? Come to think of it, you let everyone know. So what was originally something between you and us is now everybody's business.

I don't get it though. Sure your time is valuable. It's so valuable in fact that you chose to avoid the various systems we invested significant time and money in to address these types of issues. Hey, our time is valuable too. That's why we spent millions on technology to automate our systems and responses. We didn't divert profits toward this expensive voice recognition software because we didn't want to be close to you or talk to you live, but to make it a more efficient process. That says something about how much we value you, right?

If you make your way through the series of prompts and redirects, we've hired and trained a staff of people who are prepared to address you directly. And guess what . . . if they can't fix your problem, they have backup resources in locations all around the world to step in and attempt to resolve the issue. Sure each individual will ask you to start from the beginning and retell your story, that is, if you do make it to one of them, and assuming you do not get disconnected. They do, after all, want to make sure to hear every detail of your experience from the very beginning. Also, please excuse their brashness. Everyone works hard, we all have somewhere to go, and you're probably not the only one having a hard day.

So, next time you think about Tweeting, blogging, Facebooking, Googling, YouTubing, Pinteresting, Yelping, Foursquaring, or whatever social whatchamacallit-dot-com you decide to vent on, remember, if you want resolution, the best path between two points is a straight line. Call us. E-mail us. Fill out a trouble ticket on our website. We're here to help. This is an "A" and "B" conversation so your so-called social network friends can "C" their way to funny cat videos instead.
—From the Foreword to *@YourService*

MAKING THE RIGHT INVESTMENTS

On average, companies invest 1.7 percent of revenues on information technology and 2.8 percent of revenue on R&D. Across the board, there is an expectation by supply chain leaders that projects must drive a return on investment (ROI). But does this stunt the potential of the supply chain? The data in the first three decades of supply chain leadership says yes.

For leaders like Dell, Procter & Gamble, and Toyota, there is an understanding that there is also a need for investment in process innovation in supply chain teams to drive business differentiation. There are active teams to find, to source, and to evaluate new technologies and approaches to improve the supply chain potential.

We now have the teams in place to work on process innovation. We need to give them the financial resources to make a difference. Five years ago, fewer than 15 percent of companies had a dedicated team to work on global supply chain practices in a center of excellence (COE). The functions of the team are shown in Figure 6.6 while the performance gaps are shown in Figure 6.7.

Today, 65 percent of manufacturing companies have a COE. The greatest gap is in the building of strong horizontal processes. These teams are hamstrung by the lack of global governance models, the lack of clarity on supply chain excellence, and the lack of a multiyear

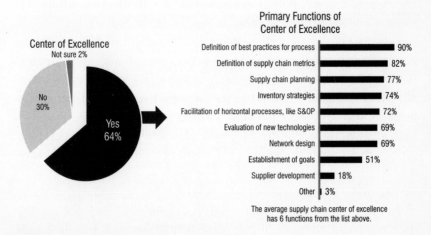

Figure 6.6 Supply Chain Center of Excellence

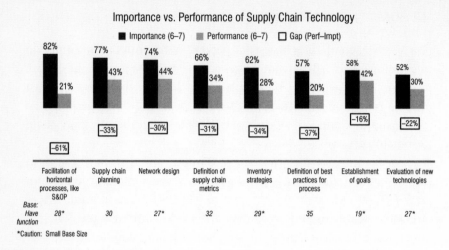

Figure 6.7 Current Gap in Supply Chain Processes in the Center of Excellence

road map. They are plagued by always having to have a definitive ROI and the traditional project approach.

To break the cycle, companies should task their COE with actualizing the supply chain vision through a multi-year road map. They should be embraced as a critical piece of the guiding coalition. To support the team, companies should merge the efforts of continuous improvement groups, training resources, R&D teams, and change management experts to actualize the potential. This multifaceted coalescence focused at driving horizontal, outside-in process improvement is needed to run the race for Supply Chain 2020.

Throughout the first three decades of supply chain leadership, the greatest advancements in business results were made by companies that could invest in process innovation holistically and cross-functionally. As we get ready to run the race for Supply Chain 2020, we are at a juncture where process innovation is needed. There is more unknown than known. New data, new technologies, and market changes make process innovation an important element of readiness to run the race.

SUPPLY CHAIN 2020

As the curtain rises on Supply Chain 2020 and the fourth decade of supply chain management, the rate of change accelerates. There is a new clock speed. Trading lanes will morph and change. Supply chain processes will be redefined. Constraints are many. They will increase. No longer will manufacturing be the primary constraint to manage. Labor rates across countries will reach new equilibriums. Protectionism will reign. As a result, the supply chain will be continually designed and redesigned to take advantage of ever-changing labor arbitrage and tax efficiency scenarios. It will be a new age of compliance. Increasing governmental regulation will redefine quality and change the focus of the extended supply chain. Safe and secure supply chains that maximize the impact on social responsibility will grow in importance.

The roles of individual companies in value chains will also be transformed. Power will shift between players and the focus will be on value-based outcomes. Some examples are:

- Health care will shift from a focus on efficient sickness to effective wellness. The Internet of Things coupled with mobility will enable real-time sensing of wellness. The focus of the supply chain will shift from the patient in the hospital to an individual's home.
- Within the consumer value chain, power will continue to shift to the shopper. Shopping anytime and anywhere is becoming a new reality. The convergence of mobility, social, and e-commerce technologies will redefine the moments of truth.
- Transportation value chains will be transformed by smarter city initiatives. Green legislation will become a reality and monitoring the true carbon footprint will become a new modeling constraint in network design activities.

The supply chain is a complex system with complex processes and increasing complexity. As we approach 2020, business complexity will continue to increase, putting pressure on the supply chain system. Some general trends are clear:

- **Advancements in predictive analytics**. The rate of technology change for advanced analytics is staggering. Through investments in new technologies, companies will be able to get better answers quicker. This will allow leaders to better understand the supply chain effective frontier in the face of rising complexity.

- **Shorter life cycles**. Product complexity will continue to increase. It will be driven by microsegmentation in global markets with shorter product life cycles.
- **Reduced latency of data**. Through the use of mobility and data sharing, the data latency of the supply chain will decrease up to five times in the next three years. Companies will get massive amounts of data faster. In existing IT architectures, there will be no place to put the data resulting from the outside-in redesign.
- **Greater availability of data**. Ninety percent of the world's data has been created in the past two years and 80 percent of it is unstructured.[5] Supply chain applications have not been built to harness the power of unstructured data. Over time, it will increase in variability, velocity, and variety. The past practices for master data management will become obsolete.
- **Ongoing network design**. Historically, the design of the supply chain has been an ad hoc process. Typically project-based, the design was not holistic and ongoing. Today, there is an increasing need to continually redesign the supply chain based on tax, labor, raw material, and market inputs. These supply chain inputs will continually change, and the physical supply chain will need to adapt to the changes.
- **Greater outsourcing**. Because of the explosion in the number of products in the portfolio, and the introduction of new underlying technologies in new product launch, outsourcing will play a key role in getting products to market faster.

While only a soothsayer can predict the future, based on our interviews with the supply chain pioneers, we project seven plausible tipping points for the supply chain for the next decade (shown in Figure 6.8).

In the development of the supply chain strategy, a useful exercise for supply chain leaders is to contrast the first three decades of supply chain management (reference Chapter 1) with their own future view. In the dialogue, think back. Remember how these early tipping points fundamentally changed the span of control, the design and capabilities of organizations, and the speed of decision making. Then, project forward to understand how fast these changes will affect your organization.

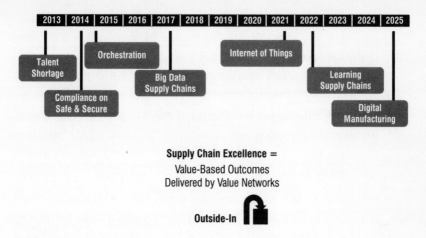

Figure 6.8 Supply Chain 2020 Tipping Points

Organizations adapt at different rates. Looking back and mapping the organization's adoption will help predict the rate of adoption of future tipping points. Companies typically fall into one of five categories:

1. **Innovator**. The innovator wants to be on the bleeding edge of technology adoption. They are frequent drivers of process innovation. They will often participate in codevelopment and may invest in best-of-breed solutions. These companies drive the organization's rate of change. The teams tend to be smaller in size, readily embrace technology, and have a clear road map for the future. This organization is more open to failure with mechanisms in place to fail forward.

2. **Early adopter**. The early adopter is on the leading, not the bleeding, edge of technology adoption. These companies wait for the first wave of adoption, learn the pitfalls and quickly follow. These companies will lag the projected supply chain tipping point by one year.

3. **Mainstream adopter**. These companies find themselves in the middle of the pack. They learn from those that have gone before them and they cautiously find their way. These companies will lag the supply chain tipping point by three to five years. They invest only with a guaranteed return on investment (ROI).

4. **Late follower**. The late follower is slow to adopt new technologies and concepts. Very conservative in approach, these companies will lag the supply chain tipping point by five to seven years. They will drive painstaking evaluation processes. They will be slow to make a decision. ▪

5. **Laggard**. The laggard will stand at the back of the pack watching technology adoption and taking a wait-and-see attitude. This type of company will lag the supply chain tipping points by six to eight years.

While these future road map views will vary by adoption rates, they also may vary by other factors. This includes the industry, the design of the supply chain strategy, and the number of supply chains. Using these inputs, leadership teams should project their view of what they believe the rate of change will be for their supply chain. The highest success happens when this road map is cross-functional with a forward-looking duration of at least three years.

Supply Chain Talent Shortage

In 2012, one in four demand planning positions were open. Supply chain talent in emerging markets is a barrier to growth. Universities in Europe and North America today support the development of supply chain talent for the world. This model is not sustainable.

By 2020, university programs in Brazil, Russia, India, and China (or BRIC countries) will mature and support the growing need for talent, but this transition will happen slowly. The burden today and the burden of the future, for training global supply chain professionals, will fall squarely on the leadership team. Although there will be some relief through hiring and outsourcing, it will be temporary and short-lived. It will not solve the problem. Organizations need to own talent development. The only real option is to train. In the words of one supply chain procurement leader in South Africa, "Skill shortages abound. I could chose to fire my team due to skill gaps; but when I looked at talent available in the market, I decided that a more prudent course of action was to invest in training. I took the responsibility to build my supply chain team. I am convinced based on the talent that is available that we do not have another option."

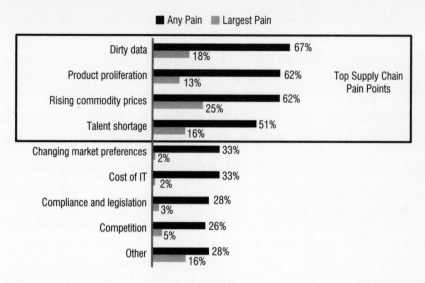

Figure 6.9 Supply Chain Pain Points: All vs. Largest

Supply chain talent, as shown in Figure 6.9, ranks fourth as a gap in priority for supply chain executives today. It follows dirty data, product proliferation, and commodity price escalation. As the first generation of supply chain pioneers continue to retire through 2012, it will become a more pressing issue. To solve it, a new industry will evolve to support the development of company-specific training. To help companies understand the complexity of supply chain systems, new forms of experiential training programs will evolve.

Within the next year, it will become more critical. The race into BRIC countries, the acceleration and adoption of planning technologies, and the pending retirements of the first generation of supply chain pioneers will make this a mission-critical issue. It is one that will need to be tackled head on.

In the development of this training, organizations will encounter new challenges. Companies will find that the majority of the fourth generation of supply chain pioneers will come from a business background. They are not engineers well-grounded in system theory. They may have never experienced work in a manufacturing setting. With the increased outsourcing, they may never experience manufacturing operations. As a result, companies will need to build simulation exercises. They will need to model and simulate the factory, determine choices in manufacturing and distribution, and learn how to make the right trade-offs for the supply chain's effective frontier. The understanding of the supply chain as a system will either come through hands-on training, simulation activities, or gaming.

Compliance: Safe and Secure Supply Chains

Government compliance is increasing. In 2020, the food, pharmaceuticals, high-tech, medical device, and chemical supply chains will look nothing like they do today. They will be permanently changed based on governmental compliance. The change will be pervasive, but it will happen bit by bit. Like waves lapping the shore, the legislation will slowly change the supply chain, but each country's regulation will be slightly different.

Traditionally, the supply chain was designed to track lot or pallet level information for chain of custody. Tomorrow in chemical, food, toy, and pharmaceutical supply chains the chain of custody will be defined by tracking *each*. Each item will have a unique identifier that will be traced across the end-to-end supply chain. This is termed *serialization*.

Five years ago, pharmaceutical executives discussed serialization. It was feared. Companies did not think that it would become a reality. The pace of change and adoption of serialization has moved faster than they originally believed. Today, it is a requirement for shipments into Turkey, Venezuela, or China.

CASE STUDY

PHARMACEUTICAL SERIALIZATION

This case study of supply chain tenacity is a story where a company went slow to go fast and delivered big results in the market. When we visited the team, the members had constructed a timeline on brown paper that stretched the length of the conference room. It depicted the history of the project over the past 15 years.

Right in the middle of the first sheet of the timeline was a research note from the Gartner Group on radio frequency identification (RFID). It brought back memories of the go-go years of RFID. In those years, RFID was riding at the top of its hype cycle with companies betting large sums of money on RFID investments for their supply chain. It was not so for this company. The company took a more conservative and a wiser approach. It sidestepped the hype and kept focused on the goal.

In 2002, the company started work on projects to improve product traceability. The U.S. Federal Drug Administration (FDA) report of 2002 was the catalyst. However, at the start, the team could not do much. The company could only analyze the marketplace. So it became an avid student. The company sent executives to attend conferences and put together cross-functional teams. However, at that time, most of the discussion was between the original team and the FDA.

Then, five years ago, the industry focus on serialization accelerated. The emphasis shifted to product pedigree and lineage. The initial team was then forced into action. It was asked to solve the technology issues to make serialization a reality.

As the team worked the problem, it realized that the members were spread out too far across the organization to have a concerted effort. So the team leaders went to senior management with a proposal to centralize resources and fund a pilot center for active project work. They asked for a test center to be sure that the output of their efforts could be retrofitted to any packaging line in the company.

For a global initiative like this, the team members felt that it was important to have a healthy dose of skepticism. They believed that any time they had a technology vendor calling them saying that the vendor had an answer—but they didn't know what the question was—that they needed to be skeptical.

In the early days, they worked hard to understand the marketplace. They participated in all the trade associations. The goal was to be more knowledgeable than the vendors trying to sell their solutions. They took the time to read vendor information and to ask hard questions.

They also looked for luminaries—great minds—within industry associations. In their words, "After a while, you know who they are. When they speak, you want to listen. It helped us separate ourselves from all the noise."

They were uncertain in uncertain times. During the project, there was more confusion than certainty. They decided that they did not want to

(Continued)

lead the pack. They did not want to be the slowest to adopt or the fastest. As a result, the team watched these industry trends closely:

- **1988:** The Prescription Drug Marketing Act (PDMA) is passed, giving responsibility to the FDA for minimum guidelines of product tracking (paper based).
- **2003/2004:** Florida-Pharmaceutical Wholesaler Reform legislation along with Walmart's RFID mandate for pharmaceutical suppliers coupled with California's pedigree law moves forward.

In this same period, the FDA also published the *Combating Counterfeit Drugs Report*: "Mass serialization is the single most powerful tool to secure the U.S. supply chain. RFID tagging of products by manufacturers, wholesalers, and retailers appears to be the most promising approach to reliable product tracking and tracing. . . . The adoption and common use of reliable track and trace technology is feasible by 2007."

- **2005:** Pfizer began RFID tagging of Viagra bottles with two-dimensional Data Matrix codes on each label for redundancy and the Department of Defense began the RFID tagging initiative. Amgen publically questions RFID for use on biologics.

In Italy, the Ministry of Health initiates a decree for use of serialized stickers to track pharmaceutical products, and Katherine Eban's book, *Dangerous Doses: How Counterfeiters Are Contaminating America's Drug Supply* sends shock waves through the industry.

On September 21, 2005, Scott Gottlieb, FDA deputy commissioner, admits, at the National Council for Prescription Drug Programs, "More research is needed into RFID and other track and trace technologies before such expensive safeguards against counterfeit drugs are deployed. . . . Validation of these technologies remains a problem."

An IBM executive testifies to the FDA that the pharmaceutical industry was rallying around RFID technology.

- **2006: Glaxo Smith Kline** commits to a six-month trial of RFID on an HIV drug. **AstraZeneca** began a multiphase project toward serialization for Nexium—with 14 packaging lines. Florida repeals the July 2006 wholesaler reform implementation date. California pedigree law is delayed until 2009 with extra provisions that pedigree must be electronic and needed to track the smallest package/container.

An EFPIA white paper (European Federation of Pharmaceutical Industries and Association) recommends the use of two-dimensional Data Matrix codes, including unique serialization numbers for each secondary packaging unit distributed and sold in Europe: "It would enable the identification and verification across the entire supply chain, therefore improving transparency and patient safety, and helping fight serious problems like counterfeiting. It will lend to harmonization of technologies used in EU and worldwide."

- **2007:** Pfizer and GSK publically questions the use of RFID for serialization. Pfizer was quoted publically saying, "RFID is a long way from being deployable. It's very expensive and, for it to work, you have to have technology deployed at every point along the supply chain."

A U.S. federal judge's injunction of the FDA's product tracking requirement is issued for secondary wholesalers. Animal health industry manufacturers embrace a global product identification standard. The pharmaceutical industry rushed to meet Turkey's serialization requirements for all products sold in the country.

- **2009:** California pedigree law is delayed again. The ruling would have mandated that 50 percent of pharmaceuticals have to meet serialization requirements by 2015; the other 50 percent of pharmaceutical manufacturers' portfolio must be serialized by 2016. Wholesalers and retail pharmacies will need to utilize electronic pedigrees by 2016.

Brazil serialization requirements (ANVISA), approved and applicable, are to be on all pharmaceutical products by 2012.

- **2010:** AstraZeneca publically shares its learning from the Nexium coding effort. "Serialization is not as easy as it sounds. . . . Early experimentation was really critical. Our rollout will be phased and will depend in part on risk-based decision as well as on emerging market (regulatory) requirements."

The FDA released voluntary guidance in a document called "Standards for Securing the Drug Supply Chain—Standardized Numerical Identification (SNI) for Prescription Drug Packages," which outlined the FDA's recommendation to use a serialized national drug code (sNDC) as the package level SNI. Note: the SNI structure is harmonized with GS1's standard for a Global Trade Item Number (GTIN).

Brazil delays its serialization implementation date.

(Continued)

- **2011:** France passes a law for lot level Data Matrix codes required on all products by January 2011. In parallel, Korea issued a mandate for lot level DataMatrix codes required by January 2012.

China announces serialization requirements for the first group of pharmaceutical products. Meanwhile, the European Union passes the Falsified Medicines Act, which could lead to harmonized serialization requirements in Europe by the middle of this decade. In the United States, the FDA conducts the Track and Trace Public Workshop: PRMA (Pharmaceutical Research Manufacturers Association), advocating for national preemption of state pedigree laws.

Through all the changes, the team went forward by going forward. As a guiding coalition, the members tried to learn from the industry and focus using a slow methodical approach. They were careful to not overreact to increasing public pressure.

The goal was to build a core system to improve the delivery method. The team wanted to deploy serialization with minimal impact to current production and with minimal implementation time. So, they focused on different approaches for different types of markets while focusing on the commonality of the systems. While the legislation was different in each locale, all requirements focused on unique identification of the package, followed by inspection and recording the data into a database. The team's goal was to configure and validate the working solutions so that it could adapt to the country-by-country legislation.

With a global approach, the team wanted a systematic approach to enable flexibility to meet ever-changing global requirements. It was pleased with the success. Within a week of a new serialization requirement in Serbia, the team met the challenge.

The first step was recognizing the need to make it a concerted effort for the company. It took the team four years to gain the sponsorship of the global executive group and drive a guiding coalition. The first year, the members spent time identifying the players and the issues. They then got executive alignment by breaking the effort into three smaller focus areas:

1. **Packaging:** How does the team design the package to embrace the pending changes in serialization?
2. **Technology:** What does the team need to do with enterprise systems and modifications/co-development with technology partners to trace and record serialization records?
3. **Distribution:** How do the requirements change distribution activities of pick/pack ship?

Four years previously, when the team was trying to get sponsorship, the members were fortunate to work for an enlightened supply chain leader. In their words, "He allowed us to bump into walls, and to find a place within the walls." For the first couple of years, it was informal. As the team gained momentum, it then became a more formal organization. The core team was eight people across the three functions of supply chain, manufacturing, and packaging research and development.

The movement of GS1 standards to health care was also a big help. They were excited to see so many people and countries adopting them. In their words, "The GTIN gives a basis for data exchange." The team believes that more than 80 percent of the channel will be GTIN compliant by the end of 2012.

In the words of the team, "On a technology level, no company was ready to tackle serialization in a serious way until the last several years. We worked with technology providers in codevelopment. It is still an opportunity, but it is being worked.

"In the next few years, the systems that enterprises will use will control and transmit data into cloud-based architectures. We have to decide who will access the data. And how will it be controlled? Who hosts it? There are a lot of questions. We have to work together to answer them one step at a time."

Safe and secure supply chain regulation is increasing for all supply chains. As legislation is passed, it spawns new technologies. It happens bit by bit. When the final changes are made, the impacts are far-reaching.

With every new technology, there is a hype cycle. Smart supply chain leaders will shepherd their teams through the transition. However, doing so requires skepticism, patience, and organizational support. It requires a guiding coalition. Problems such as this cannot be solved in functional silos.

This level of product tracking will slowly be applied to other industry value networks. For food and beverage, the focus will be a new chain of custody from field to fork. The solutions will focus on tracking manufacturing product transformation in drying and blending operations. It will be across trading partners. As a result, the quality information, warehousing, shipping, and reporting systems will need to be transformed.

For the chemical supply chain, the focus will be on biohazardous waste and the reduction of bioterrorism. Packaging and transportation policies will be transformed. For high-tech and electronics, it will be about waste and disposal. This will be an impetus for remanufacturing processes.

Slowly, supply chains will be transformed by many layers of compliance. Success will only come when teams work the evolution systemically. Getting ready will be a multiyear journey. The team will need to be thorough and aligned cross-functionally as the legislation transforms the supply chain bit by bit.

DEMAND ORCHESTRATION

In the first three decades of supply chain process evolution, demand was primarily used vertically within a function. It was seldom used to stretch horizontally to align the value network. In the definition of Supply Chain 2020, this will change.

Historically, the terms *demand* and *forecasting* were synonymous. It was passive. Not so anymore. In market-driven value networks, demand becomes a new and more powerful signal. Demand will be translated and orchestrated market-to-market bidirectionally.

In network design, this will be modeled through the use of the probability of demand and supply. In tactical planning, this will happen through the use of S&OP scenario planning. In the operational time period, this planning will happen through the sensing of demand and supply variability and shifts in bill of materials (raw material substitution, alternate formulas, and recipes), and an intense focus on revenue management in demand shaping.

This functionality will redefine price management and sourcing. New technology platforms for demand and supply sensing will enter the market. Companies will focus on the use of sensing from new data sources, the translation of demand across the organization, and the rationalization of the demand signal into a more profitable response.

BIG DATA SUPPLY CHAINS

Ninety percent of the world's data was generated in the last two years, and 80 percent of that data is unstructured—presentations, e-mails, audio files, and video files—and will not fit neatly into transactional systems. The use of unstructured data for early market sensing could have prevented 60 percent of the major supply chain disruptions outlined in Chapter 1.[6] In Figure 6.10, we share an overview of the changes with big data supply chains.

Big data supply chains and their impact on business will redefine supply chain applications. It will enable sensing and predictive analytics that were previously only dreamed of by the early supply chain pioneers. It will make traditional supply chain technologies obsolete, or legacy, applications.

It will happen over the course of the next five years as companies question why they cannot use new forms of data to improve their supply chains. Examples of use cases currently being worked in big data supply chains include:

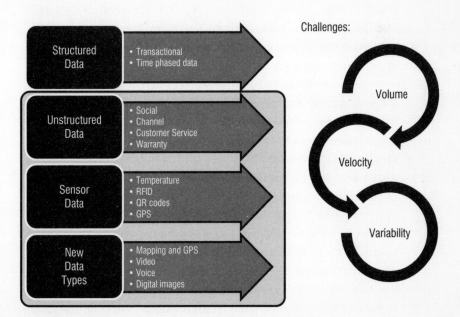

Figure 6.10 Big Data Supply Chain Evolution

■ **Freshness**. Depending on the food supply chain for fresh vegetables or protein products, 20 to 30 percent of products are thrown
away as waste. Fifty percent of this waste is due to temperature
variation. This is happening in a time when more and more consumers want fresh products at a more reasonable cost. The use of
RFID devices on pallets and streaming temperature data in handling and storage will be used to redefine the path or flow that
the product should take to maximize yield and minimize waste.

■ **Health and wellness**. Sensor data of the human body to alert
the physician and dispatch special medications and services will
be used to redefine the health-care supply chain. This at-home
sensing using new devices will allow physicians to monitor
the body in near real-time and will improve disease prevention. This will redefine the moment of truth for the health-care
supply chain. Whereas the traditional supply chain has always
questioned, "Who is the customer? Is it the patient? Is it the
hospital?" The use of sensor technologies and the redefinition
of big data supply chains will serve the patient that is fighting
to prevent illness.

■ **Cold chain**. Biologic medical products are created through
biologic processes versus chemistry. They are more temperature sensitive and require careful shipment through refrigerated storage called cold chains. They include vaccines, blood,
gene therapy, tissue, or living cells. RFID sensors on pallets with
streaming data can be used to more effectively process materials
through the value network to improve product efficacy. This is
a big data supply chain problem.

■ **Digital path to purchase**. In consumer products, there are
four moments of truth of purchase: the list, the basket, the
checkout, and the usage. Each of these components of
the shopping experience has digital inputs and outputs.
Consumer products companies are defining new processes to
translate these digital signals into action to affect the supply
chain experience.

■ **Supply chain risk management**. The combination of structured and unstructured data on suppliers can improve the time
to sense a supplier risk. The translation of this data for early
warning is a big data supply chain opportunity.

In big data supply chains, data increases in velocity, variety, and variability. The architectures to use this influx of new and very valuable data have names that the supply chain team is just now learning. Start with a cross-functional team to understand its importance and grow from there.

Mobility and the Internet of Things

Today, there are more mobile devices than toothbrushes in the world. The use of mobility in supply chain management changes the signal from a near real-time to a real-time signal enabling anytime and anywhere interaction. While the impact currently is limited due to the lack of rugged devices, this situation will change over time. Mobility in combination with the Internet of Things will change the face of supply chain management. In retail today, as shown in Figures 6.11A and B, the average North American retailer has 3.7 Facebook sites, 2.1 e-commerce sites, and 1.6 mobile applications. In this recent survey of 40 North American retailers, 53 percent of the retailers are starting to use Twitter for customer service. This represents a major shift for the retail industry.

While retailers are focusing on the use of mobility for channel automation, the impact of mobility in manufacturing and operations is pervasive. It is powered by the Internet of things, which is formed from objects having virtual and physical identities that interact with supply chain networks. This will give a new definition to event processing by redefining signaling from a time-based to an event-based trigger. The list of possibilities and the future impacts are endless. Here are some examples:

- **Plant maintenance**. Instead of scheduling pump maintenance based on hours used, the pump will broadcast status on a real-time basis. Maintenance will move from a time-based model to real-time sensing based on needs.
- **Replenishment**. Vending machines will broadcast real-time signals. Replenishment will be based on the rate of actual consumption. The consumer's refrigerator can transmit inventories and integrate replenishment with a virtual list.
- **Service**. Heavy equipment servicing will be monitored and repairs will be scheduled based on machine sensing. Automobiles will be monitored in real-time to drive new design ideas.

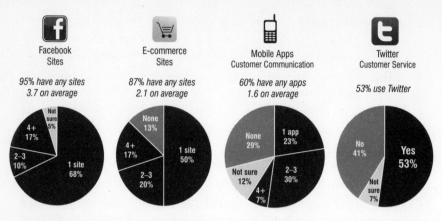

Figure 6.11A   Mobile and Social Presence

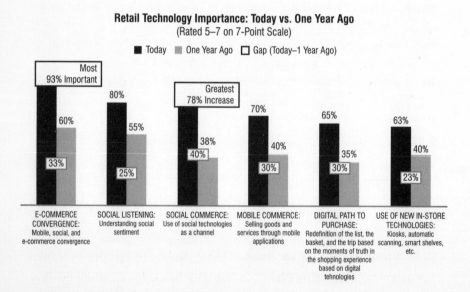

Figure 6.11B   Retail Technology Trends

To prepare for this tipping point, companies must list all of the critical devices and inputs in their supply chain. Business leaders have to postulate on how mobility and the Internet of Things can change the face and future of their supply chain, and then they can form a cross-functional team to work the most actionable use cases.

Learning Systems

The IBM Watson winning of *Jeopardy* in 2011 was a demonstration of an artificial intelligence computer system capable of answering questions posed in a natural language. To win the game, the Watson computer had access to 200 million pages of structured and unstructured content consuming four terabytes of disk storage. Watson consistently outperformed its human opponents on the game's signaling device, but had trouble responding to a few categories, notably those having short clues containing only a few words.

The supply chain learning system is in our future. Rules-based ontologies, sentiment analysis, learning algorithms based on industry benchmarking in the cloud, and real-time learning systems for supply chain planners are all possibilities. Within 10 years, companies will systemically test and learn based on real-time data. While today's supply chain response is a fixed and often a dumb response based on historic data, the supply chain of the future will listen, test, and learn in real time.

Digital Manufacturing

Three-dimensional printers will be used to build products in make-to-order processes layer by layer. It will have smart machines that can sense defects. It will have machinery that learns and transmits status. The cost of setting up a machine is the same whether the order is for 1 or 1,000. Machinery will require less human intervention and more and more companies will operate factories remotely. In our interviews of the first generation of supply chain pioneers, one bragged that his new manufacturing plant in Germany has one operator that sits at home in his pajamas. Pharmaceutical companies are envisioning smaller, regional factories and discrete manufacturers are designing for efficient production of units of one.

Manufacturing is coming full circle. It originated as a craft focused on the production of individual units. It was mechanized to improve quality and reduce labor. Through digital manufacturing, we are returning to the unit of one with the potential to improve supply chain agility.

The embracing of digital manufacturing is a step change. It will be the complete overhaul of manufacturing systems and paradigms. It will not happen quickly, but the change will be pervasive.

WINNING THE RACE

Make-to-order supply chains will be redefined by digital manufacturing. Process supply chains will be redefined by mobility and the Internet of things. With both, data explodes and data latency is reduced. These tipping points make the technology and processes of the first 30 years obsolete in the areas of planning, scheduling, and supply chain execution. The processes of demand and supply sensing, revenue management, risk management, and manufacturing reliability will see a step change. It will become easier and easier to link supply chains together. It will no longer be about transactions; instead, as contrasted in Figures 6.12A and B, it will be about predictive analytics and the use of new signals to connect customers' customers to suppliers' suppliers.

With the introduction of these new manufacturing techniques, co-location will become the norm. Supply chains will shorten, become more intricate, and new forms of networks and relationships will emerge. Market-driven value network will become a business differentiator for leaders and an Achilles' heel for laggards.

While the tipping points for Supply Chain 2020 seem far off on the horizon, now is the time to prepare. The supply chain of the future cannot be built overnight and there is substantial momentum in today's organization that must be overcome. To drive success, build momentum by following this nine-step process:

1. Build a three-year road map that outlines supply chain excellence.

2. Train the organization on the road map and why it matters.

3. Tie projects and initiatives to this three-year road map. Make it holistic and overarching.

4. Build a guiding coalition to enable success. Make sure that it has the right mix of leaders and managers.

Figure 6.12A   Historic View of How to Connect the End-to-End Supply Chain

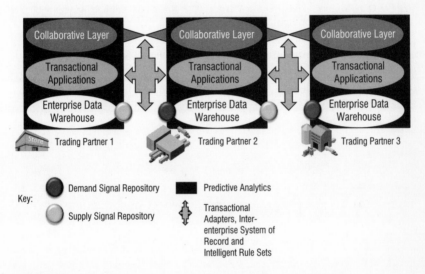

Figure 6.12B   Future View of How to Connect the End-to-End Supply Chain

5. Align organizational behaviors to value strength, balance, and agility. Train for the Supply Chain Race of 2020 by building these capabilities.

6. Learn to listen to the consumer outside-in. Build systems to use the voice of the customer outside-in.

7. Using the three-year road map, build capabilities to embrace new opportunities for the upcoming tipping points. Evaluate how each can build business differentiation

8. Invest in process innovation.

9. Win the race for Supply Chain 2020.

Good luck on your journey. In the words of Keith Harrison, former product supply officer of Procter & Gamble, remember, "It is a journey, not a sprint. And it must be based on a firm foundation of operational excellence."

NOTES

1. Quantitative Studies, "Supply Chain Insights," 2008–2012.
2. Yr Gunnarsdottir and Brenton Harder, "CI? Not Good Enough Anymore?" *Lean Management Journal*, April 2012.
3. Supply Chain Insights Research, 2012.
4. Supply Chain Insights, "Quantitative Study on Agility," March 2012.
5. IBM, "What Is Big Data?" CSCMP Conference, 2011.
6. "Where Angels Will Tred," *The Economist*, November 2001.

About the Authors

Lora Cecere is the founder of the research firm Supply Chain Insights, which is paving new directions in building thought-leading supply chain research. She is also the author of the enterprise software blog *Supply Chain Shaman*. The blog focuses on the use of enterprise applications to drive supply chain excellence. As an enterprise strategist, Lora focuses on the changing face of enterprise technologies. Her research is designed for the early adopter seeking first mover advantage. Current research topics include the digital consumer, supply chain sensing, demand shaping and revenue management, market-driven value networks, accelerating innovation through open design networks, the evolution of predictive analytics, emerging business intelligence solutions, and technologies to improve safe and secure product delivery. With more than 30 years of diverse supply chain experience, Lora spent 9 years as an industry analyst with Gartner Group, AMR Research, and Altimeter Group. Prior to becoming a supply chain analyst she spent 15 years as a leader in the building of supply chain software at Manugistics and Descartes Systems Group, and several years as a supply chain practitioner at Procter & Gamble, Kraft/General Foods, Clorox, and Dreyers Grand Ice Cream (now a division of Nestlé).

Charles Chase is the principal industry consultant of the manufacturing and supply chain global practice at SAS. He is the primary architect and strategist for delivering demand planning and forecasting solutions to improve supply chain efficiencies for SAS customers. He has more than 26 years of experience in the consumer packaged goods industry and is an expert in sales forecasting, market response modeling, econometrics, and supply chain management. Prior to working as the principal industry consultant at SAS, Chase led the strategic marketing activities in support of the launch of SAS Forecast Server, which won the Trend-Setting Product of the Year award for 2005 by *KM World* magazine, and SAS Demand-Driven Forecasting. He has also been involved in the reengineering, design, and implementation of three forecasting and marketing intelligence processes/systems. Chase has also worked at the Mennen Company, Johnson & Johnson, Consumer Products Inc., Reckitt & Benckiser, the Polaroid Corporation, Coca-Cola, Wyeth-Ayerst Pharmaceuticals, and Heineken USA.

Chase is a former associate editor of the *Journal of Business Forecasting* and is currently an active member of the practitioner advisory board for *Foresight: The International Journal of Applied Forecasting*. He has authored several articles on sales forecasting and market response modeling. He was named a 2004 Pro to Know in the February/March 2004 issue of *Supply and Demand Chain Executive* magazine. He is also the author of *Demand-Driven Forecasting: A Structured Approach to Forecasting* (Wiley, 2009).

Index

NOTE: Page refers in *italics* refer to tables and figures.